'Til Freedom Came

Slaves in Allen County, Kentucky

1815 - 1865

'Til Freedom Came

Slaves in Allen County, Kentucky
1815 - 1865

GLEN CONNER

Acclaim Press
MORLEY, MISSOURI

Acclaim Press
— Your Next Great Book —
P.O. Box 238
Morley, MO 63767
(573) 472-9800
www.acclaimpress.com

Design: Tiffany Glastetter
Cover Design: M. Frene Melton

Library of Congress Cataloging-in-Publication Data

Conner, Glen.
'Til Freedom Came: Slaves in Allen County, Kentucky 1815-1865 / by Glen Conner.
p. cm.
Includes bibliographical references and index.
ISBN-13: 978-1-935001-50-8 (alk. paper)
ISBN-10: 1-935001-50-7 (alk. paper)
1. African Americans--Kentucky--Allen County--Genealogy. 2. Slaves--Kentucky--Allen County--Genealogy. 3. Slaves--Kentucky--Allen County--Registers. 4. Freedmen--Kentucky--Allen County--Genealogy. 5. Freedmen--Kentucky--Allen County--Registers. 6. Registers of births, etc.--Kentucky--Allen County. 7. Allen County (Ky.)--Genealogy. 8. Allen County (Ky.)--Census. I. Title. F457.A5C66 2010
929'.3769732--dc22

2010019354

Cover: Group of contraband at Follers House, Cumberland Landing, Virginia, May 1862. Library of Congress photograph LC-DIG-cwpb-01005

First Printing: 2010
Printed in the United States of America
10 9 8 7 6 5 4 3 2 1

Contents

Acknowledgments

This document was inspired by a recent visit to the Allen County Historical Society by an African American who had traced her roots to our area. Her ancestors were slaves who had lived in the Gainesville area. The amount of information that was readily available to help her was embarrassingly meager. From that encounter came a resolve to discover and present the history of both slaves and slavery in Allen County, Kentucky to assist future researchers in their search for slave ancestors. This document is the result. Particular effort was made to identify and record the names of the slaves and of the slave owners. Both are necessary to follow the thread of ancestry back through the slave era.

Compilation of data from existing documents, such as the census, tax records, death records, and other such tabulations, is tedious and seldom spurs excitement or produces joy. The docents of the Allen County Historical Society endured many hours of such tedium to extract data and to proofread the tables that were prepared from them. To the docents individually and collectively who worked on the project, my admiration and appreciation is given.

There must be an acknowledgment of the enormous contribution of slaves to Allen County's history and heritage. Their contributions were, in most cases, in the form of involuntary labor. Most are omitted in previous written histories. Their contributions were vital in every aspect of the development within every community of the County.

In a few cases, the contributions of slaves were both voluntary and recorded in histories. For example, slaves were charter members in several of our early churches. They attended and participated in church services, all while remaining enslaved. They must have influenced the opinions of their fellow members about slaves and slavery.

Perhaps no contributions by Allen County-born slaves were more remarkable than those by the thirty-eight of them who volunteered for the army to fight for the preservation of the Union during the Civil War. We must acknowledge their service under the most trying of circumstances. Ten of them died while on active duty of non-combat causes, mostly from disease. Two more were killed in action, both with the 6th U.S. Colored Cavalry. Their ultimate sacrifices in defense of our country must be acknowledged and honored: Private James Sears killed in the battle at Saltville, Virginia and Private John Sears killed in the battle at Marion, Virginia.

It is as difficult to imagine life as either a slave or as a slave owner as it is to understand how slavery was tolerated or accepted. But, judgment must come from the reader. The purpose of this document is to record our history and heritage, whatever it was and as it was, to help us to identify and learn more about our ancestors.

Glen Conner

Allen County, Kentucky

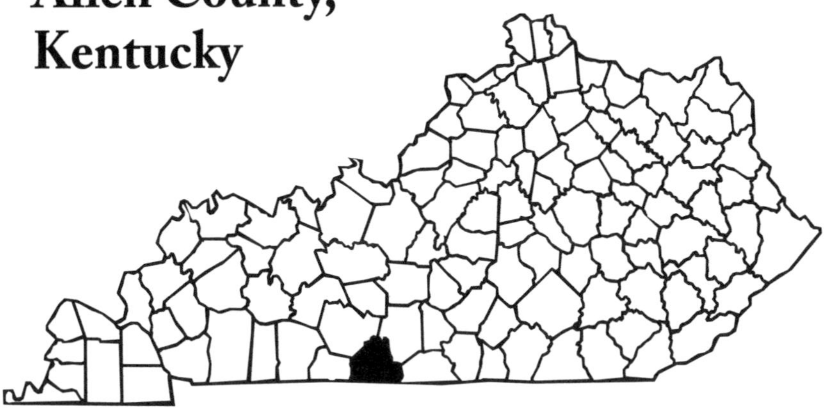

Preface

Freedom! The word stirs our hearts when we say it. To the 864 enslaved African Americans in Allen County in 1830, there was little hope for the freedom we cherish so much. They had been born into slavery and they expected to die as slaves. The possibility of freedom was sometimes used as an incentive for hard work but it was seldom given as a reward. The truth was that their freedom was highly improbable and not one of them could reasonably expect to join the five African American men and two African American women in the County who were free at that time.

Samuel E. Carpenter was born into a North Carolina family that owned eleven slaves. He moved to Kentucky prior to 1810 and married Sarah Downing in 1814. All of their children were born in Kentucky. He owned 300 acres of land in the Long Creek area of Allen County near what is now the village called Holland. The tax rolls of 1831 recorded the value of his property at $5,095, an amount exceeded by only eight other Allen Countians. Like those other wealthy men, most of his wealth was in the value of the fifteen slaves he owned. Among those slaves were one boy and four girls younger than ten years old; four young men and two young women younger than twenty-four; one man and one woman younger than thirty-six; and a man and a woman younger than fifty-five.

Samuel's oldest enslaved male was named Dick, but like other slaves, he wasn't allowed to have a last name. He was born into slavery in 1789, one of eleven slaves owned by the Carpenter family in North Carolina. Dick and the oldest female were two of seven slaves that Samuel brought with him to Kentucky. She and Dick likely considered themselves man and wife although slave marriages were not recognized as legal in Kentucky.

July 16, 1832 was to become a memorable day for Dick. On that County Court Day Monday, he accompanied Samuel to the octagonal courthouse in the middle of Scottsville to appear before the July Session of the Allen County Court.

It was not unusual for Samuel E. Carpenter to make an appearance in the Courthouse because he was one of the Justices who met there each month to administer the activities of the County. This time though he appeared in front of the Court. The Court's Order Book reported that Thomas Caruth, John Whitney, Thomas Sutton, Robert McCleary and John Caruth were seated as Justices that day. All but Sutton were slave owners like Samuel and now these Justices had a slave and a slave owner standing before them. That was unusual because Kentucky law limited slave testimony to confessions of wrong doings or to provide evidence against other slaves. One can imagine that Dick was apprehensive about these unfamiliar proceedings but his heart must have been pounding with excited expectation.

Standing there in open court with Dick at his side, Samuel declared that he freed Dick. The Justices ordered that the emancipation be recorded and certified according to the law. Against all odds, Dick was free! As another African American would say 131 years later, "Free at last! Free at last! Thank God Almighty, ...free at last!"

The Court recorded a detailed description of Dick. There were Patrollers in Allen County and elsewhere who had the authority to apprehend and detain runaway slaves, slaves who were out after curfew, or those unlawfully congregating. If confronted by Patrollers, the law required Dick to prove that he indeed was a free man of color, was subject only to the laws that applied to white people and was not a runaway slave. For that purpose, the Court recorded that Dick was a mulatto with a yellowish complexion and short nappy hair. He stood about five foot six or seven, well built and muscular for a forty year old. He had three small scars on the left backside of his head, one scar behind his right ear that ran down the neck, and one scar on his right thigh that ran perpendicularly down the front side. That description would save him from harassment by the Patrollers, at least from the ones who could read.

The 1833 tax roll listed Samuel with only fourteen slaves, a reduction by one, indicating that Dick was no longer his property. In the 1840 census, the slave numbers listed by the census taker again included Dick as a slave. That mistake would be corrected in the next census.

There is no doubt about Dick in the 1850 census. He was listed as "Free Dick Carpenter." One can imagine that the emphasis on "free" was his and not that of a Methodist clergyman R. Y. McReynolds who was the census taker. He listed Dick as a head of household farmer who owned property that was valued at $200. His nearest neighbor was his former owner, Samuel, who by then had twenty-seven slaves. That indicates that his emancipation of Dick was not a result of a newly acquired leaning toward the abolition of slavery, but was a unique act.

There was a surprise in the slave portion of the 1850 census. Free Dick Carpenter was listed as a slave owner! There was a 59 year-old female slave in his household. She was part of his property that the Tax Assessor had valued at $200. She was born in North Carolina just as Dick had been. She appeared as a female slave in the appropriate age group in the 1820, 1830 and 1840 censuses in Samuel's household. Kentucky law allowed Freedmen to only purchase slaves who were family members. Therefore, one must conclude that Dick bought her because she was his wife. It was not uncommon for a Freedman to purchase his wife to assure that her owner would not sell her away from him.

Mt. Gilead Baptist Church was organized in 1829. Its first three members were Samuel Carpenter, his wife Sarah and a black woman named Dolly. In the 1870 census, Samuel appears at age 75 with a black woman named Dollie (sic) Carpenter living in his household. This Dolly, like Dick, was born in North Carolina and was 79 years old. It seems clear that Samuel brought Dick and Dolly, a man and his wife, with him to Kentucky. It is also clear that Dick had to work as a free man for eighteen years before he could buy Dolly and assure that they would be together for the rest of their lives.

We can celebrate the life of Dick Carpenter who was enslaved for forty-three years before being granted freedom by his owner. We can marvel that he shared strong bonds of mutual respect with his owner. We can be thrilled that Dick found a way to assure the freedom of the woman he loved. We can be thankful that Dolly lived to be 99, her later years living again in the household of the family that had set Dick free. Dick and Dolly's lives remind us that our heritage is worth preserving.

This study is an effort to help preserve that heritage.

Introduction

Allen County, Kentucky histories record few if any contributions of African Americans to its settlement and growth. Names of the early white settlers were mentioned, but the names of the slaves who came with them were not. Names of slave owners are known, but the names of their slaves are not. African Americans who seek their ancestors are hampered by these omissions. The purpose of this publication is to identify the slaves who were brought into our county and the names of their progeny along with historical information about them. The data and information contained herein may help those who wish to discover or to better understand the roots of our heritage within a proper historical context.

'Til Freedom Came

Slaves in Allen County, Kentucky
1815 - 1865

CHAPTER 1

Early Slaves in Allen County

Slaves Before 1815

The British Army killed three Americans in the Boston Massacre on March 5, 1770, the first casualties of what would become the Revolutionary War. One of those killed in the first volley was Crispus Attucks[1] a slave who had run away to freedom twenty years earlier. The first Africans were brought forcibly to America in 1619, 151 years before Attucks was killed. They were brought to Virginia, just twelve years after the settlement of Jamestown. Their enslavement was perpetuated through the next 244 years before President Lincoln signed the Emancipation Proclamation. An African American tracing their ancestry to that original group of Africans would have to identify ancestors through 15 generations, the earliest nine of which were slaves.

We don't know the slave owner who brought the first slave to what is now Kentucky. The owner was likely one of the first explorers, perhaps Christopher Gist in January 1751.[2] He, along with three other white men and one servant (slave), visited a French and Indian village in what is now Greenup County.[3] That servant, whose name was not recorded, was likely the first slave in Kentucky. In fact, he crossed southward over the Ohio River the day before his owner, Gist, but was not credited for being first.

We honor Daniel Boone and we recount how the Indians killed his son James in 1773. But, we seldom add that a slave named

[1] Transcript, 1824. *The trial of the British Soldiers of the 29th Regiment of Foot for the Murder of Crispus Attucks, Samuel Gray, Samuel Maverick, James Cladwell and Patrick Carr on Monday Evening, March 5, 1770.* Transcript of the hearing before the Justices of the Superior Court on 27 November 1770. William Emmons, Boston

[2] Gist, Christopher, and William M. Darlington. 1893. *Christopher Gist's journals: with historical, geographical and ethnological notes and biographies of his contemporaries by William M.* Darlington. Pittsburg: J.R. Weldin & Co.

[3] Kentucky Historical Marker Number 31, located in South Portsmouth, Kentucky on KY highway 10 in Greenup County Kentucky

Charles was killed with him and that Adam, another slave, survived to tell the story.[4]

In 1777, Harrod's Fort had 198 residents, of whom 19 (about 10%) were slaves.[5] By 1784, Kentucky had about 4,000 slaves and by the 1790 census, the slave population was about 16% of the total. By 1810, the number of slaves rose to 41,084, about 19% of the total population. At that time, about one of every five Kentuckians was black. By the time slavery ended, about one-fourth of all white households in Allen County had one or more slaves. It is highly probable that each Allen Countian has at least one ancestor who was enslaved or who owned slaves.

The date of the arrival of the first slaves into Allen County is not known, but it is certain that they were here long before Allen County was formed in 1815. One would assume that slave owners who moved to Kentucky would not have left their slaves behind. It is reasonable to assume that they would have brought their slaves along to share the strenuous work during the travel and after arrival.

There are records of Samuel E. Carpenter, James McElroy and Langston Williams being in Allen County in 1797. They had slaves in later years and it seems certain that some or all of their slaves came with them. Unfortunately, Allen County history mentions only white settlers.[6]

A few individuals had large numbers of slaves. As an example, Jeremiah Stark had 33 slaves in 1810. It seems probable that he brought the slaves with him because the purchase of that many would have been difficult before slave markets became readily accessible.

One of the early settlers who acquired slaves after arrival was Jacob Dry, a Revolutionary War soldier from North Carolina who was captured by the British when Charleston, SC surrendered. After being released, he walked back to North Carolina and rejoined the

---

[4] Addington, Robert M., 1990. *History of Scott County, Virginia*. Salem, Mass: Higginson Book Co.

[5] Kleber, John E. 1992. *The Kentucky encyclopedia*. Lexington, Ky: University Press of Kentucky.

[6] Horton, Louise. 1975. In the hills of the Pennyroyal: a history of Allen County, Kentucky, from 1815 to 1880. Austin, Tex: White Cross Press.

Revolutionary Army. He walked to Kentucky with his wife and nine children before the 1810 census. By the tax rolls of 1821, he had acquired five slaves and a farm, collectively assessed at $3,765.

The move to Kentucky was usually made on foot in late winter because travel was easier then and arrival was in time to grow food for the following winter. Trees could be deadened by cutting a notch through the cambium layer, completely around the tree trunk, interrupting the flow of water and nutrients, killing the tree thereby removing its shade, and opening the canopy to sunlight. That would permit food crops to be planted among the trees without removing the trees themselves. Slaves could have been used for that work as well as to clear small areas from the forest to build the first shelter. Likely the very first shelter was a lean-to that was quick to build but was not permanent.

The lean-to replacement could have been a structure called a "Puncheon Camp." This structure, made from small-diameter logs, could serve as an interim house during that first winter. Puncheons could be hewn to surface the roof of the puncheon camp. The puncheons were small logs hewn flat on just one side when used for a roof — or for a floor.[7] Slaves could have been used for this work too. There was a church near Holland that had the name Puncheon Camp, perhaps referring to its original structure.

The permanent house for the earliest settlers likely was a hewn-log house. That type of structure used large poplar logs, too large for one person to move and shape. That work was yet another contribution by slaves. It was common for the hewn-log houses to have a loft as a sleeping area. Trundle beds with straw ticks were common too, to save space.

One can imagine that producing enough food for the coming winter was the first priority. Building a shelter before winter arrived seems like the second priority. Building a separate building for the slaves would appear to have been a low priority, given all the intimacies of camping en route and before a more permanent shelter was built. Perhaps that came later when the increases in the size of the slave owner's and the slave's families produced overcrowding in a shared house and made a separate house necessary.

[7] Jordan, Terry G. 1994. Texas log buildings: a folk architecture. Austin: University of Texas Press.

Slaves in the US Census

The primary source for the Allen County data in this publication was the United States Census taken each decade. Data tables were prepared from the census to make it possible to compare data about slaves and slave owners. A single format for the tables was adopted for the 1830, 1840, 1850 and 1860 data to simplify the data set. A different format was necessary for the 1820 data because those data were insufficiently detailed compared to the other years.

Each census taker was a resident of Allen County and was appointed to survey people in a specific district (a voting precinct, for example) of the County. His survey was handwritten in the sequence of his visits. The census taker spelled surnames phonetically when the head of household could not provide the preferred spelling. Users will recognize modern names by those phonetic substitutions.

Censuses Before Allen County Was Formed

The 1790 census was taken before Kentucky was a state, and the 1800 census for Kentucky are unavailable. The citizens were enumerated within each county and the results published in the US Census of 1810. Because Allen County was not formed until 1815, there is no way to absolutely determine the number of slaves in the area that became Allen County from the 1810 data taken in Warren and Barren counties. However, for this study, the names of the slave owners in Allen County in 1820 were located in Warren and Barren Counties in 1810 and the number of slaves associated with those names were listed. The presumption is that the slave owners with the same names were the same persons in both lists and that they had not moved geographically. Neither of those presumptions is absolutely certain, but they provide at least some data from 1810 that may be useful.

The derived data from Warren County presented in Table 1 show 23 slaves. The derived data in Table 2 show ten in Barren County.

Table 1

Allen County slaves in 1810 reconstructed from Warren County data

Slave Owner	Slaves	Slave Owner	Slaves
Afton, Samuel		Howard, John	
Anthony, Joseph	0	Logan, Joshua	5
Baird, David		Markum, William	
Barnhart, John	4	Martin, Mary	
Barns, Stephen		McElroy, James	2
Blackburn, James		McHugh, Moses	
Blackwell, Thomas	1	Moody, Samuel	
Bradburn, William C.		Moore, Charles	
Brown, Joseph		Nanny, Uriah	2
Burris, Jacob		Ray, Baxter	
Burris,Thomas	1	Reeder, Joshua	2
Carpenter, John		Right, Henry	
Chamber, Thomas		Right, Jarrot	
Clark, John Jr.		Rion, Noah	
Claton, John		Robertson, Leroy	
Cornwell, Daniel	0	Rughly, Phillip	
Crow, William		Sears, Joseph	
Cushenberry, Vinson	1	Sledge, Miles C.	
Ellis, Thomas	1	Smith, Elizabeth	0
Follis, Mary		Thompson, Balam	0
Gaines, Edward		Trail, Elizabeth	
Gains, William		Travers, Charly	1
Garrison, Samuel		Travis, John	
Gibson, Randolph	1	Wadle, Charles	
Gibson, William		Waggoner, George	
Guy, William	1	Walker, William	
Hamm, William	0	Williams, Langston	1
Heeter, George		Williams, Mastin	
Hill, John	0	Williams, Solomon	
Hinton, Moore		Williiams, Ralph	
Hood, Bryant		Willouby, Samuel	

Table 2

Allen County slaves in 1810 reconstructed from Barren County data

Slave Owner	Slaves	Slave Owner	Slaves
Afton, Samuel		Howard, John	0
Anthony, Joseph		Logan, Joshua	
Baird, David		Markum, William	
Barnhart, John		Martin, Mary	
Barns, Stephen		McElroy, James	
Blackburn, James		McHugh, Moses	
Blackwell, Thomas		Moody, Samuel	
Bradburn, William C.		Moore, Charles	
Brown, Joseph		Nanny, Uriah	
Burris, Jacob		Ray, Baxter	
Burris,Thomas		Reeder, Joshua	
Carpenter, John		Right, Henry	
Chamber, Thomas		Right, Jarrot	
Clark, John Jr.		Rion, Noah	
Claton, John	10	Robertson, Leroy	
Cornwell, Daniel		Rughly, Phillip	
Crow, William		Sears, Joseph	
Cushenberry, Vinson		Sledge, Miles C.	
Ellis, Thomas		Smith, Elizabeth	
Follis, Mary		Thompson, Balam	
Gaines, Edward		Trail, Elizabeth	
Gains, William		Travers, Charly	
Garrison, Samuel		Travis, John	
Gibson, Randolph		Wadle, Charles	
Gibson, William		Waggoner, George	
Guy, William		Walker, William	
Hamm, William		Williams, Langston	
Heeter, George		Williams, Mastin	
Hill, John		Williams, Solomon	
Hinton, Moore		Williiams, Ralph	
Hood, Bryant		Willouby, Samuel	

Censuses After Allen County Was Formed

In the early census years 1820 through 1840, the only names recorded were the white heads of household. All other white people appeared by gender as just a number in an age category. Slaves were never identified by any name, just by age group and gender. Free Blacks, as they were called, were listed by name if they were a household head and did not live in a white household. See Freedmen of Allen County (Chapter 13) of this publication for this and other related details.

In 1850 and 1860, the census listed the surname of each white household head, and the first name, age, and gender of each white person in the household. There was a separate form called the Slave Schedule that recorded the name of the slave owner and the age, gender, and color of each slave owned, but not the names. There were some households that had more than one slave owner living there. That may have resulted from the distribution of slaves when a deceased owner's estate was divided among the inheritors. It also could have been for other reasons such as tax considerations, for example.

The 1850 and 1860 slave schedules listed the color of each slave as either black or mulatto. The word mulatto originally described the first-generation offspring of a black person and a white person. However, the census did not prescribe what definition the census taker should use. Lacking an explicit definition, the census takers applied it to any slave who they perceived to be of mixed black-white ancestry. One cannot infer that the mix had recently occurred, nor infer a relationship between the owner and the slave. Black and mulatto slaves also produced mulatto children, sometimes for many generations.

It is interesting that Kentucky had a higher percentage of mulattoes than any other slave state. In 1850, 16.4 percent of Kentucky slaves were mulatto and the percentage was 19.2 percent in 1860. The deep south percentages in 1860 were about 5 percent in South Carolina, 7 percent in North Carolina, and 8 percent in Alabama, Georgia, and Mississippi. In the 1850-1860 decade, the percentage of mulattos decreased in Arkansas and Texas as the number of slaves increased. That seems to indicate a buying preference in the south for black slaves.[8] Kentucky was an exporter of slaves to the south and, if it sold more blacks than mulattoes, its percentage of mulattoes would rise.

Previous researchers have transcribed the handwritten census forms into more easily read typewritten data. Those transcriptions of each decadal census were used for convenience in this study to compile the data shown in Tables 3 through 7. A cohort is a group determined by age.

Table 3

1820 age and gender of slaves compared to the number of slaves in a household

	Males by Age Cohort				Females by Age Cohort				
Slaves in Household	*<14*	*14-26*	*26-45*	*>45*	*<14*	*14-26*	*26-45*	*>45*	*Total Slaves*
1	5	7	6	1	11	8	5	5	48
2	9	14	7	1	17	49	5	2	74
3	15	9	2	1	15	13	4	1	60
4	11	4	5	1	12	5	5	1	44
5	17	4	4	3	16	11	12	3	70
6-10	49	28	16	3	45	18	26	2	187
11-24	44	21	22	9	54	32	17	6	205
TOTAL	150	87	62	19	170	106	74	20	688

[8] Taylor, Orville W., 1958. Jumping over the broomstick: slave marriage and mortality in Arkansas. Vol. XVII, No. 3, Arkansas Historical Quarterly, Arkansas Historical Association, Van Buren, Arkansas

Table 4

1830 age and gender of slaves compared to the number of slaves in a household

Males by Age							Females by Age						
Slaves in Household	***<10***	***10-24***	***24-36***	***36-55***	***55-100***	***>100***	***<10***	***10-24***	***24-36***	***36-55***	***55-100***	***>100***	***Total Slaves***
1	6	8	7	6	2		7	15	6	1	1		59
2	10	9	11	3	1		10	20	6	1	1		72
3	14	12	4	3	0		11	14	7	4	0		69
4	14	7	1	2	0		10	10	4	3	1		52
5	14	14	4	0	0		8	13	6	6	0		65
6-10	52	34	17	7	0		54	36	25	15	6		246
11-25	58	40	24	14	4		65	52	26	13	5		301
TOTAL	168	124	68	35	7		165	160	80	43	14		864

Table 5

1840 age and gender of slaves compared to the number of slaves in a household

Males by Age							Females by Age						
Slaves in Household	***<10***	***10-24***	***24-36***	***36-55***	***55-100***	***>100***	***<10***	***10-24***	***24-36***	***36-55***	***55-100***	***>100***	***Total Slaves***
1	9	18	6	8	1	1	5	20	4	5	5		82
2	13	8	2	1	3		11	23	8	5	2		76
3	6	10	3	2	2		20	15	7	3	1		69
4	19	17	2	3	1		12	13	8	9	0		84
5	18	17	4	3	1		15	18	5	7	2		90
6-10	62	51	11	10	7		54	45	23	25	3		291
11-25	44	45	24	10	5		44	30	22	13	7		244
TOTAL	171	166	52	37	20	1	161	164	77	67	20		936

Table 6

1850 age and gender of slaves compared to the number of slaves in a household

Males by Age							Females by Age						
Slaves in Household	*<10*	*10-24*	*24-36*	*36-55*	*55-100*	*>100*	*<10*	*10-24*	*24-36*	*36-55*	*55-100*	*>100*	*Total Slaves*
1	3	13	5	6	1		7	23	5	8	3		74
2	9	17	6	4	4		9	30	11	7	3		100
3	23	13	4	4	3		7	15	4	7	1		81
4	24	14	8	2	2		18	27	11	5	1		112
5	25	25	9	1	1	1	21	17	9	9	2		120
6-10	77	56	27	13	3		68	57	30	21	10		362
11-50	91	70	43	24	13		69	83	33	23	14		463
TOTAL	252	208	102	54	27	1	199	252	103	80	34		1312

Table 7

1860 age and gender of slaves compared to the number of slaves in a household

Males by Age							Females by Age						
Slaves in Household	*<10*	*10-24*	*24-36*	*36-55*	*55-100*	*>100*	*<10*	*10-24*	*24-36*	*36-55*	*55-100*	*>100*	*Total Slaves*
1	9	16	5	8	2		6	18	5	11	5		85
2	9	16	4	3	2		10	22	7	4	1		78
3	12	11	2	3	0		15	9	9	7	1		69
4	14	22	4	2	2		16	20	6	5	1		92
5	21	23	13	7	1		11	21	11	8	4		120
6-10	81	66	25	21	5		68	61	35	16	8		386
11-25	93	56	21	17	3		80	66	29	20	11		396
26-66	51	45	24	19	5		55	38	26	15	10		288
TOTAL	290	255	98	80	20		261	255	128	86	41		1514

The census derived slave data from each of the five decadal censuses 1820 to 1860 are contained in the next five chapters of this chapter. Each has data in tabular and graphical form, and information in narrative summaries. The tables above are discussed in those sections.

Chapter 2

Slaves in Allen County in 1820

1820 Census

The first official enumeration of slaves after Allen County was formed in 1815 was the US census of 1820. By then, 5,327 people lived in the county. Of that total, 688 were enslaved African Americans, about 13 percent of the total population. Of course, white women and children formed most of the population, and few of them owned slaves. A more accurate representation considers the 708 heads of household in the county. Of that number, 175 were slave owners. Thus 25 percent, one out of every four white households, owned slaves.

The numbers of slaves in those households varied from one to twenty-four. There were 50 households that had only one slave and 39 that had just two. At the other end of the distribution, each of 15 households had more than ten. Of them, Jeremiah Stark owned 24 slaves, James J. Foster had 20, and John Godley had 19. They were farmers who held large numbers of acres. For example, Foster's heirs sold about 2,500 acres of his farm when he died in 1821.

About one-out-of-three slave children died in infancy due to their mothers having inadequate rest and improper nutrition.[1] However, that would not have affected the normal birth pattern, one that would produce an even distribution of males and females. The pattern was not normal for the slaves in 1820. About 54 percent of them were female and 46 percent were male. Only the over-45 age group has about equal numbers. In all other categories, females outnumbered males. A comparison among those slaves showing the difference by gender is shown in Figure 1.

---

[1] Larkin, Jack. 2007. The reshaping of everyday life, 1790 - 1840. The everyday life in America series. New York, NY: Harper Perennial.

Figure 1

Allen County slaves by gender and age groups in 1820

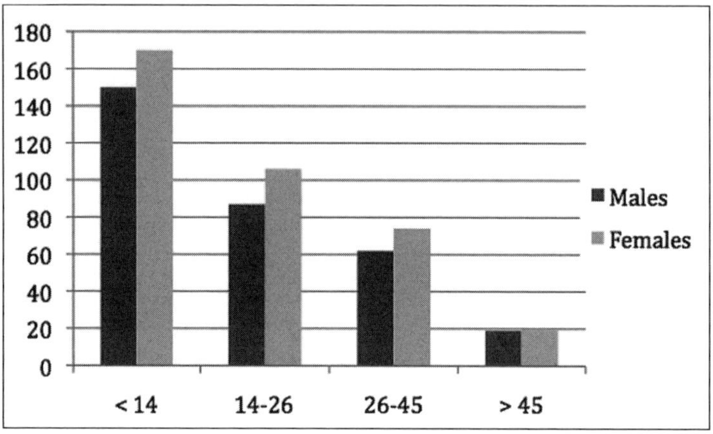

The disparity shown in Figure 1 was consistent among households having a small number of slaves but differed among households with more than five slaves. Tables 8 and 9 show that inconsistency.

Table 8

Gender disparity by age group among slaves in slave owner households in 1820

	Males by Age Cohort				Females by Age Cohort				
Slaves in Household	*<14*	*14-26*	*26-45*	*>45*	*<14*	*14-26*	*26-45*	*>45*	*Total Slaves*
1	5	7	6	1	11	8	5	5	48
2	9	14	7	1	17	49	5	2	74
3	15	9	2	1	15	13	4	1	60
4	11	4	5	1	12	5	5	1	44
5	17	4	4	3	16	11	12	3	70
6-10	49	28	16	3	45	18	26	2	187
11-24	44	21	22	9	54	32	17	6	205
TOTAL	150	87	62	19	170	106	74	20	688

The age group data from Table 8 are presented as a percent of the total slaves per household in Table 9.

Table 9

Slave gender distribution by percent of total slaves in household in 1820

Percent Males by Age Cohort Percent Females by Age Cohort									
Slaves in Household	*<14*	*14-26*	*26-45*	*>45*	*<14*	*14-26*	*26-45*	*>45*	*Total Slaves*
1	10.0	14.0	12.0	2.0	22.0	20.8	10.0	10.0	48
2	12.2	17.9	9.0	1.3	23.0	25.8	6.4	2.6	74
3	27.0	14.3	3.2	1.6	23.8	21.7	6.3	1.6	60
4	25.0	9.1	11.4	2.3	27.3	11.4	11.4	2.3	44
5	24.3	5.7	5.7	4.3	22.9	15.7	17.1	4.3	70
6-10	26.2	15.0	8.6	1.6	24.1	9.6	13.9	1.1	187
11-24	21.5	10.2	10.7	4.4	26.3	15.6	8.3	2.9	205
TOTAL	21.8	12.5	8.9	2.7	24.7	15.4	10.6	2.9	688

One-Slave Households

The disparity by gender was examined among slave owners who owned just one slave. They showed a significant preference for females. Of the fifty slaves in households with only one slave (Table 8), 29 (60%) were female. That gender difference existed in all age groups other than the 26-45 where the numbers were about the same with six males and five females. The largest disparity was among the younger-than-fourteen ages where the females outnumbered the males 11 to 5.

There are several possible reasons for the gender disparity. Speculation about those reasons is just that, but one cannot help wondering about those reasons. One may imagine that, if only one slave was to be owned, females would be selected to become a domestic servant. The domestic servant cooked, made the beds, milked the cows, dusted and swept, and could be a nanny if needed. Households with a large number of children would have imposed a heavy workload on such servants.

The data in Table 8 also show a preference for younger females, as compared to the males who had almost identical numbers in each of the three age groups younger than 45. For the females, there were twice as many in the two youngest age groups as in the group from 26 to 45. Acquisition cost may have been a factor. Female slaves could be acquired at less cost than males, and younger slaves cost less than older slaves. Value of slaves reached its peak at about age 16 and remained steady until about age 35. Value decreased afterward.

Slave children were considered to be ready to work at age eight, half-hands as they were called, but they could not yet do an adult's full day's work.[2] The preference for younger slaves may have been based on simple economics, an eight-year-old child cost half as much as a sixteen- year- old. Poor whites may have bought only what they could afford.

One-to-Five-Slave Households

The question arose, would the disparity between males and females persist in data from households with more slaves? Indeed, there were also more females than males in households that held from two to five slaves.

Figure 2

Allen County slaves by gender and number of slaves in households in 1820

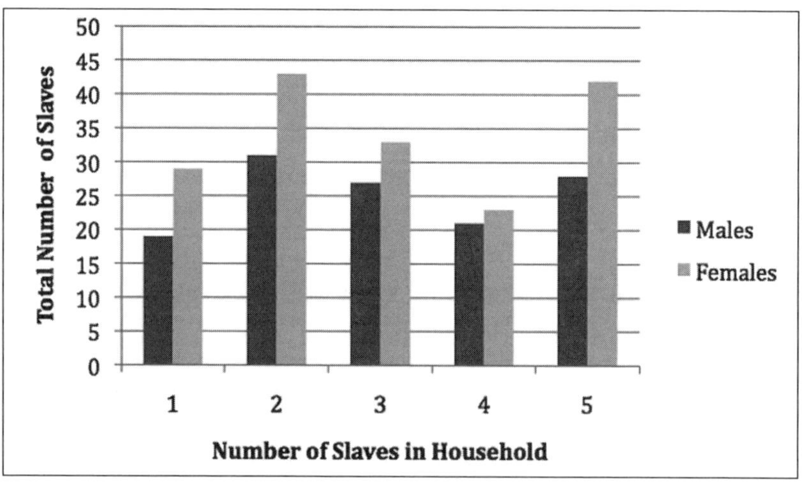

Speculation about the reason for gender disparity becomes more tenuous in households with multiple numbers of slaves because there then exists another possibility. The preferential sale of males

[2] Frankel, Noralee. 1999. Freedom's women: Black women and families in Civil War era Mississippi. Blacks in the diaspora. Bloomington: Indiana University Press.

could have produced the disparity. No data exist with which to test that possibility.

Numbers alone do not tell the full story among households with multiple slaves. The age groups were examined for gender disparity. The number of slaves who were younger than 26 remained disproportionately more than the older groups. The portion younger than 26 years old was 76 percent of the total slaves for both males and females. This was true although the number of females was 16 percent higher than the number of males.

The pie charts in Figure 3 illustrate that the age distribution of slaves in households with five or fewer slaves was about the same for males and females.

Figure 3

Gender distribution by age group of slaves in households with 1 to 5 slaves

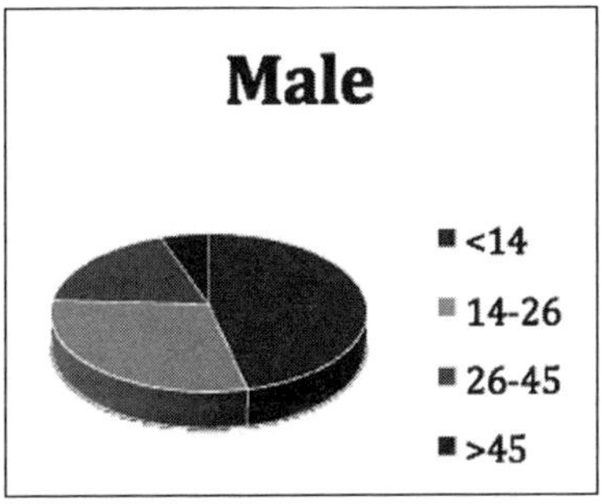

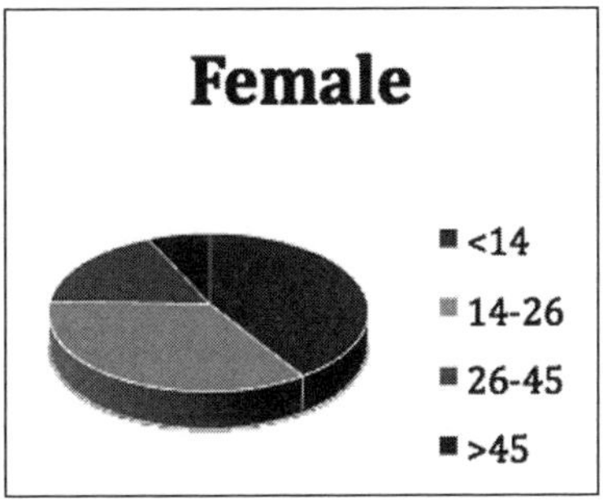

Six-to-Twenty-Four Slave Households

The gender distribution changed completely in households having six to ten slaves. Among these households, males outnumbered females and composed 55 percent of the total.

Figure 4

Gender disparity of slaves in households with 6 to 10 slaves

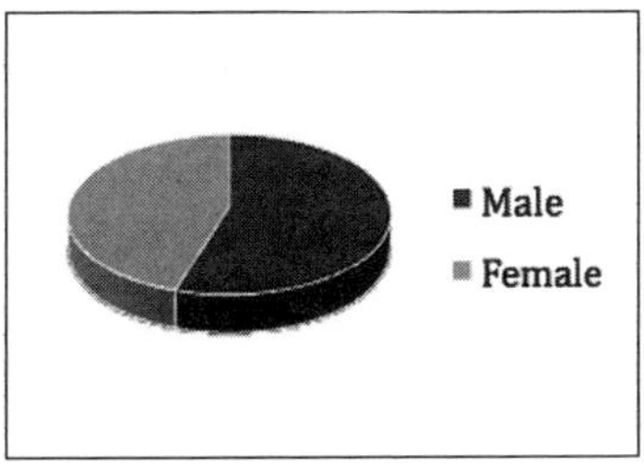

The same distribution pattern existed in the households with eleven to twenty-four slaves where males, at 57 percent, outnumbered females (Figure 5).

Figure 5

Gender disparity of slaves in households with from 11 to 24 slaves

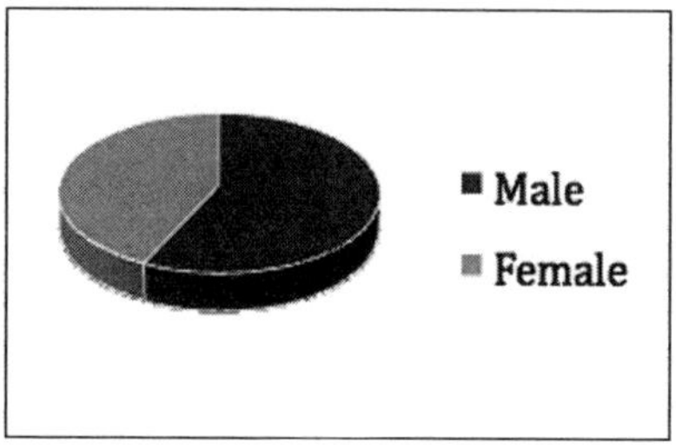

In all age groups younger than 45, males outnumbered females. There seems to have been a threshold that came into play when the total number of slaves exceeded six. At that level and beyond, a higher proportion of males in the household were common. One could speculate that labor needed by larger farms resulted in larger numbers of male slaves. In any case, the results could have been achieved by buying additional males or selling some of the females. Data were not available to examine those speculations.

Only in the over-45 age group were the genders about equal. That may be a data artifact caused by slaves and owners immigrating into Allen County together. The slaves would have been about 20 to 25 or so at the time of the long walk from their state of origin. One could speculate that they were chosen for the trip because of their age and because they were couples. Once in Allen County, the slaves could be traded or sold like any other property. Figure 6 illustrates one such sale.

Figure 6

William Flippin bill of sale of Peg and her son Burrell to John Calvert, 28 July 1819. Used by permission of Todd Calvert

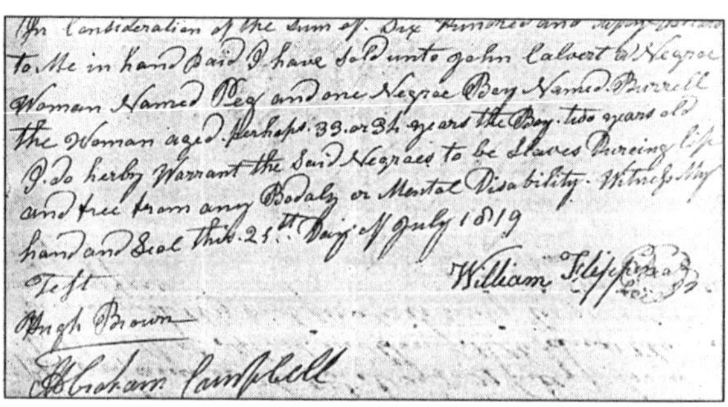

In Consideration of the Sum of Six Hundred and [illegible]
to Me in hand Paid I have Sold unto John Calvert a Negroe
Woman Named Peg and one Negroe Boy Named Burrell
the Woman aged Perhaps 33 or 34 years the Boy two years old
I do herby Warrant the Said Negroes to be Slaves Dureing life
and free from any Bodaly or Mental Disability. Witness My
hand and Seal this 25th Day of July 1819

William Flippin (Seal)

Test
Hugh Brown
Abraham Campbell

Table 10 contains data on slaves extracted from a 2002 transcription made by Roy Markham of the 1820 census.

Table 10

Allen County Slaves in 1820

Slave Owner	Enslaved Males				Enslaved Females				Total
Alphabetical by Owner	*<14*	*14-26*	*26-45*	*>45*	*<14*	*14-26*	*26-45*	*>45*	
Afton, Samuel	1				1	2	1		5
Alexander, Mary					1		1		2
Anderson, William		1							1
Anthony, Joseph	3				1		1		5
Baley, Benjamin						1			1
Barnhart, John		1				1			2
Barns, Stephen	1				3		1		5
Blackburn, James					1				1
Blackwell, Thomas			1					1	2
Bradburn, William C.				1	1	1			3
Bright, James	1	1							2
Brinson, Stout	1	2			2	1	1		7
Brown, Hugh							1		1
Burris, Jacob	3				2	1	2		8
Burris, Thomas			1						1
Burton, Cuthbert	1	1							2
Burton, Drury		2			1				3
Carpenter, Catherine			1				1		2
Carpenter, John	3	1	1		2	1	1		9
Carpenter, Stephen	3	1			2	1			7
Chamber, Thomas		1	3			1	1		6
Clark, John Jr.	4		2		1				7
Claton, John	1				1	1			3
Clayton, James		1	1						2
Cockrel, J. J.	1	1			1	1	1		5
Cockrel, Joseph					2	1			3
Cockrel, William	1								1
Collins, Henry	1								1
Collins, William					1				1
Cornwell, Daniel	1				1	1			3
Cowdin, James	1	1			1	1	1		5
Crow, William							1		1
Cushenberry, Vinson	5	2			4	3	1		15

Slave Owner	Enslaved Males				Enslaved Females				Total
Alphabetical by Owner	*<14*	*14-26*	*26-45*	*>45*	*<14*	*14-26*	*26-45*	*>45*	
Cushings, Elijah	2	1		1	2	1	1		8
Dearing, Elisha	1								1
Devasier, John				1				1	2
Dinwidy, Thomas					1				1
Dinwidy, William					1	1			2
Donan, Anac	2	2			4		1		9
Dry, Jacob	3	1					1		5
Duff, Hubbard							1		1
Ellis, Thomas		1							1
Ferril, Ann	1				4		1		6
Ficklin, Esther		1	2		1				4
Finney, William				1					1
Fishback, John	2					2	2		6
Fishburn, Peter					1				1
Follis, Mary	1		1		1				3
Foster, James J.	4	2	4	2	5	2		1	20
Foster, John			1		1	1			3
Foster, Peter B.	3	4	1	1	1	3			13
Gaines, Edward					1	1			2
Gains, William					1	1			2
Garrison, Samuel			2			2		1	5
Gatton, Thomas	2	1				1			4
Gibson, John L.		1							1
Gibson, Randolph	2					1			3
Gibson, William						1			1
Gills, And		1			3	1	1		6
Godley, John	3		3		8	3	2		19
Guy, William	1				1		1		3
Hamm, William	2						1		3
Hanes, Christopher			1						1
Hardcastle, John								1	1
Hart, John Sr.			1			1			2
Hawkins, Thomas	1					1	1		3
Heeter, George		1				1			2
Heter, Frederich		1				1			2
Hill, John								1	1
Hinton, Moore	1				1	1	1		4
Holder, William	4	1	1		3	3	1		13
Holloway, Charles					1				1
Hood, Bryant	2	1	1		4	2	1	1	12

Slave Owner	Enslaved Males				Enslaved Females				Total
Alphabetical by Owner	*<14*	*14-26*	*26-45*	*>45*	*<14*	*14-26*	*26-45*	*>45*	
Hopson, Thomas					1				1
Hopson, Zachariah	2	1			1		1	1	6
Howard, John					1	1			2
Johnson, Nat	1					1			2
Johnson, Thomas							1		1
Jones, Henreby							1		1
Kelley, James					1	1			2
Lark, John	2	1			5	4	2	1	15
Lee, Isaac			1		1	1	1		4
Lewis, Thomas	3	1	1	1	4	3	1	1	15
Long, Broomfield	2				2		1		5
Long, Burril		1			1			1	3
Lynn, John		2			1		1		4
Mansfield, G. W.								1	1
Markum, William					1	1			2
Martin, Mary	2	2	1	1	4		4		14
McCune, Wash G.		1				1			2
McElroy, James			1						1
McHugh, Moses					1		1		2
McMurry, James	1								1
Mitchell, Willis Jr.					3			1	4
Moody, Samuel	1				1				2
Moore, Charles	1		1	1			1		4
Moorehead, John	3	2	2		1		2		10
Motley, James					1	2	3		6
Nanny, Uriah	1					1			2
Noel, Lucy					1				1
Oliver, William		2							2
Parker, Lane	4	1	3	1	4	2	3		18
Parris, R. H.	1								1
Patrick, Fitz					1	1	1		3
Pitchford, Daniel						1			1
Pitchford, Eli		1			2				3
Poolom, John					1	1			2
Poolom, William		1					1		2
Porter, David		2							2
Porter, Denton	2	1			2		1		6
Porter, Edward			1	1	1	1		1	5
Pulom, Joseph			2		2	2			6
Ray, Baxter					1				1

Slave Owner	Enslaved Males				Enslaved Females				Total
Alphabetical by Owner	*<14*	*14-26*	*26-45*	*>45*	*<14*	*14-26*	*26-45*	*>45*	
Ray, Jeremiah M.					1		1		2
Ray, Mary			1	1	1	1	1		5
Reed, Theophlus	3		1	1	3	1	1		10
Reeder, Joshua	1				2	1			4
Richey, Alex						1			1
Right, Henry		2				1			3
Right, Jarrot	2					1			3
Rion, Noah					1				1
Robertson, Leroy						1			1
Rughly, Phillip	2	2			1		1		6
Satterfield, Henry	1	1			1				3
Sears, Henry	2								2
Sears, Joseph								1	1
Shipley, Nat	1					1			2
Shipley, Robert		1							1
Simons, Isaiah						1			1
Sledge, Miles C.					1	1			2
Smith, Elizabeth	3				1		1		5
Smith, Fanny		1							1
Smith, Lum	2				2	2			6
Smith, Sarah				1	1	1	1	1	5
Stark, Daniel		2			3		1		6
Stark, James	1	4	2		4	2	2		15
Stark, Jeremiah	8	2	4	3	3	3		1	24
Stark, Jessee	3		1		5	2		1	12
Stark, Raleigh	2		1		2		1		6
Stark, Thomas	1	1				1			3
Statom, Thomas					2				2
Stovall, Thomas					1	1			2
Thomas, Walter	2	3	1		1		1	1	9
Thompson, Balam			1		1				2
Thompson, Balam			1		1				2
Thrailkell, Thomas	2	1			2	1			6
Trail, Elizabeth	1					2			3
Travers, Charly								1	1
Travis, John			1						1
Vant, Fielding	2	3			2		2		9
Wadle, Charles						1			1
Waggoner, George					1				1

Slave Owner	Enslaved Males				Enslaved Females				Total
Alphabetical by Owner	*<14*	*14-26*	*26-45*	*>45*	*<14*	*14-26*	*26-45*	*>45*	
Walker, David	1				2	1	1		5
Walker, William	1					1			2
Whitney, Ann	4	2	2						8
Whitney, Jeremiah	2				1	1			4
Whitney, John		1				1			2
Whitney, Thomas					1				1
Williams, Henry		1	1						2
Williams, Langston		1							1
Williams, Mastin	2	2	1	1		1	1		8
Williams, Richard			1						1
Williams, Solomon	2		1		1				4
Williiams, Ralph	2				1		1		4
Willouby, Samuel	1	1			1				3
Willouby, Solomon	1	1			1	1	1		5
Wills, John			1						1
Witherspoon, Hardy		1							1
TOTAL	150	87	62	19	170	106	74	20	688

Chapter 3

Slaves in Allen County in 1830

1830 Census

The second official enumeration of slaves after Allen County was formed in 1815 was the US census of 1830. It revealed that over the prior decade the number of slaves had increased by 167 to a total of 864. The number of households that owned slaves increased to 198, an increase of 23 (7 percent) since the last census.

The ages in the 1830 through 1860 censuses were divided into six divisions to permit comparisons of the data. Figure 7 shows the comparison of the numbers of male and female slaves by age group for 1830.

Figure 7

Allen County slaves by gender and age group in 1830

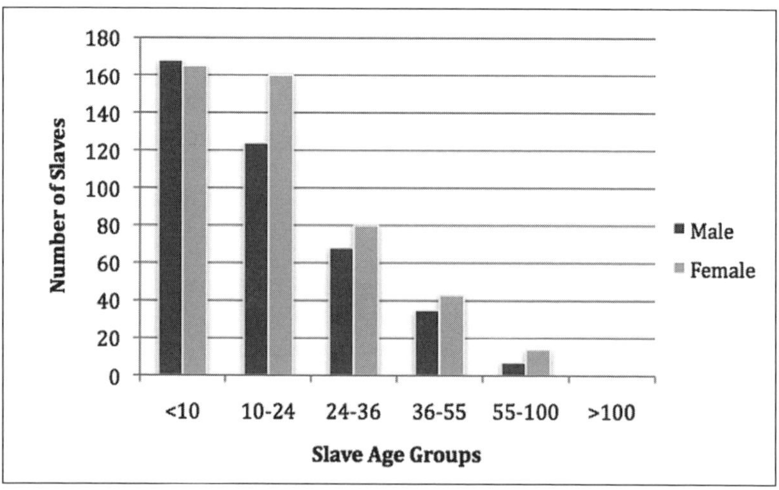

Of particular interest is that the numbers were practically equal in the under-ten-years-old group in Figure 7, just as one would expect to result from normal birth distribution by gender. The patterns for each of the other age groups reflect the significantly greater numbers of females. That was consistent with the 1820 data.

The over-55 age group in 1830 had seven males and fourteen females. That represents a loss of thirteen men and six women from the 1820 over-45 group, men and women who would have been over 55 in this census. That loss was consistent with the shorter life expectancy of slaves than that found with whites. In particular, there was even a shorter life expectancy of male slaves, thought to be the result of the more strenuous and dangerous work that they were required to do. The loss also may indicate that some older slaves had been sold while few, if any, were being purchased.

The higher numbers of females persisted in households owning fewer than six slaves (Figure 8).

Figure 8

Gender of Allen County slaves in households with fewer than 6 slaves in 1830

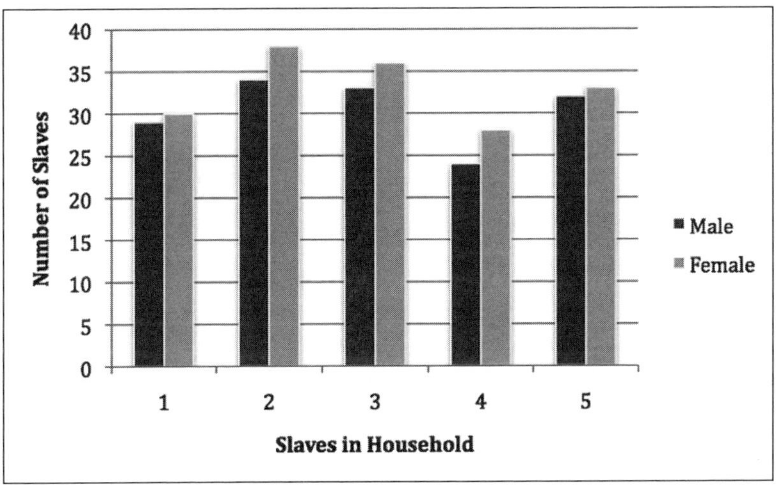

The number of slaves in households (Figure 8) with one to five slaves seemed to have a normal male-female mix.

An examination of the age distribution among the males and females compared to the number of slaves in a household is shown in Table 11.

Table 11

Gender disparity by age groups among slave owner households in 1830

	Males by Age Cohort					Females by Age Cohort					
Slaves in Household	***<10***	***10-24***	***24-36***	***36-55***	***55-100***	***<10***	***10-24***	***24-36***	***36-55***	***55-100***	***Total Slaves***
1	6	8	7	6	2	7	15	6	1	1	59
2	10	9	11	3	1	10	20	6	1	1	72
3	14	12	4	3	0	11	14	7	4	0	69
4	14	7	1	2	0	10	10	4	3	1	52
5	14	14	4	0	0	8	13	6	6	0	65
6-10	52	34	17	7	0	54	36	25	15	6	246
11-25	58	40	24	14	4	65	52	26	13	5	301
TOTAL	168	124	68	35	7	165	160	80	43	14	864

Households with only one slave revealed that their numbers of males and females were about equal overall. Within those data, there were more women in the 10-24 year group. The same was true within the households having two slaves.

Figure 9

Gender disparity in households with 6 to 10 slaves

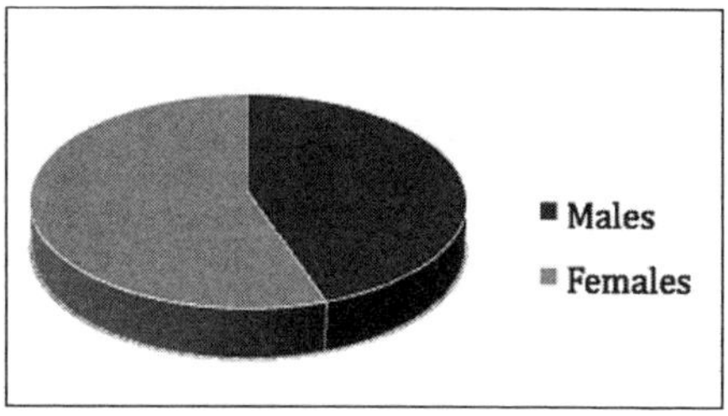

The larger numbers of slaves in a household had a different distribution. In the six to ten age group the females outnumbered the males by 136 to 110. Figure 9 illustrates that disparity.

The households with the largest number of slaves had 140 males and only 96 females (Figure 10), the opposite of the distribution found in households with smaller numbers. One could assume that the size of the agricultural activity was the determining factor although data are not available to confirm that.

Figure 10

Gender disparity in households with more than 10 slaves

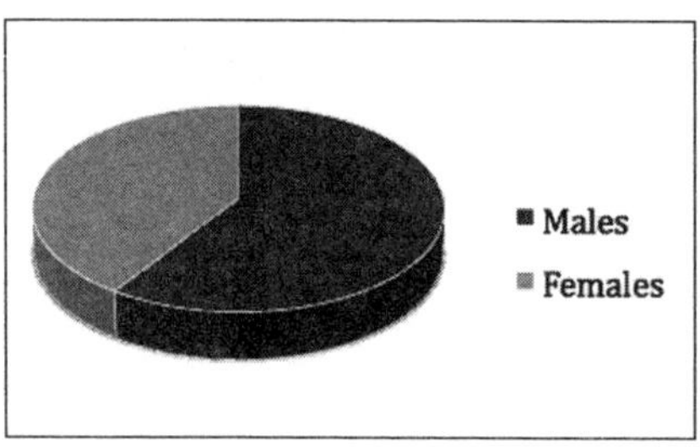

In any case, the disparity is evidence that slave families were not being preserved but were being separated to fill the demands for labor.

The data in the alphabetized list of slave owners in Table 12 were derived from the images of the 1830 slave census available from Ancestry.com.

Table 12

Allen County Slaves in 1830

Slave Owner	**Enslaved Males**						**Enslaved Females**						
Alphabetical Order	*<10*	*10-24*	*24-36*	*36-55*	*55-100*	*>100*	*<10*	*10-24*	*24-36*	*36-55*	*55-100*	*>100*	*Total*
Anderson, Samuel		1											1
Anthony, Elizabeth	1						1	1		1			4
Anthony, George		1											1
Anthony, Joseph	2	2					2	2		1			9
Bailey, Benjamin	1						1		1				3
Barlow, James		1						1					2
Barnhart, Susannah			1										1
Beheler, Jacob			1										1
Berton, Cuthbert	1						1		1				3
Blackburn, James									1				1
Boucher, Peter								1					1
Brinson, Stout		2	1					2		1			6
Brown, Henry		1						2					3
Brown, Hugh	1							1		1			3
Brown, James		1	1						1				3
Brown, Wiley	1												1
Burrows, Joseph		1											1
Burrows, Rachel	2							1	1				4
Burton, Drury Sr.			2										2
Bush, Isaac		1							1				2
Bush, Josiah	1	1					1	1					4
Bustor, John	2							1					3
Cambell, S. A.		1		1			1			1			4
Carpenter, Samuel E.	1	4	1	1			4	2	1	1			15
Caruth, John								2					2
Caruth, Mark							1						1
Caruth, Nancy	1						1						2
Caruth, Thomas	1						1		1				3

Slave Owner	Enslaved Males						Enslaved Females						
Alphabetical Order	*<10*	*10-24*	*24-36*	*36-55*	*55-100*	*>100*	*<10*	*10-24*	*24-36*	*36-55*	*55-100*	*>100*	*Total*
Chart, John Jr.	2	1		1			2	5		1	1		13
Cockrell, J. L.		1					4	1	2	1			9
Colbert, Mrs. Margaret									1				1
Coleman, William			1										1
Collins, Henry		1											1
Cowden, James W.	1	1	1				1	1	1				6
Cushenberry, D.		1											1
Cushenberry, Mary	1		1				2	1	1				6
Davis, John							1						1
Dawson, Anah	3	3	1				1	3	1				12
Deering, William								1					1
Denson, T. F. W.	2			1			2	1		1			7
Deverma, John C.					1						1		2
Doors, James		1					1		1				3
Dotson, Charles	1												1
Dotson, Dillingham			1										1
Downing, Benjamin	1		1				3		1	1			7
Drye, Jacob	7	3						1	1				12
Dunn, T. A.	2	4	1				2	2	1				12
Dye, Isaac				2									2
Dye, James									1				1
Edwards, W.			1						1				2
Emberson, John			1					1					2
Enlow, Enoch	1						1	1					3
Fant, John S.	2	4						3		1			10
Finney, Henry			2							1			3
Finney, John			1										1
Fishback, John	3		4				2	2	2				13
Fishburn, Peter	1	2						2					5
Fitzpatrick, P. W.								1					1
Fitzpatrick, William	1	2					4		2	1			10
Foster, Mary	2		1	2	2		3	3	2	1	1		17
Foster, Sarah							3	2	1				6
Foster, William	1	1						1					3
Gaines, John								1					1
Garrison, Kiah				1									1
Gibson, William		2							1				3
Godley, Elizabeth	3	2	2				5	4	2				18
Godley, Jesse	1	3					4	5					13

Slave Owner	**Enslaved Males**						**Enslaved Females**						
Alphabetical Order	*<10*	*10-24*	*24-36*	*36-55*	*55-100*	*>100*	*<10*	*10-24*	*24-36*	*36-55*	*55-100*	*>100*	*Total*
Graham, Ellis									1				1
Graham, Green	2						1	1					4
Guines, W.	2												2
Haines, Christopher				1									1
Hanes, Samuel							1						1
Harriss, David	2			1			1			1	1		6
Heeter, George			1					1					2
Herrin, George	6	1		1			2	3					13
Hickman, Jesse L.								1					1
Hinton, Moore	3						4	1	3	1			12
Holder, W.	4	2					4	3	1		1		15
Holland, Major		1		1				1		1			4
Hood, Bryant	3	2	4	1			3	4	1	2			20
Hopson, Z.	2	3					4	2					11
Horn, Thomas		2					1						3
Houser, Warner		1					1		1				3
Hughes, Elizabeth	1	1					1	1	1				5
Hunt, John									1				1
Hunt, William C.	1	1											2
Jackson, Benjamin								1					1
Johnson, Henry			1										1
Johnson, John	2	1							1				4
Johnson, M.	1	1					1	1		1			5
Kelly, John	1						1	1					3
Kelly, Miles	1	2						2					5
Landers, Isaac	2												2
Landers, William	1						1	2					4
Lee, Isaac			1	1			2	2	1				7
Logan, Robert A.		1											1
Logan, Young		1											1
Long, Barton								1		1			2
Lynn, John	1		2					1		1			5
Mannion, Able	1												1
Mannon, Ambrose	1	2	1							1			5
Mayhew, R. T.								1					1
McClary, R.	2	2					1	1	1				7
McElroy, James Sr.					1								1
McFarland, Jonathan							1	1					2
Meridith, A.								1					1

Slaveowner	Enslaved Males						Enslaved Females						
Alphabetical Order	*<10*	*10-24*	*24-36*	*36-55*	*55-100*	*>100*	*<10*	*10-24*	*24-36*	*36-55*	*55-100*	*>100*	*Total*
Meridith, T. W.								1					1
Milligan, James			1				1		1		1		4
Mitchell, Hry E.		1											1
Mitchell, Thomas							1	1					2
Mitchell, Willis		1	1				1	3			1		7
Moody, Nancy		1						1					2
Morehead, Hugh	2	1						1		1			5
Motley, James	2	1					2	1	2	1			9
Motley, John				1									1
Motley, Matthew				1									1
Motley, Thomas							1		1				2
Murray, James M.	2	4	1					3					10
Nerney, Uriah	1												1
Noel, Lucy									1				1
O'Banion, George	1							1		1			3
Oliver, Price							1						1
Oliver, S. W.				1				1		1			3
Oliver, William Sr.				2			1						3
Oxford, Samuel	2	1						1	1				5
Parish, Jefferson								1					1
Pinson, Josiah	1												1
Pitchford, Eli Sr.	1	1					1	1					4
Poe, Benjamin			1						1				2
Poe, William	1	1						1					3
Porter, D. S.	3	3					4	1	1				12
Porter, David A.	1		1					1					3
Porter, Edward	2		1	1			2	1	1				8
Porter, P. D.	1							1					2
Proctor, Nathaniel								1					1
Pruit, Abraham								1					1
Pulliam, Henry	2												2
Pulliam, John	2						2		1		1		6
Pulliam, Joseph	1		3				3	2	2	1			12
Pulliam, Robert F.	2						1		1				4
Pulliam, William	1	1	1				2	2	1	1			9
Raleigh, Philip	1	1	1				1	2	1	1			8
Ray, Baxter							1	1					2
Ray, Jerimiah R.	1							2	1	1			5
Ray, William					1								1

Slave Owner	Enslaved Males						Enslaved Females						
Alphabetical Order	*<10*	*10-24*	*24-36*	*36-55*	*55-100*	*>100*	*<10*	*10-24*	*24-36*	*36-55*	*55-100*	*>100*	*Total*
Read, George D.							1						1
Read, Peggy	1	3		1	1		4		1	2			13
Read, Richard C.							1						1
Rhea, Charles	2	3						1	1				7
Rhodes, James							1						1
Right, Janett	3	1		1			1		1				7
Rose, John C.								1					1
Sear, Joseph	1												1
Sears, Francis	3	1		2			2	4	3		1		16
Sears, Henry	2	2					2	1					7
Sears, William	3		2				2	1					8
Short, Lamond										1			1
Showell, Rolley				1					1				2
Siddens, J. S.								1					1
Siddens, W.	1		1				2	1					5
Smith, Samuel	2	2					2	1					7
Smith, Sarah	1						1	1	1	1	1		6
Snow, John							2	1					3
Spillman, Levi			1				1						2
Stark, Sarah	1	2	1	1			5	1		1			12
Stark, James	4	3	4	1	1		2	3	3	3	1		25
Stephens, Thomas			1										1
Stovall, George							1		1				2
Stovall, Nancy	1						2	1	1				5
Strait, William											1		1
Stubblefield, Robert	1	1					2	1		1			6
Thomas, Isham							1	1					2
Thomas, William	3		2	3			5	1	1				15
Thompson, Baylem			1					1					2
Travis, Susannah			1					1					2
Waggener, Mrs. M.		1					1						2
Waggoner, Ephriam								1					1
Waggoner, George	1						2	1					4
Walker, Jacob W.			1					1					2
Walker, Mrs. P.	1		1				3	1	1	1			8
Walker, William Jr.	2	1					2		1				6
Wayan, Willis H.		1						1					2
Weaver, Joel	1	1						1					3
Weaver, William	1	1						1					3
Whitney, J. G.	1	2						1					4

Slave Owner	**Enslaved Males**						**Enslaved Females**						
Alphabetical Order	*<10*	*10-24*	*24-36*	*36-55*	*55-100*	*>100*	*<10*	*10-24*	*24-36*	*36-55*	*55-100*	*>100*	*Total*
Whitney, John	3		1	1			1		1				7
Whitney, Mary	2		2					1	1				6
Whitney, Uriah	2	1	1				2		1		2		9
Wickwire, Samuel		1					2		2				5
Willaby, Samuel		1	1										2
Williams, Henry							1	1					2
Williams, James P.	1	3								1			5
Williams, Langston				1									1
Williams, Mastin	4	1		1			1		1	1			9
Williams, R.		2											2
Willmott, Richard				1									1
Witherspoon, Hardy	1							1					2
Withot, R.R.								2					2
TOTAL	168	124	68	35	7		165	160	80	43	14		864

Chapter 4

Slaves in Allen County in 1840

1840 Census

The third official enumeration of slaves after Allen County was formed in 1815 was the US census of 1840. It revealed that over the prior decade the number of slaves had increased to a total of 936. The number of households that owned slaves increased to 238, an increase of 40 during that period.

The numbers and the near equality of male and females in the 10-24 year old group appears to be a residual from the under ten group in 1830. It seems likely that the 1833 ban on the importation of slaves into Kentucky produced that effect. The numbers appear as if there were no imports or exports of slaves in that age cohort (Figure 11). The strong abolitionist movement had lobbied for that ban and it certainly constrained slave trading. Given those constraints, one would expect the male-to-female ratio to be about equal, as it was, if births had been the only source for new slaves.

Figure 11

Allen County slaves by gender and age groups in 1840

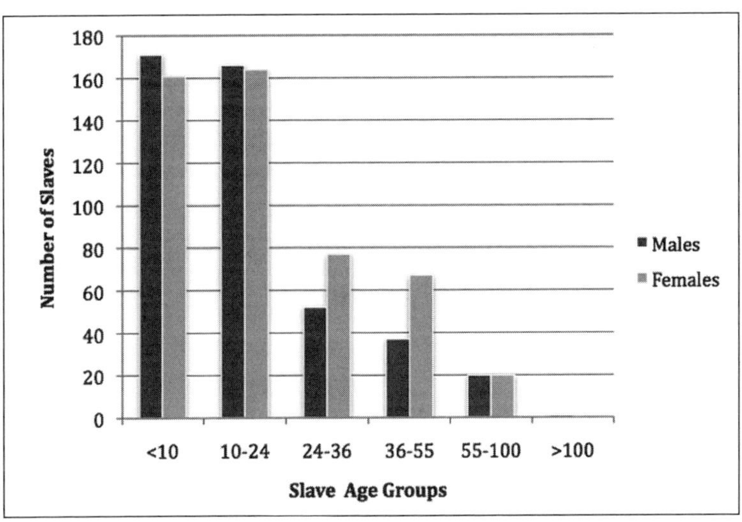

The under 10 years group mimicked the numbers in the 10-24 age group. That provides further support for the conclusion that their births had occurred locally during most of the decade.

The over-24 age groups preserve the attribute of having higher numbers of females than males that were seen in the 1830 data. The numbers in each of those cohorts had increased, an evidence of the aging of the slave population. Older slaves were not as easily marketed as the younger ones.

In 1830, the number of slaves in a household had little effect on the gender of those slaves. Gender numbers were about equal in all households with fewer than six slaves. However, in the 1840 census, in households with either two or three slaves (Figure 12), there were almost six percent more females as males in them. The reason for this inconsistency is not apparent.

Figure 12

Gender distribution of slaves in households with fewer than six slaves in 1840

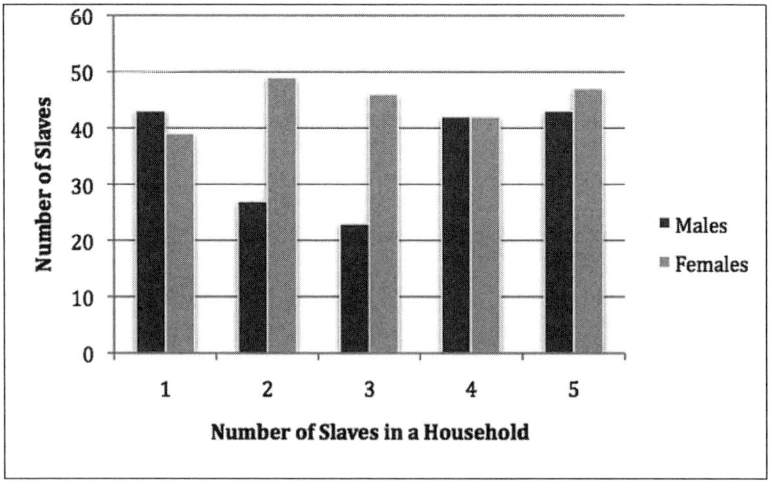

Gender distribution by age cohort was calculated for 1840 and is presented in Table 13.

Table 13

Gender disparity by age group among slave owner households in 1840

Males by Age Cohort							Females by Age Cohort						
Slaves in Household	*<10*	*10-24*	*24-36*	*36-55*	*55-100*	*>100*	*<10*	*10-24*	*24-36*	*36-55*	*55-100*	*>100*	*Total Slaves*
1	9	18	6	8	1	1	5	20	4	5	5		82
2	13	8	2	1	3		11	23	8	5	2		76
3	6	10	3	2	2		20	15	7	3	1		69
4	19	17	2	3	1		12	13	8	9	0		84
5	18	17	4	3	1		15	18	5	7	2		90
6-10	62	51	11	10	7		54	45	23	25	3		291
11-25	44	45	24	10	5		44	30	22	13	7		244
TOTAL	171	166	52	37	20	1	161	164	77	67	20		936

Just 4 percent of the slave population in Allen County in 1840 were older than 55. There were equal numbers of males and females within that group. The slave population was aging but had not yet passed 55 years in large numbers. For comparison, in the year 2000, 21 percent of Americans were 55 or older.

Overall, there were more females than males in the 1840 households with fewer than ten slaves (Figure 13).

Figure 13

Gender disparity of slaves in households with fewer than ten slaves in 1840

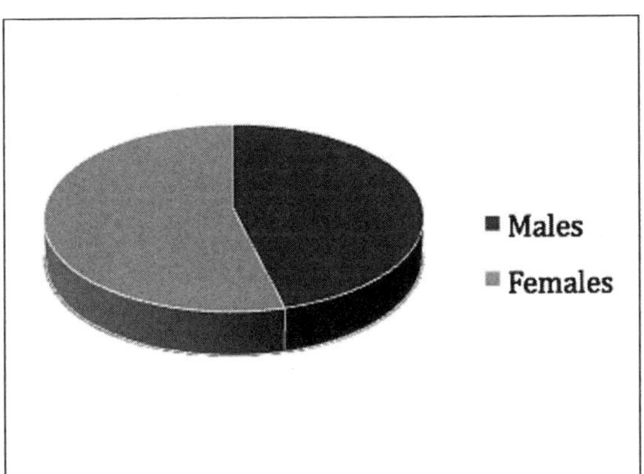

In households that owned more than ten slaves, the number of males exceeded the number of females (Figure 14).

Figure 14

Gender disparity of slaves in households with more than ten slaves in 1840

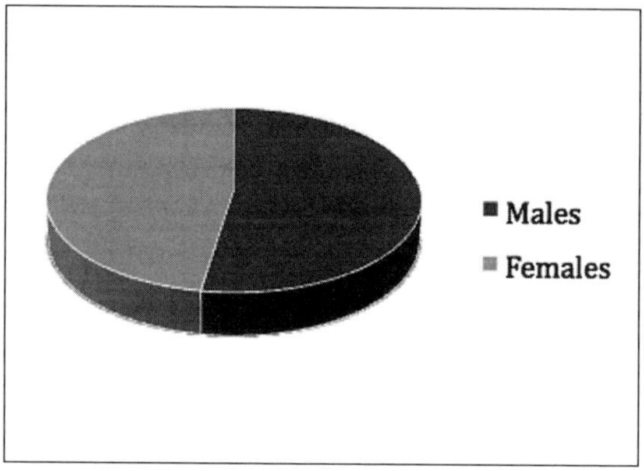

In 1840, most slaves who were sold remained in the local area.[1] Even so, the slaves were traded away from their families. Figures 13 and 14 show that families had to have been separated by sales or other actions that resulted in dislocations. Otherwise, the inequality in gender shown in the graphs would not have been produced.

The slave data shown in Table 14 were derived from the images of original census records taken in 1840 and available through Ancestry.com.

[1] Lucas, Marion B., 1992. *A history of Blacks in Kentucky*. Kentucky Historical Society, Frankfort, Kentucky

Table 14

Allen County Slaves in 1840

Slave Owner	Enslaved Males						Enslaved Females						
Alphabetical Order	*<10*	*10-24*	*24-36*	*36-55*	*55-100*	*>100*	*<10*	*10-24*	*24-36*	*36-55*	*55-100*	*>100*	*Total*
Alexander, Anzi C.									1				1
Allen, Lee	1	1						3		1			6
Allen, Luke P.	1	1					1	1					4
Anderson, James		2						1					3
Anderson, Samuel	1								1				2
Anthony, Elizabeth	1			1			1	1			1		5
Anthony, George	3	1							1				5
Anthony, Henry S.		1						2					3
Anthony, Joseph		1	2				1	2		1			7
Aspley, Sam							1						1
Austin, Willis		1						2					3
Barlow, Joseph H.	2	2	1				2		1				8
Barnes, Joseph	1						1	1					3
Beard, Davis		1	1					1					3
Beheler, Jacob				1									1
Benedict, Ben		1											1
Berry, Eph.								1					1
Berry, John A.	1												1
Blackburn, James										1			1
Boren, James								1					1
Boren, Varleton								1					1
Boucher, Peter										1			1
Bridges, Samuel		1											1
Bright, George			3					2					5

Slave Owner	**Enslaved Males**						**Enslaved Females**						
Alphabetical Order	*<10*	*10-24*	*24-36*	*36-55*	*55-100*	*>100*	*<10*	*10-24*	*24-36*	*36-55*	*55-100*	*>100*	*Total*
Bright, Mary		1											1
Brown, Alsey							1						1
Brown, Burton								1					1
Brown, Henry							1		1				2
Brunson, Johnathan			1										1
Burnes, Rachel		1						1					2
Burton, Byrd	2	1						1		1			5
Burton, Caleb		1					1			1			3
Burton, Mary				1									1
Burton, Thomas S.	1		1					2					4
Bustor, John	1	2							1				4
Carpenter, F. A.				2	1		1	1		1			6
Carpenter, Samuel E.	1	2	3	1			2	4	1	2			16
Carruth, H. C.								1		1			2
Carruth, John		2					4	2					8
Carruth, Thomas		1		1				1		1			4
Carter, Joseph	1							1					2
Caruth, Mark		1						1					2
Chapman, James	1												1
Clark, John					1			3		1			5
Cobb, Lebbrus							2			1			3
Cockerville, Johnson J.		1		1			2	1	1				6
Colbert, John	1	3			1			2		1			8
Colbert, Robert W.										1			1
Collins, Henry			1										1
Cowden, Lucy	2		1				2	1					6

Slave Owner	Enslaved Males						Enslaved Females						
Alphabetical Order	*<10*	*10-24*	*24-36*	*36-55*	*55-100*	*>100*	*<10*	*10-24*	*24-36*	*36-55*	*55-100*	*>100*	*Total*
Cusenberry, Harrison			2		1			2		2			7
Cusenbery, Daniel								1					1
Davis, Johnathan	3	2	1		1		2	1	2				12
Devasher, Daniel		1					1		1				3
Devasher, Elizabeth									1				1
Devasher, John H.								1					1
Dodson, Assenth		1											1
Downing, Ben		2	1	1			4	2	1		1		12
Drane, Anthony								1					1
Dry, Jacob	2	5	1				1	1		1			11
Dunn, Margaret	1	1					3	1					6
During, William									1				1
Dye, Carroll								1					1
Dye, James		2						1		1			4
Edmonds, Samuel								1					1
Evans, James B.	1						1	1					3
Evans, W. F.	2						1		1				4
Fikes, Malachi								1					1
Finney, Henry					1						1		2
Fishback, John	2	1	1	4			3	1	1				13
Fitzpatrick, William	2	1	2				1	3	1		1		11
Follis, George	1	1											2
Ford, Richard S.	1		1						1	1			4
Foster, George B.			1				1						2
Foster, Price								2					2

Slave Owner	Enslaved Males						Enslaved Females						
Alphabetical Order	*<10*	*10-24*	*24-36*	*36-55*	*55-100*	*>100*	*<10*	*10-24*	*24-36*	*36-55*	*55-100*	*>100*	*Total*
Foster, R. J.								2					2
Gaines, John T.											1		1
Garrison, Eli D.							2			1			3
Gibson, Elizabeth		1											1
Gibson, Randolph							1	1					2
Gilliam, James							1						1
Godley, Elizabeth	2	2					1			1			6
Godley, Jesse S.	2	1	2				3	2	2	1			13
Griggs, A.		1						1					2
Griggs, W. M.							1			1			2
Guy, William		1											1
Haines, Chris				1									1
Haines, John				1									1
Haines, Sam	1												1
Halter, Asa								1					1
Hamet, James				1									1
Hamet, William	1												1
Hand, Riley	1							1					2
Hannah, William							1	1					2
Harris, Amos	1										1		2
Harris, David	2	1			1		1	1		1			7
Harston, William		1											1
Harvey, A. A.		1											1
Harvey, Charles F.										1			1
Hector, Frederick	4						2	1	1				8

Slave Owner	**Enslaved Males**						**Enslaved Females**						
Alphabetical Order	*<10*	*10-24*	*24-36*	*36-55*	*55-100*	*>100*	*<10*	*10-24*	*24-36*	*36-55*	*55-100*	*>100*	*Total*
Hector, George T.			1						1				2
Hector, James W.	2						2		1				5
Herrell, Raby		4								1			5
Hickman, Jesse L.	2						2		1				5
Hinton, John							1	1					2
Hinton, Temperance		5						1		1	1		8
Holder, Edward	6	1	3				6	2	3	1			22
Holder, John	1						1		1				3
Hollaway, Henry M.	1						2	1	1				5
Horn, Thomas		1					1	1		1			4
Hughes, Elizabeth	1						3		2				6
Hughes, John P.								2					2
Hughes, Thompson	1												1
Hunt, James			1										1
Hurston, Thomas		2		1				1		1			5
Jackson, Ben		1											1
Jenkins, Daniel K.	1	2					1	1					5
Johnson, Matthew	1	2						1	1	1			6
Lane, Samuel		1						1					2
Lang, Rob M.	1	1	2				2	1	1	1			9
Lee, Isaac	1	1		2			2	1	2	1			10
Lindsey, Rachel	1						1						2
Linn, John	2			2			1		1				6
Loafman, Ed											1		1
Lodge, Thomas J.		1											1
Logan, Young		1											1

Slave Owner	Enslaved Males						Enslaved Females						
Alphabetical Order	*<10*	*10-24*	*24-36*	*36-55*	*55-100*	*>100*	*<10*	*10-24*	*24-36*	*36-55*	*55-100*	*>100*	*Total*
Lynch, Frederick C.										1			1
Mansfield, G. W.			1				1	1	1		1		5
Mansfield, William		1											1
Marrions, Pheriba	2	3					1			1			7
Marshall, John C.	1												1
Martin, James W.	1							1			1		3
Mayhew, Lucas	1						1	1		1			4
Mayhew, Woodford	1												1
McElroy, William B.					1					1			2
McReynolds, Robert	1							1					2
Meredith, T. A.					1			1					2
Mitchell, H. S.			1										1
Mitchell, Willis	4		2				3	1	2				12
Morehead, Raleigh	1	1			1			1					4
Morehead, Thomas J.		1					1	1					3
Motley, Francis		1					1						2
Motley, Henry		1											1
Motley, James	1								1				2
Motley, John			1										1
Motley, Matthew								1					1
Motley, Pattey		2		1	1		1	1	2				8
Motley, Thomas	2							1	2	1			6
Motley, Zack	1						1	2					4
Mulligan, James C.	2	1					2	1	2				8
Oliver, William				2				1					3

Slave Owner	Enslaved Males						Enslaved Females						
Alphabetical Order	*<10*	*10-24*	*24-36*	*36-55*	*55-100*	*>100*	*<10*	*10-24*	*24-36*	*36-55*	*55-100*	*>100*	*Total*
Oxford, Samuel		3								1			4
Paris, Robert H.							1		1				2
Parker, Ed	4	2		1	1			1		1	1		11
Pitchford, Orange D.							2	1					3
Poe, William Sr.	4	1					1		1				7
Pope, N. K.			1										1
Porter, David A.	1			1			1		1				4
Porter, Denson, S.	2	1					1	1		1			6
Porter, Uriah		3						1					4
Porter, William R.	1							1					2
Pulliam, Ben	1								1				2
Pulliam, Henry	1							1					2
Pulliam, William	4	5					3		1	1	1		15
Pullium, Joseph	1	1		1				1		1			5
Pullium, Robert	2	1						1					4
Read, Charles D.	2			1			1	1	1				6
Read, Francis A.								1					1
Read, George D.								1					1
Read, Samuel J.	2	2			1		2	3			1		11
Richards, William							1						1
Rinnick, Payton	1	1							1				3
Ritchey, Alex										2			2
Ritchey, Solomon L.									1				1
Roberson, Jordan	3	2					1			1			7
Sanders, Hez	1												1
Sanders, Isaac	2	1					3	2	1	1			10
Sears, Austin		1	1				3	1					6

Slave Owner	Enslaved Males						Enslaved Females						
Alphabetical Order	*<10*	*10-24*	*24-36*	*36-55*	*55-100*	*>100*	*<10*	*10-24*	*24-36*	*36-55*	*55-100*	*>100*	*Total*
Sears, Henry	2	2					4	2					10
Sears, Samuel	1	6	1				5		2				15
Sears, William	3	1		1			1	1	1				8
Seay, Joseph R.							1	2					3
Shickels, Samuel			1				1	1					3
Shields, Elijah											1		1
Siddens, James S.	1			1			1			1			4
Smith, Sarah	2	1						1		1	1		6
Spillman, James H.								1					1
Stark, Festus		2						2		1			5
Stark, James	8	6	5	2	1		6	3	6	5	1		43
Stark, Lucy	1						1	1		1			4
Stark, Sarah		2	1		1		1	2	1	1			9
Staton, Joseph								1					1
Stinson, Lovie				1									1
Stoval, Nancy	3	1						2		1			7
Stovall, Daniel		1											1
Stovall, George		2					1		1				4
Stovall, James	1								1				2
Strait, William						1							1
Strait, David								1					1
Stubblefield, Sarah	4	1						1		1			7
Sulser, Hardin		2					2	1					5
Swearingen, Lemuel							2		1				3
Thaxton, Z. B.	2						1		1				4
Thomas, Isham	2	1					1	1					5
Thomas, Walter		5	1	1	1		1	3		1			13

Slave Owner	**Enslaved Males**						**Enslaved Females**						
Alphabetical Order	*<10*	*10-24*	*24-36*	*36-55*	*55-100*	*>100*	*<10*	*10-24*	*24-36*	*36-55*	*55-100*	*>100*	*Total*
Thompson, Sarah	1		1						1				3
Tinsley, Elijah	1												1
Trant, Francis	2	1					2		1		1		7
Venable, Joseph		1			1		1						3
Waggoner, Edward							1		1				2
Waggoner, George	1	1					3	2	1				8
Waggoner, Matthew		1						1					2
Walker, A. S.		1						1					2
Walker, William		2					1	3		1			7
Weaver, John								1					1
Weaver, William		1											1
White, James	3	1						1					5
Whitney, Jeremiah	1						1						2
Whitney, John	3	3	1				1	1		1			10
Whitney, S. W.		1											1
Whitney, Uriah	3	4	1				2	3			1		14
Wilbor, W.		1											1
Wildman, Jonah											1		1
Williams, Asbury	2								1	1			4
Williams, Henry								1					1
Williams, Langston				1									1
Williams, Mary A.	1						2		1				4
Williams, Mastin	2	1			1			1		2			7
Williams, Ralph		1											1
Willoughby, Daniel				1				1					2
Wilmot, E.					1								1

Slave Owner	**Enslaved Males**						**Enslaved Females**						
Alphabetical Order	*<10*	*10-24*	*24-36*	*36-55*	*55-100*	*>100*	*<10*	*10-24*	*24-36*	*36-55*	*55-100*	*>100*	*Total*
Wilson, Ben								1					1
Wilson, George					1		1		1				3
Wishman, Elijah G.							2		1				3
Woodcock, G. B.							1						1
Wright, Elizabeth							3	1		1			5
Wright, Griffin				1									1
TOTAL	171	166	52	37	20	1	161	164	77	67	20		936

Chapter 5

Slaves in Allen County in 1850

1850 Census

The fourth official enumeration of slaves after Allen County was formed in 1815 was the US census of 1850. Kentucky's 1833 prohibition against importation of slaves into Kentucky from other states had been eradicated by its new constitution in 1849, the year before the census. It is clear that slavery in Allen County had been expanding. The census revealed that over the prior decade the number of enslaved African Americans had increased by 375 to a total of 1,312. That increase of 28.6 percent was the largest of any decade. Natural increases would have accounted for only about 2.1 percent.[1] The number of households that owned slaves increased to 278, an increase of 40 (14.4%) since the last census.

The 1850 gender disparity differed from the previous censuses in some cohorts, but overall there were still 4% more females than males (Figure 15).

Figure 15

Allen County slaves by gender and age group in 1850

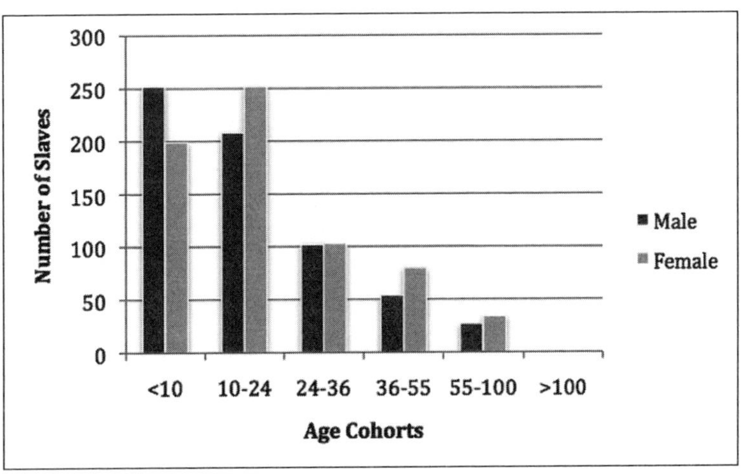

Males outnumbered females only in the under-ten age cohort. They were 59 percent of the total in that group, an 8 percent difference. The same disparity existed ten years earlier in this group although the difference then was only 4 percent.

The opposite was true with the ten to twenty-four cohort that contained 56 percent females (Figure 15). There had been equality (166 males and 161 females) ten years earlier in this group. During those ten years, 42 males and 88 females were added. Even if there were imperfections in the census data, that number represents significant purchases and importation into Allen County. During the 1850s, Kentucky sold and exported about 2,500 to 4,000 slaves per year to the states that would form the Confederacy ten years later. Slave traders were often social outcasts, avoided by all but fellow traders. To prevent runaways, traders operating near the Ohio River kept slaves shackled together in pens when not being displayed to buyers.[2] One of those pens is preserved at the National Underground Railroad Freedom Center in Cincinnati, Ohio.

The gender disparity of slaves among households persisted (Figure 16).

Figure 16

Gender distribution of slaves in a household in 1850

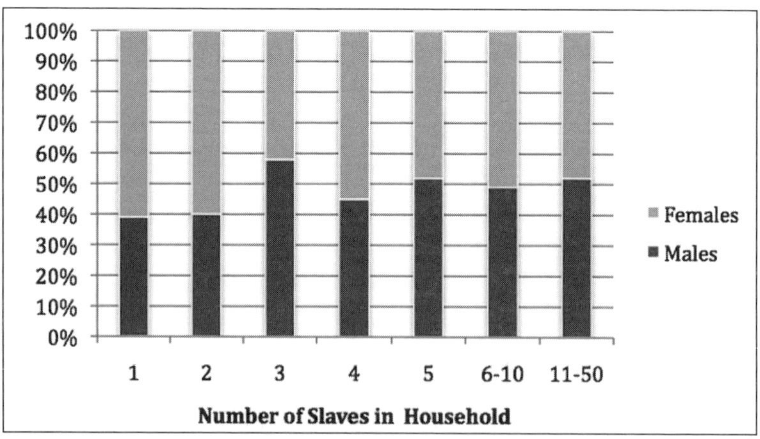

[1] McClelland, Peter D., and Richard J. Zeckhauser. 2002. Demographic dimensions of the New Republic: American interregional migration, vital statistics, and manumissions, 1800-1860 Cambridge: Cambridge University Press.

[2] Kentucky Historical Marker # 1990, located at 2nd and Main Streets in Louisville, KY

The gender disparity was particularly noticeable with those who owned four or fewer slaves. The number of females in households with one or two slaves was significantly higher than males. There were more males than females in households with three slaves. As the numbers increased, the percentage of males increased (Figure 17).

Figure 17

Gender disparity by number of slaves in a household in 1850

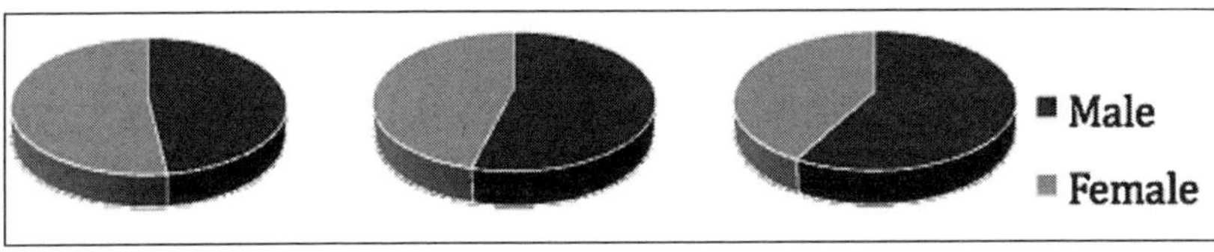

1 – 10 Slaves **11-20 Slaves** **21-50 Slaves**

The raw numbers in Table 15 show how the slave population was changing.

Table 15

Gender disparity by age cohort among slave owner households in 1850

Males by Age Cohort						**Females by Age Cohort**							
Slaves in Household	*<10*	*10-24*	*24-36*	*36-55*	*55-100*	*>100*	*<10*	*10-24*	*24-36*	*36-55*	*55-100*	*>100*	*Total Slaves*
1	3	13	5	6	1		7	23	5	8	3		74
2	9	17	6	4	4		9	30	11	7	3		100
3	23	13	4	4	3		7	15	4	7	1		81
4	24	14	8	2	2		18	27	11	5	1		112
5	25	25	9	1	1	1	21	17	9	9	2		120
6-10	77	56	27	13	3		68	57	30	21	10		362
11-50	91	70	43	24	13		69	83	33	23	14		463
TOTAL	252	208	102	54	27	1	199	252	103	80	34		1312

Only 5 percent of the slaves were older than 55 years of age, still far short of the 21% percent of our day, but an increase from 41 in 1840 to 62 individuals in this census. As in the other census years, the slave population did not have the pyramidal shape seen in stable populations.

This census recorded one slave centenarian, a rare occurrence to say the least.

The data in Table 16, and those on the alphabetized list of slave owners were derived from the transcription of the 1850 slave census made by Sharon Tabor in 2002.

Table 16

Allen County Slaves 1850

Slave Owner	**Enslaved Males**						**Enslaved Females**						
Alphabetical Order	*<10*	*10-24*	*24-36*	*36-55*	*55-100*	*>100*	*<10*	*10-24*	*24-36*	*36-55*	*55-100*	*>100*	*Total*
Ackerman, Jacob							1		1				2
Alexander, A. C.											1		1
Allen, A. P.									1				1
Anderson, Sampson	1												1
Anderson, Samuel	2									1			3
Anthony, George	1	2		1			4			1			9
Anthony, H. S.	4							1	1				6
Anthony, Joseph	2		1				2		1		1		7
Anthony, W. F. & J. J.	1	3					1	2	1				8
Arnold, W .E.								1					1
Ashford, William	1									1			2
Atwood, L. S.			1					1					2
Atwood, T .J.	2							1	1				4
Austin, William								1					1
Austin, Williamson		1											1
Austin, Willis	2	1					3	1	2	1			10
Ayers, John	1												1
Bailey, F.		1											1
Beheler, J.					1								1
Beheler, William								1					1
Benedict, Mary			1							1			2

Slave Owner	Enslaved Males						Enslaved Females						
Alphabetical Order	*<10*	*10-24*	*24-36*	*36-55*	*55-100*	*>100*	*<10*	*10-24*	*24-36*	*36-55*	*55-100*	*>100*	*Total*
Blackburn, William	3				1					1			5
Boren, James	1						1	1					3
Boucher, Peter							1						1
Bracken, Green	1							1					2
Bradley, E.		2						1		1			4
Bright, James A.	1						1	1					3
Bright, John	1						1	1					3
Brown, Alsey		1								1			2
Brown, Burton	1	1	1					1					4
Brown, H.	2	2						1	1				6
Brown, H.								2					2
Brown, J. R.	1								1				2
Brown, John H.										1			1
Brown, O.							1						1
Brown, R.								4					4
Burruss, J.		1					2		1				4
Burton, Cuthburt		3					2	1		1			7
Burton, John	1	2	1					1	1				6
Burton, Mary				2									2
Burton, Thomas	1		1	1	1		5	2	3	1	1		16
Carlock, G. W.				1				1					2
Carpenter, L.	1			1				1					3
Carpenter, Dick Free Dick											1		1
Carpenter, J. D.			1					1					2
Carpenter, James		1						1					2
Carpenter, R. D.	2		1				3		1		1		8
Carpenter, S. E.	9		2	2	1		5	2	4	1	1		27
Caruth, Mark	2	1					1		1				5
Caruth, Thomas		1						1	1		1		4
Caruth, John	2	2					3	4	2				13
Celsor, Harden				1	1					1			3
Chaney, W.	2						1						3
Chaney, W. B.							1						1
Chaney, William			2		1			1					4
Clark, Susan	1								1				2
Cockrill, J. J.	1	1	1				1	1		1			6
Colbert, Jessee	1												1
Colbert, John	6	1	3				8	1	3	1	1		24

Slave Owner	**Enslaved Males**						**Enslaved Females**						
Alphabetical Order	*<10*	*10-24*	*24-36*	*36-55*	*55-100*	*>100*	*<10*	*10-24*	*24-36*	*36-55*	*55-100*	*>100*	*Total*
Collins, H.				1									1
Cowden, J. M.	2	1					1	1					5
Crow, Joseph	1			1			4	1		1			8
Crowder, Currance		1											1
Cushenbery, Harrison	2			1			1		1	1			6
Dance, J. E.		1	1						1				3
Davis, Jonathan	6	4	2		1			4		1			18
Davis, S.		1						1					2
Davis, Wyley		2											2
Dawson, A.			1					1					2
Dering, M.		1											1
Devasier, John H.					1			1					2
Dodson, Dillingham	4			1					1				6
Downing, B.	1	1	1	1				5			1		10
Downing, W. R.								1					1
Drane, A.		1					2	3					6
Dry, Jacob	3	3	4	1			1	2			1		15
Dunn, M.	2	1	1	1			2	3		1			11
Dyer, Elizabeth										1			1
Edmunds, R. W.	2							1		1			4
Ellis, R. T.								1					1
Eubanks, Carson								1					1
Evans, J. B.	1		1							1			3
Evans, S. K.								2					2
Evans, W. F.									1				1
Fant, F.	2		1				1	2		1	1		8
Finney, Henry					1						1		2
Fishback, James	1						1	2					4
Fisher, Thomas	1						1						2
Fitzpatrick, William	1	1	1	2			2	1		1	1		10
Follis, G.	2	1						1					4
Follis, R. S.		1						1					2
Ford, A. M.		1					1	1					3
Foster, B. A.	2							1					3
Foster, Price	2						1		1				4
Foster, R. J.	1	2	1	2	1		5	4	1				17
Foster, William	4	3	2				1	3	2				15

Slave Owner	Enslaved Males						Enslaved Females						
Alphabetical Order	*<10*	*10-24*	*24-36*	*36-55*	*55-100*	*>100*	*<10*	*10-24*	*24-36*	*36-55*	*55-100*	*>100*	*Total*
Frances, J. A.		1						2	2				5
Franklin, S. H.		1						1					2
Gaines, B. J.	1	1					1	1	1				5
Garrison, A. W.		4		1				1					6
Garrison, Eli D.		1								1			2
Gatewood, F.	1						2	1					4
Gipson, D.				1									1
Gipson, Randolph		1					1	2					4
Gocer, B. W.								1					1
Godley, John		1						1		1			3
Godly, J. S.	5	3		2			1	3	1	2			17
Goodnight, Isaac	2	1					1			1			5
Greer, J. J.		1											1
Griggs, A.		2	1										3
Guy, William			1										1
Hagar, J. J.		1						1					2
Hammett, James M.										1			1
Hammond, J. E.		1											1
Harrell, Raba			4							1			5
Harris, A.	1	1	1					1			1		5
Harris, J. F.					1						1		2
Harris, S. W.	1	1							1				3
Harston, Samuel			1							1			2
Harston, Thomas	3	2					1	2	1				9
Harston, William	2	1					2		1				6
Harvey, A. A.	1		1				1		1				4
Harvey, C. F.	2							1					3
Harvey, F. G.								1					1
Haynes, Tillitha	1				1						1		3
Heeter, C. Baston			1	1				2					4
Heeter, J. W.							1	1					2
Henderson, J. W.	1	2					1	1					5
Henderson, Sarah	1	1					1		1				4
Hickman, M. A.		2						1		1			4
Hinton, John								1					1
Holder, Edward	4	1	1				3	4	1	1			15
Holder, John	4	3	1	1			5	2	1	1			18
Holland, M. Y. H.								1					1

Slave Owner	Enslaved Males						Enslaved Females						
Alphabetical Order	*<10*	*10-24*	*24-36*	*36-55*	*55-100*	*>100*	*<10*	*10-24*	*24-36*	*36-55*	*55-100*	*>100*	*Total*
Holland, Mary			1										1
Horn, Thomas	1	1	2	1			3	2	1		1		12
Howel, James								1					1
Hudson, H. W.		1							1				2
Hughes, E.	3							2		1			6
Hughs, A. P.								1					1
Hughs, T. R.		1											1
Hunt, Riley	1						2		1				4
Jackson, Benjamin	1		1				2	1					5
Johnson, Henry								1					1
Johnson, M.	1	2	1				4		2		1		11
Landers, Hezakiah		1											1
Landers, Isaac	2	1	1					3	1	1	1		10
Lee, Isaac		2			1			1	1	1			6
Logan, Robert				1									1
Long, G. P.	1		1				2	1	1				6
Long, Thomas A.									1				1
Lyles, Thomas H.	1									1			2
Manion, F.	1	2	1					1		1			6
Mansfield, G. W.										1			1
Mansfield, William		1											1
Martin, J. M.		1											1
Mayhew, R. L.	1						1	1					3
Mayhew, W.								1	1				2
McClary, J.							1						1
McClary, R.	1	1	1				2		1	1			7
McClary, Samuel		1											1
McElroy, A.	1						1						2
McElroy, William	1	2					1			1			5
McMurry, Isaac	1	1							1				3
Moor, James								1					1
Moor, Sympson	1			1	1				1				4
Moore, E. C.										1			1
Moorhead, T. J.		1					2		1				4
Morrison, F. J.	1	2						1		1			5
Motley, J. T.		1						1					2
Motley, John				1									1

Slave Owner	Enslaved Males						Enslaved Females						
Alphabetical Order	*<10*	*10-24*	*24-36*	*36-55*	*55-100*	*>100*	*<10*	*10-24*	*24-36*	*36-55*	*55-100*	*>100*	*Total*
Motley, Matthew								1					1
Motley, Patsy	2	1			1		2	3		3			12
Motley, Zachariah	1	1	2				1	1					6
Motley, Lynn			1										1
Motley, Thomas		3	1	1	1			1	1	1			9
Mulligan, G. M.		1						1					2
Mulligan, J. C.	4	3					2	2		2			13
Napier, Thomas	1	1								1			3
Neal, B. F.				1					1				2
Neal, Berryman	1							1					2
Neal, E. P.		1	1					1					3
Neal, William		1											1
Oliver, William					1				1				2
Orr, William								1	1				2
Page, John	6	6	3	4	1		3	7	4	2			36
Paris, R. G.	2						1	1					4
Paris, R. H.	2	1		1			1	1	1		1		8
Parish, Elizabeth							2						2
Pettie, J. W.								1					1
Pettie, James		1						3		1			5
Pettie, M. M.							1	1					2
Pinson, James	1	1					1	1					4
Poe, William	3	2						1					6
Pope, N. K.		1		1				1					3
Porter, Denton S.		1	2					1			1		5
Porter, P. W.			1										1
Porter, Uriah	4	6	2	1	1		1	2					17
Pruit, Elijah								2					2
Pulliam, B.	1	1	1							1			4
Pulliam, H. C.	2	2					3	1	1				9
Pulliam, J. B.	2	1					1	1					5
Pulliam, R. F.	3	1	2				1	3					10
Pulliam, William	2		3				1	1		2	1		10
Read, E. D. F.	1		1				4	1	1				8
Read, F. A.											1		1
Read, Samuel J.		3					1		1				5
Richey, Soloman							4	1	1				6
Richey, W. C.	1								1				2
Richey, William	2	1					1	1					5

Slave Owner	Enslaved Males						Enslaved Females						
Alphabetical Order	*<10*	*10-24*	*24-36*	*36-55*	*55-100*	*>100*	*<10*	*10-24*	*24-36*	*36-55*	*55-100*	*>100*	*Total*
Robe, T. F.										1			1
Russell, Gregory								1	1				2
Sarver, Wyat							1						1
Sears, Albert		1						1					2
Sears, Austin				1									1
Sears, F. A.								1					1
Sears, Jr. Henry	2							1					3
Sears, Samuel	2	2	3				1	4		2			14
Sears, Sr. H.	3	1	1					4	1	1	1		12
Sears, William		2	1				1	1		1			6
Settle, Thomas J.		1									1		2
Sey, Joseph R.	1						1	1	2				5
Shultz, Juliet A.										1			1
Smith, H. T.									1				1
Smith, H. T.	1						2	1					4
Smith, Sanford								1		1			2
Spencer, William		1			1			1					3
Stark, Amanda	2				1		1		1	1			6
Stark, C. D. J.							1	1					2
Stark, D. G.	2	1					1	1		1			6
Stark, J. D.	1		2	1			3	1					8
Stark, James	7	12	6	2	3		6	6	3	1	4		50
Stark, Jemma								3		1			4
Stark, L.	1	1						1	1				4
Stark, Sally	2		2	1	1		4	2	1	1	1		15
Staton, E. J.	3	2					1	1	1				8
Stinson, Mary										1			1
Stoval, Daniel		1		1						1			3
Stoval, James	1	3					1	1	1				7
Stoval, Nancy	3	3						1	2		1		10
Straight, William	1					1	2		1				5
Syddens, James C.	1	5					2	2	1	1			12
Syddins, John	3	1		2					1		1		8
Tapscot, G. A.								1					1
Thackston, Z. B.									1				1
Thomas, Alexander		1						1					2
Thomas, Isham	2		1				2	2	1				8
Thomas, W.	1	2	1	1	2		2	2			1		12

Slave Owner	Enslaved Males						Enslaved Females						
Alphabetical Order	*<10*	*10-24*	*24-36*	*36-55*	*55-100*	*>100*	*<10*	*10-24*	*24-36*	*36-55*	*55-100*	*>100*	*Total*
Thomas, Wesley			1										1
Thompson, Sarah		1						1		1			3
Tinsley, John M.								1					1
Tucker, J. N.								1					1
Venable, Joseph	1	1	1				4	1					8
Waggoner, George	1	2					2	3		1			9
Waggoner, Samuel			1						1				2
Walker, A. S.	1	1	1				3	1		1			8
Walker, William		2					2			1			5
Waters, A.	2							1					3
Weathered, W. Y.		1											1
Weaver, Elizabeth								1					1
Whitney, H.	1	4	1	2				2		1			11
Whitney, J.	1	1					2		1				5
Whitney, Jeremiah	2		1					1					4
Whitney, M.	3		1				1	2	2				9
Whitney, M.							1						1
Whitney, Uriah	1	2	3	2				5	2		1		16
Whitney, Uriah	8							6					14
Williams, Edward		1					1						2
Williams, H.	1	1	1					1		1			5
Williams, J. F.							1						1
Williams, J. R.		1						1					2
Williams, Ruth				1									1
Williams, S. S.	1						1		1				3
Williams, A. G.	1	2					1			1			5
Willoughby, William	1			1			2	1					5
Witt, James								1					1
Woodcock, G. B.								1					1
Wright, N.V.	1		1				1		1				4
TOTAL	252	208	102	54	27		199	252	103	80	34		1311

Chapter 6

Slaves in Allen County in 1860

1860 Census

The US census of 1860 was the fifth and the last official enumeration of slaves after Allen County was formed and before slavery ended. The winds of war, the strengthening abolition movement, the preservation of the union, and the presidential campaign kept the topic of slavery as the center of attention and conversation. The census data may hold evidence of the mixed emotions that no doubt existed in Allen County. It revealed that over the prior decade, the number of slaves had increased by 202 to a total of 1,514. However, the number of households that owned slaves had increased by only four since the 1850 census, to a total of 282 (Figure 18).

Figure 18

Allen County slaves by gender and age cohorts in 1860

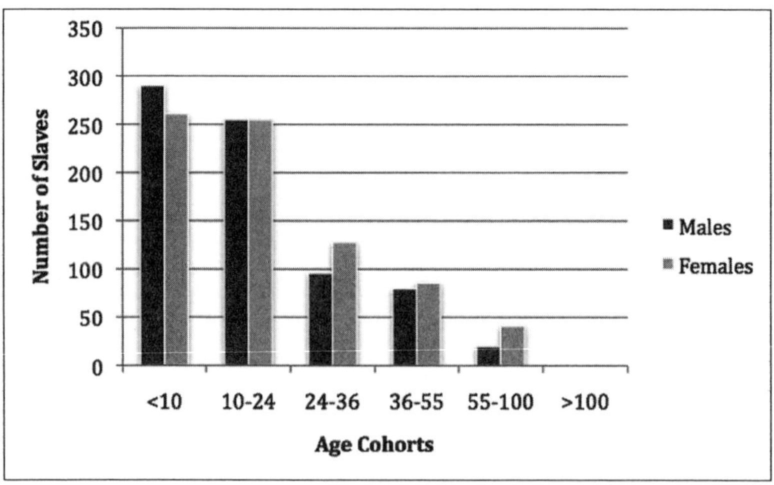

The increase of in the number of slaves was evenly divided by gender. There were 99 more males and 103 more females than in the previous decade. Nevertheless, the total of 771 females and 743 males reflected the same ratio that had existed in 1850.

The number of slaves who were older than 55 was exactly the same as in 1850, but the gender distribution was very different. There were twice a many women over 55 as men. That resulted from seven fewer males and seven more females in that cohort. That result may be the effect of the shorter life expectancy among male slaves.

Only 16 percent of the slaveholding households had more than 8 slaves. Allen County did not have the large acreages of the plantations that were common in the deep south, but its larger ones held the larger numbers of slaves. For example, there were nine households with more than 20 slaves. Of them, the largest numbers were owned by Uriah Porter with 71, James Stark with 66, Samuel Sears with 36, J. H. Page with 31, and S. E. Carpenter with 29.

More common were households with eight or fewer slaves. Households with just one slave continued to the most common circumstance in Allen County. Of the 282 households with slaves, 30 percent had only one. Just 14 percent had two (Figure 19).

Figure 19

Slaveholding households with eight or fewer slaves

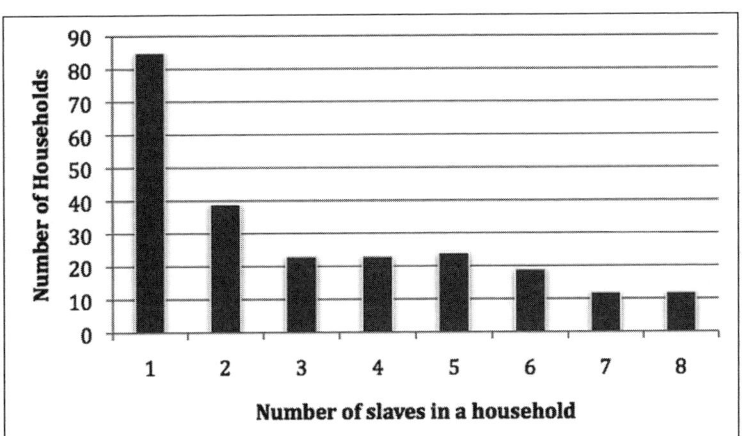

Table 17

Gender disparity by age cohort among slave owner households in 1860

Males by Age Cohort						Females by Age Cohort							
Slaves in Household	***<10***	***10-24***	***24-36***	***36-55***	***55-100***	***>100***	***<10***	***10-24***	***24-36***	***36-55***	***55-100***	***>100***	***Total Slaves***
1	9	16	5	8	2		6	18	5	11	5		85
2	9	16	4	3	2		10	22	7	4	1		78
3	12	11	2	3	0		15	9	9	7	1		69
4	14	22	4	2	2		16	20	6	5	1		92
5	21	23	13	7	1		11	21	11	8	4		120
6-10	81	66	25	21	5		68	61	35	16	8		386
11-25	93	56	21	17	3		80	66	29	20	11		396
26-66	51	45	24	19	5		55	38	26	15	10		288
TOTAL	290	255	98	80	20		261	255	128	86	41		1514

The households with the six to ten slaves (Table 17) had 147 males (53%) and only 129 females (47%) in the under 24-year-old group. Although not greatly different, that represents the opposite of the distribution found in most households and age cohorts. One could assume that the size of the agricultural activity was the determining factor, although data are not available to confirm that.

The slave data and the alphabetized list of slave owners (Table 18) were extracted out of the 2002 transcription of the 1860 slave census made by Sharon Tabor.

Table 18
Allen County Slaves 1860

Slave Owner	**Enslaved Males**					**Enslaved Females**					
Alphabetical Order	*<10*	*10-24*	*24-36*	*36-55*	*55-100*	*<10*	*10-24*	*24-36*	*36-55*	*55-100*	*Total*
Ackerman, Jacob							1	1			2
Alexander, A. C.		1								1	2
Alexander, C. H.							1				1
Allen, C. E.						1					1
Allen, E. S.						1					1
Allen, J. M.	1										1
Allen, Su			2				1		1	1	5
Allen, Y. S.							1				1
Allen, W. G.		1									1
Anderson, J. A.							1				1
Anderson, J. J.	1					1			1		3
Anderson, Sampson								1			1
Anthony, B. F.	1										1
Anthony, George		3	1	1		1	4		1		11
Anthony, H. S.	2	3					1				6
Anthony, J. G.	3	1				1	1	1			7
Anthony, Joseph				1							1
Anthony, Lee	1					1	2	1			5
Anthony, R. D.		1									1
Anthony, W. H.	1				1	1		1			4
Anthony, W. T.	1		1			1	1				4
Asply, R. L.							1				1
Atwood, J. S.		1									1
Atwood, Jett									1		1
Atwood, Lemuel						3	1				4
Atwood, T. J.							1				1
Austin, Eliza & 5 others			3			1		1			5
Ayers, Elizabeth						1		1			2
Bailey, Catharine			1								1
Behuler, Samuel	1										1
Behuler, Susan					1						1
Benedict, Mary				1					1		2
Blackburn, William		2				1			1		4
Booker, Freeman		2					1		1		4
Borger & Simpson		2									2
Bracken, Green	2	1				2	1	2	1		9

Slave Owner	Enslaved Males					Enslaved Females					
Alphabetical Order	*<10*	*10-24*	*24-36*	*36-55*	*55-100*	*<10*	*10-24*	*24-36*	*36-55*	*55-100*	*Total*
Bradley, Edward		1	2				1				4
Bright, J. A.	2	2				1	1	1			7
Britt, W. A.							1				1
Brown & Mulligan				1							1
Brown, Alsy			1				1				2
Brown, Anny	2	1		1		1	1	1			7
Brown, Harrison						2		2			4
Brown, Henry		3	1			1			1		6
Brown, Oliver							1				1
Brown, Robison	2	1				2	2	1			8
Burton, Adaline	6			1	1	2	2		2	1	15
Burton, C.						1	1				2
Burton, Cuthbert			2			3	1	1		1	8
Burton, John	2	1	2			3		2			10
Burton, T. W.					1		1				2
Calvert, J. C.						2	1				3
Calvert, Jessee	1	2		1					1		5
Carpenter, Adaline			1								1
Carpenter, Benjamin	4	1					2				7
Carpenter, J. D.	1			1		1		1	1		5
Carpenter, S. E.	6	6	1	2	1	6	2	4		1	29
Carpenter, Samuel		1					2		1		4
Carpenter, W. C.	1	1			1	1		1		1	6
Caruth, Thomas		2	1			2		1		1	7
Chaney, Washington	1	1			1	1	1	1			6
Chany, W. B.						1	1				2
Claypool, S. D.							1				1
Cockrill, J. H.							1				1
Collins, Henry				1							1
Collins, J. H.		1									1
Cook, Green	1										1
Cook, Leonidus	1										1
Cook, Samuel		2				1	1		1		5
Corder, J. M.	1	3					1		1		6
Crow, Nancy		1									1
Cushenberry, W.	1					2	1	1		1	6
Dance, J. E.				1							1
Davasier, J. H.		1				1		1			3
Davis, Jonathan	3	6	3	1		6	1	4	1	1	26

Slave Owner	**Enslaved Males**					**Enslaved Females**					
Alphabetical Order	*<10*	*10-24*	*24-36*	*36-55*	*55-100*	*<10*	*10-24*	*24-36*	*36-55*	*55-100*	*Total*
Davis, Susan	2	1					2				5
Deane, Jr. N.			1								1
Dixon, T. R.	4	2				2	2	1	1		12
Dodds Estate		1					1				2
Dodson, J. S.	2					2		1			5
Dodson, Synatha	1			1		3		1			6
Downing, Benjamin	6	1	1	2		7	2	2		1	22
Downing, Benjamin Jr.		1									1
Downing, W. R.	2	1	1				1				5
Dunn, John							1				1
Dunn, Margaret	5	1		2		3	1	1	1		14
Dye, Elizabeth									1		1
Dyre, Squire							1		1		2
Edmunds, R. W.	2	1				1					4
Ellis, James		1									1
Ellis, Robert F.	1					1		1			3
Ellis, T. E.						1					1
Ellis, W. J.				1							1
Elllis, W.J. & W. Martin									1		1
Etherly, William							1				1
Eubank, C. T.	1	2					1	1			5
Ewing, J.	2						2				4
Fishback, Joseph	2	2				6	3	1			14
Fisher, Thomas	2	2				1		1			6
Fitzpatrick, J. N.									1		1
Fitzpatrick, William		1	1	3			1		2		8
Follis, George		1				1		1			3
Follis, R. S.				1							1
Foster, A. S.	1					1					2
Foster, B. A.	1	1				3	1	1			7
Foster, J. W. & 6 others	8	3	1	2		6	2	1	3		26
Francis, Addison	5	1	1	1		1	3		1		13
Francis, Joseph						1		1			2
Franklin, Samuel	2	4	1			1		1			9
Gains, T. F. M.	3	1	1	1			2	1			9
Gains, T. H.	2		1			1	4				8
Garrison, E. D.	1	1					1			1	4
Gatewood, F.	2	3				2	2	1	1		11

Slave Owner	Enslaved Males					Enslaved Females					
Alphabetical Order	*<10*	*10-24*	*24-36*	*36-55*	*55-100*	*<10*	*10-24*	*24-36*	*36-55*	*55-100*	*Total*
Gibson, J. H.	1			1							2
Gibson, Randolph	5	1	1			4	1	1	1		14
Glasenflo, Sara		1							1		2
Glover, Jane	1	1					1				3
Godley, J. S.	2	5	1	1		3	2	2	1	1	18
Godley, John S.								1			1
Goodnight, Isaac	1	2	1			3	1		1		9
Goodnight, T. M. C.		1		1							2
Gosaney & Wollis		1				1					2
Guy, William					1						1
Guy, William	1										1
Ham, M. F.				1							1
Ham, S. W.		1					1				2
Hammet, James										1	1
Haral, Rola				3			1			1	5
Harris, Amos		2				1		1			4
Harris, S. H.		1	1	1			1	1			5
Harston, A. A.	1						1				2
Harston, Reca									1		1
Harston, Rot							1				1
Harston, Thomas	7	1	1	2		2	5	2			20
Harston, William	2	2	1			1	2	1			9
Heeter, J. W.	2			1		1	1		1		6
Heeter, Sebaston	3		1		1	1	1				7
Hill, Nancy		1					1				2
Hinton, W. G.	5		1					1			7
Hobdy, M. C.	1					1		1			3
Holder, John	5	2	1		1	1	5	3		1	19
Horn, F. Estate									1		1
Horn, Thomas	3	6	2			3	3	1		1	19
Howards Estate			1								1
Howards Estate		1									1
Hower, James	3							1			4
Hudson, Huey	3	1				2			2		8
Hughes, Elizabeth	3					1	3		1	1	9
Hughes, T. R.	1		1	1		2	1	1			7
Hughs, A. P.	4							1			5
Hunt, C. D.			1				1				2
Ingram, J. A.	1			1		1	1				4
Jackson, Benjamin						1	2		1		4

Slave Owner	Enslaved Males					Enslaved Females					
Alphabetical Order	*<10*	*10-24*	*24-36*	*36-55*	*55-100*	*<10*	*10-24*	*24-36*	*36-55*	*55-100*	*Total*
Jackson, John										1	1
Jackson, John S.		1									1
Jewel, G. W.			2						1		3
Jewel, W. H.	1	2	1					1			5
Jimerson, J. A.						2			1		3
Jimerson, M.D.	1						1				2
Jimerson, Nancy	1	1				2		1			5
Johnson, Henderson									1		1
Johnson, Mathew		1									1
Johnson, Nancy									1		1
Johnson, W. V.	1	1			1		1				4
Kiger, C. C.		1									1
Landers, Patsy	2	2	3			2	3			2	14
Lewis, William									1		1
Long, G. P.	1	1	1			2	1	1			7
Manion, Phenba		1	1	2			1	1			6
Manion, Tomtson	2	1		1		1		1			6
Mansfield, William									1		1
Marcrum, Peter									1		1
Martin, James W.		1							1		2
McElroy, Burnett		1									1
McFarland, J. B.							1				1
McLary, Daniel		1									1
Meridith, A.		1					1				2
Milleken, J. H.		1		1		2					4
Moore, E. C.										1	1
Moore, Joseph W.		1			1						2
Moore, Simpson		2		3				1			6
Moorhead, E. S.								1			1
Moorhead, T. J.	2		1			1	1	1			6
Morgan, Jackson						1		1			2
Morgan, John M.						1					1
Morrison, F. G.	1	1					1				3
Motley, John				1							1
Motley, Joseph	1	3				1	3		1		9
Motley, Lynn	2							1			3
Motley, Martha								1			1
Motley, Narcissa	1							1			2
Motley, Patsy	1	2				1	1	1			6
Mulligan, G. M.	1	1							1		3

Slave Owner	Enslaved Males					Enslaved Females					
Alphabetical Order	*<10*	*10-24*	*24-36*	*36-55*	*55-100*	*<10*	*10-24*	*24-36*	*36-55*	*55-100*	*Total*
Mulligan, J. C.	4	2				5	1	1		1	14
Napier, Thomas		1									1
Neal, Benjamin	1					1	1	1			4
Neikirk, William	1						1				2
Oliver, William	2							1			3
Orr, William		1	1			1	1		1		5
Page, J. H.	9	4	5	1		4	4	2	2		31
Paris, G. P.						1					1
Paris, R. H. & M. Russle										1	1
Petty, James							1				1
Petty, James	2		1			8	1	2		1	15
Pinson, J. W.	2	5					3	1	1		12
Pitchford, Cyrus	1										1
Pitchford, J. F.	1										1
Pitchford, W. F.						1		1			2
Poe, Delany	1		1								2
Pope, N. K.		2	1	1		1		1			6
Pope, S. H.						1					1
Porter, E. W.	1		2			4	1				8
Porter, Frank			1								1
Porter, Luther	2	5	2			4	1	1	1		16
Porter, Uriah	7	9	3	2	1	10	6	3	2		43
Porter, Uriah	3	5	2	2		8	5	4	2		31
Porter, W. R.	1	3	1		1	2	1				9
Pruitt, Elijah		2					2				4
Pulliam, Benjamin	1	1	1	1						1	5
Pulliam, J. C. C.	3	2	1			3	2	1	1		13
Pulliam, James P.		2					2				4
Pulliam, R. F.	1			1			1				3
Pulliam, W. P.		2				1	1		1		5
Read, G. D.						1	1				2
Read, S. J.	3		2			3	1	1	1		11
Richey, A. J.						1	1				2
Richey, S. S.							6		1		7
Richey, Thomas						1	2				3
Richey, William		1				1	1				3
Roark, Henry	4							1	1		6
Robb, R. D.	2					2	2				6
Russell, George								1			1

Slave Owner	Enslaved Males					Enslaved Females					
Alphabetical Order	*<10*	*10-24*	*24-36*	*36-55*	*55-100*	*<10*	*10-24*	*24-36*	*36-55*	*55-100*	*Total*
Sarver, Wyett							1				1
Satterfield, Henry	2	1					1		1		5
Sears, Albert		2	1			1		1			5
Sears, C. C.	1							1			2
Sears, Henry		3				3		1			7
Sears, Henry	2	3		2		3	3	1			14
Sears, Samuel	8	3	3	2		7	6	4	1	2	36
Sears, William	2	1				1	3		1		8
Seay, J. R.							1	1	1		3
Settle, T. J.				1		1	1				3
Shaford, W. R.							1				1
Smith, Sandford		2				1	1				4
Stark, Amanda	1	1	1			2	1	1	1		8
Stark, C. D. J.		2	1				1				4
Stark, J. D.	1	1		4		1	1				8
Stark, James	7	9	6	7	3	8	12	4	4	6	66
Stark, Lucy	4	1				3	2		2		12
Stark, Sally	2			3		2	4	2	1	1	15
Staton, E. J.	2	3	1			2	3		1		12
Stephens, Mary		1									1
Stevens, William	2				1		2				5
Stone, John	1	2							1		4
Stovall, Daniel		1				1	2	1	1		6
Stovall, James	2	2	1	1		2	2				10
Stovall, Nancy	6	3		1		2		2	1	1	16
Street, C. J.						2		1			3
Sulser, Jefferson		1					1				2
Sydens, J. S.	2	3		1				1		1	8
Sydens, James		1					1				2
Sydens, Sampson Estate	1										1
Tabor, George	1						1				2
Thomas, Walter		2					2			1	5
Tompson, Sally		1					1				2
Travelstead, John							1				1
Tucker N. J.		1									1
Wagoner, W. S.		2							1		3
Walker, A. S.	2		1			4	5	1	1		14
Walker, William			1				1				2
Weaver, Elizabeth	1					1		1			3

Slave Owner	**Enslaved Males**					**Enslaved Females**					
Alphabetical Order	*<10*	*10-24*	*24-36*	*36-55*	*55-100*	*<10*	*10-24*	*24-36*	*36-55*	*55-100*	*Total*
Whitney, Herman	5	2	1	1	1	2	2	1	1		16
Whitney, Reaves	1	1			1	1	3			1	8
Whitney, S. W.		2					2		1		5
Whitney, W. T.		1					1				2
Willams, A. G.		3					1	1		1	6
Williams, J. R.	3		1			2	1	1			8
Williams, Nancy		2								1	3
Wilson, B. P.							1				1
Woodcock, G. B.			2				2	1			5
Worley, M. B.										1	1
Wright, Nancy V.		1		1					1		3
TOTAL	290	255	98	80	20	261	255	128	86	41	1514

Chapter 7

Slaves from Allen County Tax Records 1825-1838

Slaves as Taxable Property

Slaves were property in a legal sense and were taxable as were other properties. In 1649 in Virginia, most of the labor was from indentured white servants rather than from the some 300 blacks. There was a tax on indentured servants but the number of African slaves was thought to be too small to produce much revenue.[1] As African slave numbers increased, the tax became more attractive. In the deep southern states, the value of slaves exceeded the value of the land. In 1858, Georgia's land was valued at just 67% of the value of its slaves. That was not true in Kentucky where the land value was 65%, more than the value of its slaves.[2] Allen County's value ratio appears to be smaller.

Allen County Tax Records

The tax records contain the name of the property owner; the number of acres of land; the watercourse (creek, river, etc) that drains it; whether it had been entered, surveyed, and patented; the number of white males who were 21 or older; the number of blacks who were 16 or older; the total number of blacks; the number of horses; number of town lots; number of white children; and the total assessed value of the property.

The number of white males of 21 years or older was recorded, but there was no count of white females. For blacks, both males and females were included, but the age was 16 or older, the age at which they were expected to do an adult's full day of work. The total number of blacks (male and female of all ages) was included.

[1] Columbia University. 1891. Studies in history, economics, and public law. New York: Columbia University Press

[2] Watson, Thomas E. 1916. Political and economic handbook. Thomson, Ga: Jeffersonian Pub. Co.

Tax Assessed Value of Slaves

One of the arguments against the abolition of slavery was the tax revenue that it generated. At the time, when Kentucky's constitution was being revised, the tax on slaves as property produced $70,000 for the state, $40,000 for the counties, $35,000 for the sinking fund [to pay off debt], $14,000 for the school fund, and other taxes for a total of $173,000 per year. In addition, slaves were forced to work on roads ($40,000). That entire income from slavery was just $13,000 less than the tax on land. Not only were slaves valuable to their owners, they were also valuable to the local and state governments.[3]

The total value of the property in Allen County is interesting. For example, in 1825, one white property owner with no land, no slaves, and two horses was assessed at $50. Another with no land, two slaves, and two horses was assessed at $500. The difference was slaves.

The value of slaves often exceeded the value of the land that they tilled. James Stark's property was assessed at $24,374. He owned 1,673 acres in the Difficult Creek area. He owned 48 slaves and 42 horses. Table 19 presents the property owners who had 1,000 acres or more in 1838.

Table 19

Value of property of the Allen County landowners who held 1,000 acres or more in 1838

Property Owner	Acres	Slaves	Horses	Total Value
James Stark	1,673	48	42	$24,374
Mary S. Walker	3,053	19	5	$18,728
Thomas Walker	1,890	13	26	$13,400
John Calvert	1,007	6	11	$8,100
Robert McCleary	1,705	11	11	$7,360
Alfred Payne	1,940	0	18	$5,000
Matthew Johnson	1,000	5	7	$2,920
William Spenser	1,313	2	1	$2,150

[3] Thorpe, Francis Newton. 1898. A constitutional history of the American people, 1776-1850. New York: Harper & Brothers

Not all large landowners owned large numbers of slaves. William Spenser was such a man with just two slaves.

Not all slave owners owned taxable land. In fact, 169 (32%) of them had zero acres of land according to the tax records. Of those landless owners, twenty (12%) were women. That percentage was slightly lower than that of the entire list of 531 owner names. Of that total, 78 (15%) were women. These landless owners had 394 slaves, averaging 2.3 slaves per owner. About 56 percent of those slaves were younger than 16 years old.

Slaves Numbers Compared with Acreage by Slave Owner

Thirteen slave owners had 1,000 acres or more, with Mary S. Walker topping the list at 3,053 acres. Of those thirteen, only five held ten or more slaves. The other eight held seven or fewer.

The number of slaves owned by a person increased in direct proportion to the number of acres of land he or she owned (Figure 20). The relationship reflects the rural nature of Allen County during these early years of our history.

Figure 20

Relationship between the number of slaves and the number of acres owned

There were only 14 slave owners who owned more than 1,000 acres, an insufficient sample size to continue the graph in Figure 20 to the top number of acres of 3,053. Nevertheless, the relationship between slave numbers and farm size in Allen County is clearly established for 1,000 acres or less.

It is clear that the wealth identified by the assessed tax represented the value of both the land and the slaves. There are insufficient data in this study to distinguish between the two.

Slave Owners Surname List 1821 through 1838

The published extracts of the early Allen County tax records[4] were used to compile a list of slave owners from the available years 1825 through 1838. Data were extracted for slave owners from the tax records from 1821 and 1824 that are held by the Allen County Historical Society. The data from these two sources were merged to produce tables for this study. The objective of the data collection was to compile a list of different owner names to aid slave genealogical research, rather than to account for the numbers of slaves year by year. Therefore only the data from the earliest appearance of a name were used.

A total of 617 different people were identified as slave owners in one or more year for the available tax years 1821 through 1838. The 186 owners listed in 1825 are a bit fewer than the 198 the census counted in 1830. However, the numbers are close enough to give confidence in both the tax counts and the census counts.

Names of owners that did not replicate the 86 names from 1821 were added to the list in subsequent available tax years: 86 in 1824, 44 in 1826, 51 in 1827, 51 in 1829, 59 in 1831, 28 in 1833, 48 in 1835, 33 in 1827, and 35 in 1838. The two most likely causes of these additional owners were acquisition by inheritance or by purchase. There is surprising consistency in the variations, perhaps because the period 1821-1838 is so short.

Table 20 presents the accumulated list of slave owner names from tax records. The year listed is the year in which that owner's name first appeared in the tax record. The slave numbers and other

---

[4] Gardner, Jeanetta S., 1999. Allen County tax records. Jeanetta Steenbergen Gardner, Collierville, Tennessee

data are for that first appearance year only. Each owner name and the related data appear only once in Table 20.

Allen County slave data in Table 20 were compiled by B. S. Chambers and Lou Nell Rayner.

Table 20

Allen County slaves from tax records 1821-1838

Year	Slave Owner	Slave Numbers Age <16	Slave Numbers Total	Land in Acres	Total Land Value	Total Taxable Value
1825	Alexander, Andrew	1	2	65		
1826	Alexander, Anzi C.	1	1			1035
1825	Alexander, Samuel	1	4	300		1045
1837	Allen, Lee	7	5			1530
1831	Anderson, Jonathan	1	1			4167
1825	Anderson, Peter Jr.	1	1	100		425
1825	Anderson, Samuel	1	1			500
1829	Anderson, William	1	1	75		650
1825	Anthony, Elizabeth	1	3	100		665
1829	Anthony, George	0	1	50		1155
1836	Anthony, Henry S.	1	2			
1825	Anthony, Joseph	1	8	900		2130
1838	Anthony, W. L.	0	2	135		4785
1833	Anthony, Will	0	2			4105
1836	Ashley, John L.	1	1			500
1838	Aspler, Samuel	0	1	138		150
1825	Austin, Charles	1	3	80		910
1836	Austin, Willis	0	3			1930
1829	Austin, Wilson	1	1	280		4349
1833	Ayers, John	0	1	182		1190
1825	Bailey, Benjamin	1	1	60		796
1829	Barlow, James	1	5	400		850
1829	Barnes, Willis	0	1	544		2675
1825	Barnhart, John	1	1	150		1230
1829	Barnhart, Susannah	1	1	100		1170
1838	Barton, Mary	2	2	395		600
1837	Beheler, Jacob	1	1	220		2482
1831	Benbrook, George W.	1	1			1080

Year	Slave Owner	Slave Numbers		Land in Acres	Total Land Value	Total Taxable Value
		Age <16	Total			
1831	Benedict, Benjamin	1	1	200		435
1833	Benedict, Lindsey	0	1	75		1350
1821	Bennedict, B.	1	1			1650
1825	Blackburn, James	1	1	100		900
1831	Blackburn, Robert	0	5	297		425
1827	Blankenship, Elijah	1	1	208		1000
1827	Bonner, Henry	1	2	195		1300
1838	Boren, James	0	1	100		1300
1838	Boren, Talton	0	1	100		825
1826	Boucher, Peter	1	3	189		1600
1837	Brian, Tarlton	0	1	320		
1836	Bridges, Samuel	0	1	50		2040
1825	Brinson, Stout	3	6	114		390
1824	Brite, Albertus	1	1	150	400	
1824	Brite, George	1	1	30		400
1824	Brite, James	1	1		80	1635
1833	Brite, Mary	1	1	220		500
1824	Brite, Polly	1	1		500	660
1831	Brown, Allen	0	2	22		1630
1825	Brown, Alsey	1	1	455		185
1826	Brown, Henry	0	2	93		2110
1821	Brown, Hugh	1	1	505		
1825	Brown, James	1	1	225		2665
1824	Brown, Jonas	1	1	226	1350	2156
1831	Brown, Mary	0	1			
1826	Brown, Rachel	1	4	300		10
1831	Brown, Wiley	1	3	115		2300
1836	Brunson, Johnathan	1	1	262		383
1833	Brunson, Moses	1	1	114		1000
1824	Brunson, Stout	3	6	164	696	3295
1821	Buford, W.	2	7			3222
1824	Buley, Benjamin	1	1		260	
1831	Bunten, John	1	3	250		2600
1829	Burris, Joseph	0	1	325		1800
1827	Burris, Rachel	1	4	660		60
1825	Burris, Thomas	2	4	600		1700
1824	Burton, Cuthburt	1	1	540	576	

Year	Slave Owner	Slave Numbers		Land in Acres	Total Land Value	Total Taxable Value
		Age <16	Total			
1824	Burton, Drury	2	3	300	1500	3364
1824	Burton, Drury	2	4			1400
1829	Burton, Drury Jr.	2	3			3550
1824	Burton, John	1	2		625	
1825	Burton, John	0	1	250		1575
1833	Burton, Mary	2	2	300		1875
1829	Bush, Isaac	1	1	220		1800
1829	Bush, Josiah	1	2	134		1500
1838	Calvert, John	4	6	1007		993
1827	Carpenter, A. F.	1	1	139		1200
1821	Carpenter, Catherine	2	2			980
139	Carpenter, Frederick	1	2	139	1112	2312
1831	Carpenter, James Y.	0	1			1545
1829	Carpenter, John	4	10	465		300
1837	Carpenter, Rachael	3	4	150		3456
1836	Carpenter, Richard	0	4	100		3340
1821	Carpenter, Samuel E.	2	6	300		2800
1836	Carpenter, William D.	0	1	75		4450
1831	Carpenter, Wilson	1	1			800
1829	Carruth, John	0	2	173		1225
1829	Carruth, Mark	0	1			1236
1826	Carruth, Nance	1	3	160		130
1831	Carruth, Thomas	1	3	170		355
1831	Caruth, Samuel	1	1	260		1095
1833	Carver, James Sr.	4	6	217		600
1827	Cayton, George W.	1	1	50		
1836	Celsor, Hardin	1	2	400		600
1824	Chambers, Franky	1	1		1200	1500
1831	Chambers, Frederick	2	2	275		5025
1827	Clark, John Sr.	5	15	65		1457
1825	Clark, Marshall	4	18	750		5850
1829	Clark, Micajah	3	10	750		8825
1821	Clayton, John	1	3	249		1700
1833	Clibrun, Barbara	5	1	75		2365
1829	Clowden, Reaves	1	1			
1836	Cobb, Lebbrus	1	1	140		400
1827	Cockrill, J. Ishman	3	7	505		600

Year	Slave Owner	Slave Numbers		Land in Acres	Total Land Value	Total Taxable Value
		Age <16	Total			
1825	Cockrill, J. Johnson	3	7	850		3884
1821	Cockrill, John T.	3	5			
1824	Cockrill, Johnson	2	5		1000	
1825	Colbert, Francis	1	1			5675
1827	Colbert, Margaret	1	1	140		200
1829	Colbert, Peggy	1	1	100		600
1824	Coleman, William	1	2	200	1500	
1821	Collins, Henry	0	1	200		
1829	Collins, William	0	1			1395
1825	Conaway, Catherine	3	4			0
1821	Conniway, Thomas	2	2			980
1831	Cornwell, Elisha	1	1	324		1630
1824	Cornwell, Mary Ann	1	4		1400	2610
1825	Cornwell, Polly	1	4	200		300
1824	Cosby, Nathan	1	1			700
1837	Cosby, Nathan Y.	1	2			3420
1821	Covington, E.	1	2			610
1821	Cowden, James	3	5	585		
1831	Cowden, James Sr.	3	6	537		4325
1836	Cowden, Lucy	2	4	204		2900
1831	Cowden, Reeves	0	1			2734
1824	Crow, William	1	1	407	800	
1831	Crowder, Sarah	2	2	120		2756
1824	Cushenberry, C.	4	10		750	
1829	Cushenberry, Daniel	0	1	249		420
1821	Cushenberry, Elijah	2	6	226		3516
1837	Cushenberry, Henry	2	5	125		4547
1829	Cushenberry, James	1	5	170		3375
1827	Cushenberry, Mary H.	1	1			1265
1825	Cushenberry, Polly	2	3	75		600
1836	Cushenberry, William	1	3			1050
1826	Dalton, Phebe	2	4	200		1100
1826	Davis, James	1	2			2276
1838	Davis, Jonathan	5	12	500		300
1824	Dawson, Anak	3	9	181	600	
1821	Dean, Aulsey	1	7			2475
1829	Dearing, William	1	1	225		5355

Year	Slave Owner	Slave Numbers		Land in Acres	Total Land Value	Total Taxable Value
		Age <16	Total			
1837	Devasher, Daniel M.	1	3			1225
1836	Devasher, Elizabeth	1	1	469		820
1821	Devasher, John C.	2	2	230		1536
1831	Devine, George	1	1	640		1557
1827	Dickson, John	1	2			1015
1827	Dickson, Mary	2	4			2380
1831	Dickson, William	0	1	160		1100
1825	Dillon, Phebe	1	4	200		855
1821	Dinwiddie, William	1	5	125		2110
1821	Dinwiddie, William Jr.	0	1			790
1831	Dixon, Eliza Ann	3	7	988		690
1829	Dixon, F. W.	2	3	611		3110
1831	Dixon, John	3	7	893		2938
1831	Dodson, Charles	0	1			3123
1829	Dodson, Dillingham	1	1	390		300
1829	Dodson, Thomas	0	1			1880
1836	Doors, James W.	0	1	164		330
1829	Dose, James	1	2			400
1825	Downing, Benjamin	0	1	273		350
1826	Downing, Sally	1	2	50		1865
1825	Downing, Sarah	1	2	50		950
1836	Drane, Anthony	0	1	100		1150
1831	Driver, Anthony	0	1	1		400
1821	Dry, Jacob	2	5	252		3765
1825	Duff, Fielding	0	1			4108
1836	Duff, Wesley	0	1			1180
1831	Duke, John	0	1			500
1825	Dunn, John A.	2	8	700		320
1833	Dye, Isaac	0	2			7300
1824	Dye, James	1	1		900	
1825	Dye, James Sr.	1	1	240		700
1827	Edmonds, Richard W.	1	1			2380
1827	Elliott, Alexander	0	1			300
1827	Emmerson, John	2	2	100		430
1826	Enloe, Enoch	1	1	100		1000
1827	Eubanks, Jonathan	0	1	107		840
1821	Fant, Fielding	2	6			3070

Year	Slave Owner	Slave Numbers		Land in Acres	Total Land Value	Total Taxable Value
		Age <16	Total			
1825	Fant, Francis	3	8	356		721
1831	Fant, John	5	9	356		4853
1825	Farley, Joseph	1	1			2860
1825	Farley, Mary	11	17	2200		625
1821	Farrell, Ann	1	6			1400
1825	Ferrell, Charles	0	1	490		3600
1824	Fickling, Ester	5	5	200	1600	4500
1827	Finn, John	1	2			2980
1824	Finney, John	1	1	570		730
1831	Finney, Robert	0	1			4000
1821	Finney, William	2	2			
1821	Fishback, John	6	10			5640
1825	Fishback, John V.	8	13	460		640
1821	Fishburn, Peter	0	1	705		1350
1836	Fitzpatrick, Wash	1	1			3700
1821	Fitzpatrick, William	2	6	238		2645
1827	Follis, Mary	0	1			1470
1837	Ford, Patrick	1	1			300
1836	Foster, George B.	0	1			500
1824	Foster, James	9	17		13500	
1821	Foster, James I.	9	20			21180
1821	Foster, John	2	4			1170
1825	Foster, Mary	11	17	2487		150
1836	Foster, Price	1	1			22050
1838	Foster, Robert	2	2			500
1824	Foster, Sally	1	3		315	1435
1825	Foster, Sarah	1	3	100		1900
1829	Foster, William	3	3	300		1470
1837	Gaines, John F.	0	1			1545
1825	Gaines, William	1	5	475		870
1831	Garrison, Hezekiah	1	1			2550
1836	Garrison, John M. Jr.	0	1	491		430
1825	Garrison, Mack	0	3	250		1635
1824	Gatton, Carlton	4	11		3105	8313
1825	Gatton, Carlton R.	1	4	1085		1330
1821	Gatton, Thomas	4	10			5640
1825	Gaultney, Elizabeth	7	16			6632

Year	Slave Owner	Slave Numbers		Land in Acres	Total Land Value	Total Taxable Value
		Age <16	Total			
1824	Gibson, John	1	1		1400	
1821	Gibson, John S.	3	7			5100
1825	Gibson, John S. Sr.	1	2	208		5810
1824	Gibson, Randle	1	3	300	800	
1829	Gibson, Randolph	2	3	400		1350
1827	Gibson, Robert	1	1			2100
1824	Gibson, William	1	1	200	800	1500
1821	Gills, Anderson	2	6	314		2920
1827	Godley, Elizabeth	5	10	200		2556
1827	Godley, Elizabeth (T.S. Burton)	2	7			5100
1826	Godley, Jesse S.	3	7			3355
1821	Godley, John	7	21			10976
1826	Graham, Edward	0	2			2100
1825	Graham, Green	0	1	33		700
1825	Griggs, William	0	1			
1825	Guy, Nancy	0	1	65		870
1831	Guy, Richard	0	2	229		725
1836	Guy, William	0	1	180		1147
1837	Hagan, John	0	1	249		1200
1821	Haines, Christopher	1	1	220		1890
1831	Haines, Samuel	0	1			1640
1837	Ham, David Sr.	2	7	885		270
1837	Ham, Thomas	0	1			4082
1836	Hammett, James	1	1			625
1836	Hannah, William	0	1	100		300
1831	Harris, Amos	1	2			
1826	Harris, David	2	3	976		600
1831	Harris, Fleming	1	4			2733
1825	Harris, Robert	1	1			540
1827	Harris, Thomas	1	1			700
1827	Harris, Warren	1	1	375		200
1833	Harrison, Thomas	2	2	50		2583
1837	Harrison, William	0	1	250		300
1833	Harston, Samuel (for G. Foster)	0	2			700
1825	Hart, John	1	1	184		1400

Year	Slave Owner	Slave Numbers		Land in Acres	Total Land Value	Total Taxable Value
		Age <16	Total			
1821	Hart, John Sr.	1	1			111
1837	Harvey, James T.	2	2	371		1250
1826	Hatler, Will	7	17	425		2600
1821	Hawkins, Thomas	1	1			420
1821	Heeter, Frederick	2	2	42		2054
1825	Heeter, George T.	2	2	150		900
1831	Heeter, Zachariah	1	3	60		110
1825	Henderson, Bennett	1	1	1003		750
1831	Henderson, Samuel	1	2			4762
1829	Henderson, Samuel C.	1	2			345
1825	Henderson, Will T.	4	4	369		300
1825	Henry, George	2	7	500		3478
1831	Hern, Thomas	1	2	250		5000
1826	Herring, George	2	8	362		1500
1825	Herrington, Mimick	0	1			4655
1824	Heter, Frederick	1	1		250	850
1824	Hickman, Joseph	1	1		500	1300
1825	Hickmen, Jesse L.	1	1	100		650
1824	Hinton, George	2	2		456	1600
1837	Hinton, John	0	3			1550
1824	Hinton, Moor	3	5	160	500	2845
1827	Hinton, Moses	5	9	160		3640
1836	Hinton, Temperance	3	13	250		3360
1837	Hinton, Willis	1	1			4350
1837	Holder, Edward	1	4	240		760
1836	Holder, John	0	2			1200
1833	Holder, Peggy	6	20	350		700
1821	Holder, William	6	14	400		5196
1821	Holiday, Charles	0	1			1630
1837	Holland, Elizabeth	1	1	68		7100
1824	Holland, Major	2	5	165	800	
1826	Holland, Richard	1	2			4190
1831	Holland, Wesley	0	1	151		500
1837	Hollaway, Henry M.	0	1	190		552
1824	Hood, Bryan	5	16		2000	
1825	Hood, Bryant	5	16	625		1000
1831	Hood, William	3	6	316		7625

Year	Slave Owner	Slave Numbers		Land in Acres	Total Land Value	Total Taxable Value
		Age <16	Total			
1838	Hopson, Elizabeth	4	5	177		2222
1821	Hopson, Zackariah	2	5	200		3310
1836	Horn, Thomas	0	1			4000
1833	Houser, Nicholas	2	5	250		400
1825	Houson, Warner	1	1	225		780
1826	Howard, Amasa	0	1			5000
1831	Howard, Thomas	0	3	250		400
1821	Howell, Raleigh	2	2	540		2054
1833	Hudson, John	3	8			1480
1831	Hughes, Elizabeth	2	4	100		1950
1825	Hughes, Richardson P.	1	5	590		1125
1827	Hunt, John	1	1	100		5400
1825	Hunt, Riley	0	1			972
1825	Jackson, Benjamin	0	1			500
1825	Jackson, John	0	1			625
1826	Jackson, Wills	0	1			475
1824	Jamison, Achilly	1	9	385		1250
1836	Jennings, William M.	0	1	75		4325
1827	Johnson, Charles M.	0	2	50		694
1827	Johnson, John	1	4			465
1825	Johnson, Matthew	1	4	250		975
1821	Johnson, Nathan	1	2	100		700
1821	Johnson, Thomas	1	1	95		586
1825	Jones, Leaner	1	1	100		800
1825	Kelley, James	3	6	110		400
1831	Kelley, John	0	1	295		4390
1838	Kelley, Miles	8	18	412		1210
1824	Kelly, James	2	3		400	2465
1826	Kennedy, David	0	1	116		17025
1826	King, Aquilla	0	4	98		380
1831	Landers, Isaac	1	6	403		900
1831	Landers, William	0	1	50		2354
1833	Lane, William	2	3	100		200
1838	Leder, Wiliam	1	1	100		2864
1837	Lee, H. L.	0	1			925
1821	Lee, Isaac	2	4	275		2460
1836	Lewis, George	1	1	50		

Year	Slave Owner	Slave Numbers		Land in Acres	Total Land Value	Total Taxable Value
		Age <16	Total			
1826	Lindsey, Rachel	1	1			200
1821	Linn, John	3	3	100		1525
1825	Linn, Joseph	2	2			1176
1828	Lodge, Thomas G.	1	1	33		1200
1825	Logan, Robert S.	1	1	200		418
1831	Logan, Young	1	1	160		1500
1827	Long, Benjamin	0	1	13		715
1821	Long, Brittian	2	3	75		1950
1821	Long, Brumfield	1	5			2050
1826	Long, Nelson	0	1	118		2525
1837	Lynch, Frederick C.	1	1	100		335
1824	Lynn, John	3	3	100	200	1250
1824	Lynn, Joseph	2	2			1200
1837	Lynn, Moses	1	2			1100
1824	Lynn, Robert	1	1		532	1200
1825	Manion, Ambrose	1	1	240		700
1838	Manion, P. & F. B., & G., Exe	2	8	406		1940
1838	Manion, Pheriba	2	2	244		5135
1825	Mansfield, George	2	2	30		2705
1821	Mansfield, George W.	1	1			1260
1825	Mansfield, Robert	0	1	370		2620
1824	Mansfield, Washington	2	2			4500
1838	Marshall, Joel	2	4	435		2400
1838	Martin, James W.	3	3	370		4850
1826	Mayhew, Lucas	0	1	167		1400
1831	Mayhew, Reason L.	1	2	167		715
1838	Mayhew, Woodford	0	1			700
1825	McClary, Robert	1	4	440		360
1824	McElroy, James	1	1	200	1200	2000
1825	McElroy, John	0	1	100		1720
1836	McElroy, William	1	1			900
1824	McMurry, James	1	5	184	628	4423
1836	McReynolds, Robert	1	1	370		4837
1831	Meridith, Armsted	0	4	0		2025
1837	Meridith, Frederick	0	1	300		300
1825	Miller, Christopher	1	4	1300		1500

Year	Slave Owner	Slave Numbers		Land in Acres	Total Land Value	Total Taxable Value
		Age <16	Total			
1824	Mitchel, Willie	3	6		1050	4190
1831	Mitchell, Henry S.	1	1			5650
1825	Mitchell, Richard	1	3			400
1831	Mitchell, Thomas	1	2	82		1700
1825	Mitchell, Willis Jr.	1	1	130		600
1825	Mitchell, Willis Sr.	3	7	295		760
1825	Moody, Nancy	0	2	200		3560
1825	Moore, Charles	1	1	100		1700
1825	Moore, James W.	1	2			660
1827	Moore, Samuel	0	2	680		700
1833	Moore, Thomas I.	2	9			1940
1829	Morehead, Eliza	1	2			1860
1829	Morehead, Hugh	2	4	264		350
1833	Morehead, Jesse	2	2			1358
1833	Morehead, N. H.	2	4	225		920
1837	Morrison, Ambrose	5	11	644		1680
1833	Motley, Dicy	4	11	900		
1837	Motley, Doug	6	14	200		4300
1833	Motley, Edwin	5	13	555		4730
1829	Motley, Henry	1	1	103		4400
1821	Motley, James	5	7			3630
1827	Motley, John	1	1			5540
1831	Motley, Matthew Sr.	1	1	103		400
1831	Motley, Thomas	1	2			900
1825	Mulligan, James C.	1	2	84		500
1833	Nanney, Mary	2	2	200		1370
1825	Nanney, Uriah	2	2	150		1200
1824	Nanny, Uriah	2	2		600	1757
1829	Neale, Benjamin F.	0	4	130		1575
1829	Neale, Thomas	1	1			3830
1829	Neale, William P.	3	4			375
1826	Newman, Charles	1	2	424		940
1826	Nowell, Lucy	1	1			
1827	O'Banion, George	1	1	100		
1825	Oliver, Elizabeth	0	1	155		590
1824	Oliver, Thomas	2	2		735	1900
1824	Oliver, William	2	2	216	400	2025

Year	Slave Owner	Slave Numbers		Land in Acres	Total Land Value	Total Taxable Value
		Age <16	Total			
1821	Oliver, William Sr.	2	2			2200
1831	Oxford, John	1	4	329		2898
1825	Oxford, Samuel	1	4	416		2318
1836	Pace, Benjamin	2	3			3084
1825	Paris, Robert H.	1	2	335		1130
1821	Parker, Samuel	9	19	715		12498
1821	Parker, William	0	2	339		2696
1837	Patton, Berry	1	1			3940
1821	Payne, Alfred	1	2			4383
1825	Payne, Thomas	0	2	125		700
1837	Pinson, James	2	1			1264
1824	Pinson, Zephaniah	1	3	135	589	1789
1825	Piper, Asa	0	1	200		2050
1821	Pitchford, Daniel	1	1	262		1184
1825	Pitchford, Eli Sr.	2	3	153		2968
1829	Pitchford, Orange D.	0	1	53		2888
1825	Poe, Benjamin	1	2	484		715
1825	Poe, William	0	2	100		2968
1825	Pope, Jane	0	1	306		1390
1827	Pope, James	0	1	312		1132
1838	Pope, Nathan	1	1	385		837
1836	Porter, Braxton	0	1			3105
1824	Porter, David	2	2		2128	5158
1821	Porter, David A.	2	2	380		3840
1824	Porter, Denton	2	8		1680	5260
1821	Porter, Denton S.	1	6	210		2840
1821	Porter, Edward	5	6	310		4140
1826	Porter, Luther D.	1	1			3875
1838	Porter, William R.	1	2			475
1829	Preweitt, Moses	1	1			1714
1829	Procter, Nathan	1	1	100		
1838	Pulliam, Benjamin	1	2			600
1829	Pulliam, Henry C.	0	1			950
1824	Pulliam, John	2	3	552	1700	3000
1821	Pulliam, Joseph	3	6	182		2876
1827	Pulliam, Robert F.	6	8	328		3696
1824	Pulliam, William	2	4	607	2414	4000

Year	Slave Owner	Slave Numbers		Land in Acres	Total Land Value	Total Taxable Value
		Age <16	Total			
1821	Rae, Jeremiah	1	3			600
1825	Railey, Phillip	4	7	100		4500
1825	Ray, Baxter	0	1	100		3900
1824	Ray, Deccao	2	2		610	1382
1827	Ray, Jeremiah	2	6			1200
1821	Ray, Mary	4	5			80
1826	Ray, Noah	2	3	100		200
1821	Ray, William	1	4	200		1775
1824	Read, Charles	6	17			11392
1827	Read, Charles D.	0	4			3322
1825	Read, Daniel	0	1			1275
1824	Read, Dillard	4	7			3750
1838	Read, Francis A.	0	1			1000
1827	Read, George D.	1	2			530
1825	Read, Margaret/Peggy	5	16	524		1000
1831	Read, Richard	0	1			9168
1837	Read, Samuel J.	1	1			230
1821	Read, Theophilus	5	18			9050
1825	Reader, Joshua	0	1			1630
1838	Redman, John	0	1			500
1831	Reeves, Alvah	0	1	45		610
1829	Renick, Robert	0	3	1712		280
1824	Revin, Noah	1	1		500	1090
1825	Rhea, Jeremiah	2	5			1906
1826	Richards, Mitchell	1	3	113		1850
1824	Richey, Alex	1	1			1025
1824	Richmon, Thomas	2	5			1525
1836	Right, Elizabeth	1	8	350		1392
1824	Right, Jarrot	5	3		1050	2900
1829	Ritchey, Solomon L.	1	1			1550
1821	Ritchie, Alexander	1	1			1880
1825	Rives, Noah	1	2	100		325
1824	Roberts, John	1	4	86	336	2100
1833	Rodes, James	1	1	596		2058
1824	Russel, John	3	3			1150
1838	Satterfield, Isaac	0	2	150		800
1831	Saver, John B.	1	4	300		600

Year	Slave Owner	Slave Numbers		Land in Acres	Total Land Value	Total Taxable Value
		Age <16	Total			
1821	Scofield, Henry	1	3			2148
1836	Sears, Austin	1	1			1125
1825	Sears, Francis	4	8	196		550
1824	Sears, Henry	1	3	200		1550
1836	Sears, John	1	3			1975
1824	Sears, Joseph	1	3	182	786	1670
1836	Sears, Nancy	0	1			1900
1836	Sears, Samuel	4	16	120		50
1824	Sears, Thomas	1	1			675
1827	Sears, Thomas B.	1	1			5132
1824	Sears, William	3	8			2400
1838	Seay, Joseph R.	2	3			700
1825	Settle, Felix	0	1			1215
1825	Settle, French	1	1			525
1838	Sherry, Reubin	0	2	100		230
1838	Sherry, William	3	3	100		
1829	Shickels, Peter	0	3	50		
1838	Shields, Elijah	0	1	231		190
1821	Shipley, Jane	1	2			1100
1825	Shipley, Nathaniel	1	2	30		
1824	Shipley, Robert	1	2	454	1000	3490
1821	Shipley, Robert Jr.	0	1			
1825	Short, Landrum	1	2	270		3950
1827	Siddens, James S.	0	1	180		2165
1825	Siddens, William	1	7	1985		1170
1821	Simmons, Isaiah	1	1			520
1836	Simpson, Robert	1	3	45		1200
1825	Sledge, Miles C.	0	1	400		1277
1827	Smith, Fanny	1	1			1100
1824	Smith, Frances	1	1			550
1824	Smith, Sally	4	6	160	520	
1621	Smith, Samuel	2	6	162		3310
1837	Smith, Sarah	5	8	160		2938
1838	Smith, Washington	0	1			670
1829	Sneed, Elijah	1	6			2000
1827	Snow, John	2	3			1500
1837	Spenser, William	1	3	1313		1175

Year	Slave Owner	Slave Numbers		Land in Acres	Total Land Value	Total Taxable Value
		Age <16	Total			
1831	Spillman, Levi			80		
1821	Spilman, Polly	10	20			7742
1824	Stark, James	15	23		7772	16757
1836	Stark, Amanda	2	5			630
1821	Stark, Daniel	3	6			3544
1836	Stark, Festus	4	4	78		1500
1821	Stark, James	8	16			11450
1838	Stark, James	25	48			1594
1825	Stark, James (Add for John Godley)	11	29	1792		24
1825	Stark, James (Add for R. Stark)	9	15	562		15
1821	Stark, Jeremiah	14	30	188		17785
1833	Stark, Jerry	2	5			776
1821	Stark, Jessie	2	4			7590
1821	Stark, John	6	14			6255
1821	Stark, Joseph	3	4			1265
1836	Stark, Lucy	2	6			1160
1824	Stark, Sally	9	17	162	1460	9496
1836	Stark, Sarah	6	10	600		6036
1824	Stark, Theophilus	1	4			1600
1821	Staton, Thomas	0	2			2680
1826	Stevens, E. C.	0	1			2000
1825	Stevens, Elisha	1	1			790
1836	Stinson, William Sr.	1	2	935		1175
1824	Stoval, George	1	1		284	830
1821	Stoval, Thomas	1	2			790
1825	Stovall, George	1	2	71		2643
1833	Stovall, James	0	1			1025
1824	Stovall, Nancy	1	2	50	150	850
1826	Strait, Benjamin	0	1			1200
1825	Strait, David	0	1			400
1825	Strait, William	1	1	115		690
1824	Stubblefield, Robert	1	5	130	650	1850
1838	Sulser, Hardin	1	2	400		2170
1824	Sutton, Thomas	1	1		1261	2661
1827	Swearing, Lemuel	1	3			5025

Year	Slave Owner	Slave Numbers		Land in Acres	Total Land Value	Total Taxable Value
		Age <16	Total			
1826	Swearingen, Samuel	1	3			600
1825	Teeter, Robert	2	9			490
1827	Thaxton, Zadock	2	4			4050
1829	Thomas, Isham	0	1			1300
1838	Thomas, Johnson	1	5			330
1821	Thomas, Walter	6	9	1140		9470
1824	Thompson, Balaam	1	2		780	2380
1836	Thompson, John	0	1			1797
1836	Thompson, Sarah	2	2	400		390
1825	Tinsley, Mary	1	1			2010
1826	Tinsley, Polly	1	1	100		900
1827	Tinsley, T. J.	1	1			800
1821	Tinsley, William	1	2			1550
1827	Tracy, John	1	2	200		250
1824	Traverse, John	1	1		800	1600
1825	Travis, John	1	2	400		1850
1831	Travis, Susannah	1	1			2570
1821	Trilken, Thomas	2	6			3820
1825	Tuff, Richard	1	2			350
1824	Wade, Lois	1	1		500	1200
1825	Wadkins, Jacob	2	2	1904		1330
1825	Waggoner, George	1	1	200		3527
1826	Waggoner, Martha	0	2	71		1455
1833	Waggoner, Ralph	0	1	150		974
1826	Walker, Jacob W.	1	2	1304		575
1838	Walker, Mary S.	12	19	3053		2679
1826	Walker, Priscilla	3	6			18728
1825	Walker, William	1	3	316		1770
1826	Walker, David	3	5	273		1932
1831	Walthall, Burrell	1	2			7121
1825	Walthall, Mary	3	3	140		800
1824	Watts, Thomas	6	11		8500	15170
1824	Weatherspoon, Hardy	1	1		400	950
1833	Weatherspoon, Samuel	0	1			1060
1836	Weatherspoon, Younger	0	1			200
1837	Weaver, James	1	3	150		425
1831	Weaver, Joel	0	1			220

Year	Slave Owner	Slave Numbers		Land in Acres	Total Land Value	Total Taxable Value
		Age <16	Total			
1827	Weaver, John	0	1	20		230
1838	Weaver, William	1	1			420
1824	Whitly, John	3	3		575	2050
1821	Whitney, Ann	4	4	850		4975
1821	Whitney, Jeremiah	2	5			1750
1821	Whitney, John	1	21	375		1510
1829	Whitney, John G. Jr.	0	2			2000
1827	Whitney, Mary/Polly	3	7	100		
1821	Whitney, Thomas	1	2			1270
1821	Whitney, Uriah	0	1			480
1837	Wickware, Alphus	0	1			450
1829	Wickware, Samuel	0	1			900
1831	Williams, Asbury G.	0	1			300
1821	Williams, Henry	1	2	100		780
1824	Williams, James	1	4	150	520	2220
1824	Williams, Langston	1	1	200	1100	2050
1824	Williams, Mastin	3	8	71		3342
1825	Williams, Ralph	1	3	150		3655
1829	Williams, Will	0	1	450		1625
1825	Willoughby, Samuel	1	3	150		435
1824	Willoughby, Solomon	4	4	150	750	3250
1824	Wills, Eliza	2	3	209	865	3800
1821	Wills, John	1	1			2475
1824	Wilmot, Richard	1	1		1575	2155
1836	Wilmott, Eleanor	1	1	350		3200
1821	Wilmott, Richard	0	2	279		475
1824	Wilson, George	1	3		1500	2200
1826	Wilson, James Jr.	0	3	150		1470
1831	Winn, Willis	2	5	108		300
1821	Witherspoon, Hardy	1	1			950
1838	Woodcock, Green B.	0	1	140		725
1833	Woodson, Anderson	1	0			650
1837	Wright, Elizabeth	2	8	350		400
1838	Wright, Griffin	1	1			5525
1825	Wright, Jarrett	1	5	350		823
1821	Wright, Joseph	1	1			155

Chapter 8

Slaves Bequeathed By Wills

Slaves as Bequeathed Property

In 1776, Thomas Jefferson, once an owner of over 200 slaves, wrote that "all men are created equal" in the Declaration of Independence. In his earlier draft, he condemned King George III for capturing and shipping slaves to America and wrote that slavery was not a natural state for humans.[1] That portion was stricken from the final version and no specific mention of slavery was included. Patrick Henry owned slaves when he said, "Give me liberty or give me death." Jefferson's slaves were not freed until after his death.

In 1787, the Constitutional Convention convened to write the constitution of the United States of America. Just three years later, the first census of United States population was completed. Kentucky had only 61,133 white people but it already had 11,830 slaves, 16.2 percent of the total population.[2] The United States constitution did not prohibit slavery and did not free the slaves.

George Washington, Benjamin Franklin, and many other slave owners voiced strong opposition to slavery but did not free their slaves. Washington, Franklin, and others stated in their wills that their slaves were to be freed upon the death of their master. That indicated their acceptance of the slaves as property to be dispersed as the owner saw fit but their conscience must have said otherwise.

The Supreme Court upheld the view that slaves were property in the famous Dred Scott decision.[3] Scott was a slave born in Missouri who was taken by his owner to the free states of Illinois and Wisconsin. Courts, including ones in Kentucky, had held

---

[1] Cunningham, Noble E. 2000. *Jefferson vs. Hamilton: confrontations that shaped a nation*. The Bedford series in history and culture. Boston: Bedford/St. Martin's.

[2] Harrison, Lowell Hayes, and James C. Klotter. 1997. *A new history of Kentucky*. Lexington, Ky: University Press of Kentucky.

[3] Smith, Goldwin, 1893. *The United States: an outline of political history, 1492-1871*. New York, McMillan and Company

previously that slaves gained freedom when they moved to reside in free states. Scott's owner refused to free Scott or allow him to buy his freedom. Scott sued for his freedom.

The U.S. Supreme Court in 1857 held that Scott had no right to sue because he was not a citizen. Further, slave owners could not be deprived of their property and slaves were property.[4]

Perhaps many Kentucky slave owners did not share the founding fathers' abhorrence of slavery as an institution. Most shared the belief that slaves were property, not citizens. In many counties in Kentucky, slave auctions were conducted in front of the Courthouse. Sales were transacted between individuals using what amounted to a bill of sale that had witnesses to the signature. It was tidy, legal, and binding. One such bill of sale is shown in Figure 21.

Figure 21

An Elizabeth Calvert bill of sale of Burrell for $850 in 1837. Used by permission of Todd Calvert.

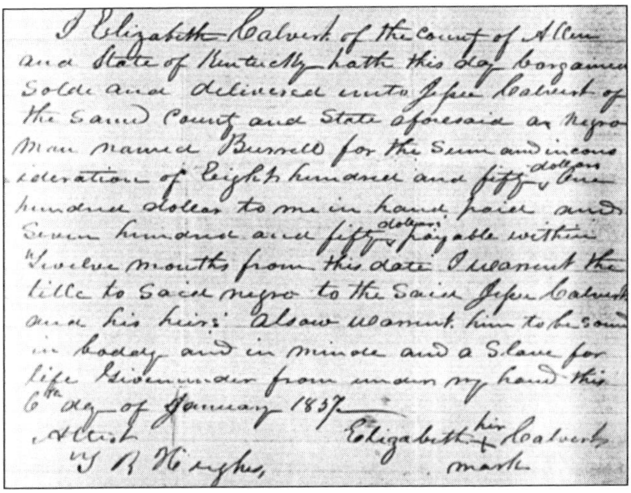
I Elizabeth Calvert of the County of Allen and State of Kentucky hath this day bargained Solde and delivered unto Jesse Calvert of the Said County and State aforesaid a negro Man named Burrell for the Sum and inconsideration of Eight hundred and fifty dollars One hundred dollars to me in hand paid and Seven hundred and fifty dollars payable within Twelve months from this date I warrant the title to Said negro to the Said Jesse Calvert and his heirs: alsow warrant him to be Sound in body and in minde and a Slave for life Given under from under my hand this 6th day of January 1837.

Attest
J R Hughes,

Elizabeth her + mark Calvert

[4] Finkelman, Paul. 1997. *Dred Scott v. Sandford: a brief history with documents*. The Bedford series in history and culture. Boston: Bedford Books

The ratification of the 13th and 14th amendments to the Constitution settled the issue and made slavery unconstitutional. After 1865, slaves were no longer property but were citizens.

Slaves' Monetary Value

Before ratification, not only were slaves property, they were expensive property. Abolition of slavery without recompense, as the Emancipation Proclamation did for slaves in the Confederate States, was a matter of great concern to slave owners. Kentucky owners would incur a heavy financial loss if emancipation without recompense occurred.

Figure 22

Inventory of the slaves owned by Daniel Hays on 14 January 1863, provided by Joyce Weaver

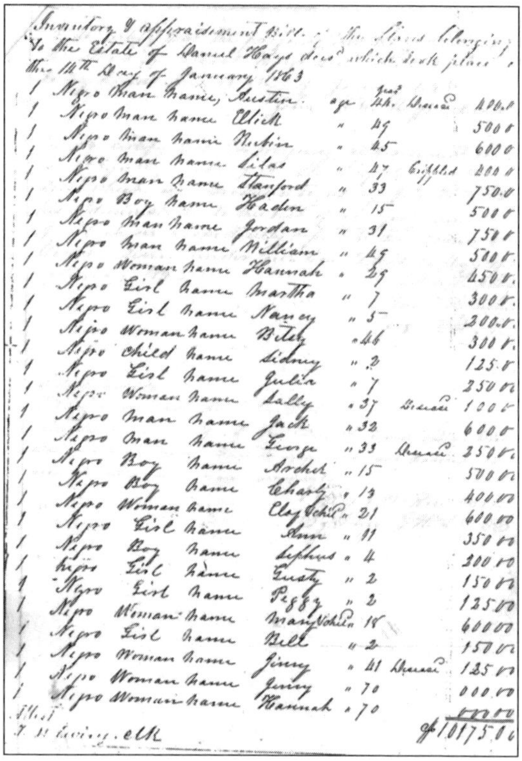

Inventory & appraisement Bill of the Slaves belonging to the Estate of Daniel Hays dec^d which took place the 14th Day of January 1863

			Age		Value
1	Negro Man name	Austin	age 44 years	Diseased	400.0
1	Negro Man name	Elick	" 49		500 0
1	Negro Man name	[illegible]	" 45		600 0
1	Negro Man name	Silas	" 47	Crippled	400 0
1	Negro Man name	Stanford	" 33	"	750.0
1	Negro Boy name	Haden	" 15		500 0
1	Negro Man name	Jordan	" 31		750 0
1	Negro Man name	William	" 49		500 0
1	Negro Woman name	Hannah	" 29		450 0
1	Negro Girl name	Martha	" 7		300 0
1	Negro Girl name	Nancy	" 5		200.0
1	Negro Woman name	[illegible]	" 46		300 0
1	Negro Child name	Sidney	" 2		125.0
1	Negro Girl name	Julia	" 7		250 00
1	Negro Woman name	Sally	" 37	Diseased	100 0
1	Negro Man name	Jack	" 32		600 0
1	Negro Man name	George	" 33	Diseased	250 00
1	Negro Boy name	[illegible]	" 15		500 00
1	Negro Boy name	Charly	" 13		400.00
1	Negro Woman name	Clay & child	" 21		600 00
1	Negro Girl name	Ann	" 11		350 00
1	Negro Boy name	[illegible]	" 4		200 00
1	Negro Girl name	[illegible]	" 2		150 00
1	Negro Girl name	Peggy	" 2		125 00
1	Negro Woman name	Mary & child	" 18		600 00
1	Negro Girl name	Bell	" 2		150 00
1	Negro Woman name	Jinny	" 41	Diseased	125 00
1	Negro Woman name	Jenny	" 70		000.00
1	Negro Woman name	Hannah	" 70		000 00
					$10175.00

[illegible] clk

An example of the value of slaves was the appraisal conducted when someone died and left slaves as part of their estate. That was the circumstance when three appraisers were appointed to value of the estate of Daniel Hayes of Warren County. Figure 22 is an inventory of his slaves and their monetary worth from that appraisal. Their total value was $10,175.00, a significant sum. That would have been $172, 457 in today's dollars.[5]

The monetary value of slaves was so high that the owners would incur an enormous loss if slavery were to be abolished. That clouded

[5] http:// oregonstate.edu/polici/faculty-research/sahr/cv2009.xis

the moral, philosophical, and religious decisions to free them. It is interesting that the Emancipation Proclamation had been issued just ten days before the appraisal of the Hays estate. There is no evidence that the appraisers knew of the proclamation or, if they had known, would have altered the values. Even after the owners knew about it, few Allen County slaves were freed prior to passing of the Thirteenth Amendment almost three years later.

The number of slaves in the Hayes household was no doubt determined by a variety of factors, but their value was the most important part of that owner's wealth. He owned fourteen male and fifteen female slaves[6] who were appraised after his death. (Figure 22).

The individual value of males peaked at about 32 to 33 years old. Three male slaves were outliers in the value curve: the 33 and the 44 year old were diseased and the 47 year old was crippled. The oldest slave men were 49 years old. Figure 23 illustrates the variation of those values for the males.

Figure 23

Value of male slaves of Daniel Hays on 11 January 1863

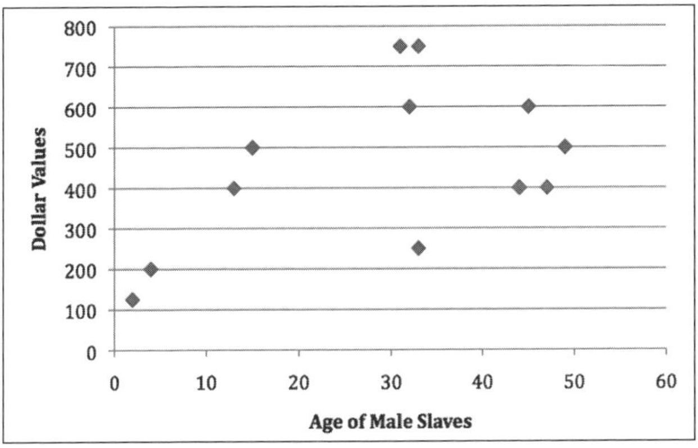

The fifteen female slaves were appraised at lower values than the males, except for the very youngest whose value at 2 years old was $125 for both genders (Figure 22). There were two 70 year old women who the appraiser determined to have no monetary value.

There were two outliers on the females' value curve (Figure 23):

[6] The Hays' slaves do not appear in the 1860 census because the enumeration occurred after he died

they were 37 and 41year old women who were identified as diseased. The peak values were for the 18 and 20 year old young women. At $600 each, their value was $100 less than the peak value of the men. In addition, the women reached their peak value twelve to fourteen years earlier than the men. Figure 24 shows the variation of value by age of the Hays' female slaves.

Figure 24

Value of female slaves of Daniel Hays on 11 January 1863

Slaves for Hire

The 1797 slave code of Kentucky law prohibited slave owners from allowing their slaves to hire themselves out to others. But, it allowed the owner to hire them out. One easily overlooked value of slaves was the income that the owner could receive from hiring out his slaves to work for others, "rent-a-slave" so to speak. These rentals were often in the form of verbal agreements if the hire was for a short period, day or week perhaps, typical of crop harvests, spring-cleaning, or clearing land. Verbal agreements were common when a neighbor or friend made the hire. No record exists for those verbal contracts.

A more formal rental was made in the form of a promissory note (Figure 25). In it, Nancy Parker hired out her slave boy, Mack, for one year ending on 2 January 1857. The hire was for the sum of $45 (payable to Ms Parker), two summer suits (sets), one winter suit (set), one pair of shoes and socks, one wool hat, and one blanket.

Figure 25

Promissory Note to Nancy Parker for the hire of her slave boy named Mack, provided by Joyce Weaver.

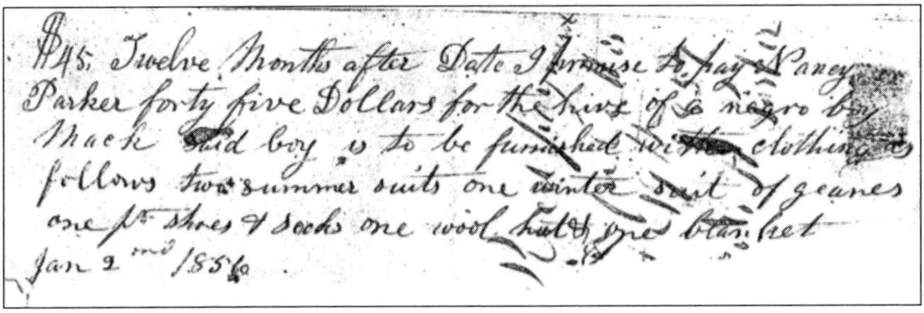
$45. Twelve Months after Date I promise to pay Nancy Parker forty five Dollars for the hire of a negro boy Mack said boy is to be furnished with clothing as follows two summer suits one winter suit of geanes one pr shoes & socks one wool hat & one blanket
Jan 2nd 1856.

Ms. Parker had previously hired-out Mack for other periods, once for four months and another for a year. There were several possible advantages that accrued to an owner who hired-out their slaves: there was no cost to the owner for feeding and boarding the slave during the period of the hire; there would be temporary relief from a recalcitrant or unruly slave who would become someone else's problem for that period; a slave could acquire a new and more valuable skill; and it provided cash income to the owner with minimal risk.[7] In the 1840s and 1850s, the typical rental fee was from twelve to fifteen percent of the slave's value. Thus, Mack's value must have been between $300 and $375. That value would indicate that Mack was a boy between 10 and 12 years old.[8]

Commonly, a hire for a year ended on Christmas Day, allowing the interval before the New Year to be used to complete another contract or allow bids at a slave-hiring auction for the coming year. The hire-out of slaves was more common in urban areas, especially for domestic help. During the Civil War in the Lexington area, hire-out slaves were used to repair a railroad. There were some who advocated that railroad companies should buy slaves.[9] In any case, wherever they were used, hire-out slaves were cheaper than free-wage white laborers.

[7] Hunter, Tera W. 1997. *To 'joy my freedom: Southern Black women's lives and labors after the Civil War*. Cambridge, Mass: Harvard University Press.

[8] Lucas, Marion B., 2003. *A history of Blacks in Kentucky from slavery to segregation 1760-1891.* Kentucky Historical Society, Frankfort, Kentucky

[9] Takagi, Madori, 1999. *Rearing wolves to our own destruction: slavery in Richmond, Virginia 1782-1865.* Carter G. Woodson Institute of Black Studies, University Press of Virginia

Rental of a slave also benefited the hirer as well. It was beneficial to those who could not afford to own a slave, those whose need was seasonal or temporary, and those who needed to assuage their moral objections to slavery.

Slave Insurance

Because of the high value of slaves, life insurance was available to mitigate loss in Virginia. Medical examination was required, and the policy did not pay if the slave was transported from or escaped from the state, or died as a result of suicide, war, riots, insurrections, or at the hands of justice or abuse by the owner. Slaves could be insured for up to two-thirds of their value.[10] About three percent of industrial slaves and an even smaller number of plantation slaves were insured.[11] In Missouri, slave insurance was unavailable for slaves under 14-years old because, according to their data, the slave youngster was twice as likely to die as a white.[12] No evidence was found that Allen County slaves were insured, but the insurance seems to have been available.

Deeds that Conveyed Slaves As Property

Deeds are used to convey property from one individual to another. We think of a deed as a tool to convey land from one owner to another, and that is the most common use. However, before the emancipation of Kentucky's slaves by the 13th Amendment, deeds were sometimes used to covey slaves from one owner to another. For example, Elizabeth Harris filed a deed with the Allen County Court on 29 April 1848 that conveyed ownership of

"…two negroes, to wit, Mary and her child James…" to children of her deceased daughter Rebecca: James M., David Wesley, Solomon H., Elizabeth J., Emily C. and Martha. C. Pope."

The slaves were to be used by the children's father, Samuel Pope, to assist in raising and educating those children.[13] This was also an example of children owning slaves.

---

[10] Jordan, Ervin L. 1995. *Black Confederates and Afro-Yankees in Civil War Virginia.* Charlottesville, Va: University Press of Virginia.

[11] Miller, Randall M., and John David Smith. 1997. *Dictionary of Afro-American slavery.* Westport, Conn: Praeger.

[12] Frazier, Harriet C. 2004. Runaway and freed Missouri slaves and those who helped them, 1763-1865. Jefferson, N.C.: McFarland & Co.

[13] Allen County Court Deed Book H, 1845-1850, page 426, provided by Harris Overholt

No extraction of slave ownership transfer by deeds has been made. Therefore, no list of them is available for inclusion in this document. However, researchers may wish to search the deeds for mention of their ancestors.

Wills that Bequeathed Slaves

Prior to December 1865, the slaves in Allen County, and elsewhere in Kentucky, were legal property. As such, they were frequently bequeathed by owners in their wills as were other forms of property. Typically, the will stated the gender and first name of the slave and designated who was to inherit him or her. These wills are sources of information for genealogical researchers searching for ancestors who were slaves before being freed.

There are several categories of wills that mentioned slaves. Some had a simple statement that bequeathed all the slaves to the spouse or child. Some wills directed that the slaves be sold and the money distributed among designated inheritors. A few of those directed that slave families only be sold as a family group.

Some wills were specific in naming to whom each slave was bequeathed. J. J. Anderson's will of 1863 gave his estate to his wife except for "two little negro children." He gave a boy named Hugh Franklin to his daughter Elnora and a girl named Laura to his daughter Malissa.

A few wills required that slaves were to be freed after the owner's death. Baxter Ray, in his 1837 will stated that he was "destitute of children" and bequeathed his land, gray mare, hogs, and furniture to Nance [Nancy], a "negro girl." He willed that "Nance and her increase [all her current and future children] be freed from yoke of bondage." In rare cases, an owner's will directed that all the slaves be freed.

Table 21 contains information that was extracted by B. S. Chambers from a compilation of wills of Allen County slave owners who had wills that mentioned slaves.[14] These data will be valuable for tracing slave ancestors through the chain of possession prior to freedom.

---

[14] Rabold, Mary M. and Elizabeth M. Price, 1972. Allen County Kentucky wills and settlements 1815-1902. Published by authors

Table 21

Slaves Bequeathed in Allen County

***Note:** Bequeathed slaves of Allen County are listed below in a list sorted alphabetically the slave owner. Slave names are shown in bold print*

Alexander, A. C., 1863: To my daughter Sarah Brown my black girl **Pat Ann**. To Almira Alexander my black **Susan Jane**.

Allen, William, 1846: To my wife Sally Allen a black man named **Frank**.

Anderson, J. J., 1863: To my wife all my estate except two little black children. To Elnora Smith, a black boy named **Hugh Franklin**. To Malissa Smith, a little girl named **Laura**.

Austin, Margaret K.: All the blacks I gave to Herman Whitney at his death goes to Margaret K. Austin

Baily, Benjamin, 1845: To daughter Nancy Margaret and her heirs my black boy named **Reuben**.

Benedict, Benjamin, 1847: To my wife Mary Benedict black man named **Burrell** and black woman named **Lucinda**. After death of wife black man Burrell to select his own master.

Blackburn, James, 1843: To my wife Elizabeth my black woman named **Gin**.

Burton, Mary 1860: To my son Francis M. Burton, my interest in **Jane** our girl of color.

Bush, Isaac, 1822: To Elizabeth Montgomery's daughter Polly Montgomery my black boy **James**.

Calvert, John, 1856: To my wife Elizabeth Calvert my black man named **Burrell** and black woman **Pheby**. To my son Jesse Calvert two black boys and a black girl. To my son Tolivar Calvert three blacks. To my son John J. Calvert two black boys and a black girl. To my son James W. Calvert three blacks.

Clark, John Jr. 1844: To free my servant **Matt** and give him fifteen acres of land, at his death the land goes to my son Adam.

Cockrill, Johnson H., 1850: To daughter Lee Ann E. Cockrill one black girl named **Mariah**. To son Sidenham P. Cockrill one black man named **Zack**. To son, Elijah M.Cockrill, one black girl. To son, Ben F. Cockrill one black girl. To daughter Mary F. Read a black woman.

Cockrill, Johnson J., 1851: One black girl **Mariah**.

Colbert, Francis, 1827: To wife Peggy Colbert black woman named **Kizzy**.

Curd, Jesse, 1851: To daughter Mary G. Pulliam my blacks.

Cusanbury, Elyah: One black woman and child **Eliza** one black boy **Riac**, one black woman **Pheve**, one black man **Thomay**, one black boy **Linus**, one black girl **Mary** one black girl **Sally**, one blind woman **Milley**, one black woman **Grun**.

Davis, Jonathan, 1862: Two blacks, **Harriett** and **George**.

Dixon, John, 1829: To my nephew, Thomas W. Dixon, my black slaves

Downing, 1834: To Rachel Proctor, my black boy named **Thomas**.

Downing, Benjamin, 1868: To Isabella Boheler, a black girl named **Angeline** and 4 other choice blacks.

Downing, Sarah, 1826: To Samuel Downing, choice of all my slaves. My old black woman, **Violet**, the choice of my children to live with.

Dye, James, 1846: **Wish**, a black person purchased for my wife

Fish, Nancy, 1835: Slave document - purchase of black woman, **Lola** $350

Fitzpatrick, 1853: To my wife, Dolly

Fitzpatrick, my black woman, **Sally** and black boy **Lewis**. To my daughter-in-law, Frances Jane Fitzpatrick, a black woman and her child, **Rachel**.

Foster, Thomas Gibson, 1843: To my brother, Robert J. Foster, my black boy, **Isaac**, age 18. To my sister, Virginia Mary Smith, my black man, **Douglas** and his wife, **Sally**. To my niece, Mary Martha J.J. my black girl named **Frances**, age 13. To Martha Jane Foster, my black girl named **Margaret**, age 6. To James J. Foster, my two black boys, **Nelson** age 18 and **John**, age 4. One black girl named **Mary**, age 2, to niece Mary Gibson Foster.

Goodrum, John J., 1860: I want the slaves sold.

Haines, Christopher, 1846: To my daughter, Christiana Haines, my black woman **Sukey** and her infant child, **Mindy**.

Haines, Malinda, 1867: To daughter, my black woman named **Evaline**. To son John, a black boy named **Henry**.

Hains, Talitha, 1851: Unjustly deprived of my black woman and $30 to my old servant, **Alexander**.

Hammond, Reubi, 1849: To my daughter, my black boy, **Alfred** and my black woman, **Louisa**

Harris, David, 1842: To my wife, all my black people.

Hickman, Jessee L., 1843: To wife, Mary Ann Hickman, all my black people

Hinton, Moore, 1832: To Tempy Hinton, my wife, my black boys and woman **Elish**, **Penny**, **Fillie**, **Silvey**, **Ewing**, **Frances**, **Fanny**, **Vilet**, **Minty** and **Elvira**.

Holder, William, 1831: To my daughter, Emaline Wade, one black slave. To Sinthy Whitney, one black slave. To John Holder, one black slave. To Edward Holder, two black slaves. To daughter, Elizabeth, two black slaves.

Hughes, T. R. L., 1891: To daughter, Belvidreda, a black girl worth $1000.

Jackson, Benjamin, 1876: A house girl living in my (papers were burned) **Hagar Hay** a woman of color.

Jameson, James A., 1863: To my wife Narcissa, my blacks, until my children come of age, then divided between my wife and children.

Johnson, Matthew, 1852: My black people, to my wife.

Landers, Isaac, 1872: Patsy Landers, $200 to the children for the emancipation of the slaves.

Lynn, John, 1849: Appraise the estate and slaves of J. Lynn.

Lynn, Moses, 1849: To Mary Ann Morrison, her dower of the slaves

McClary, Robert, 1853: To son Daniel McClary for sale of black boy named **Henry**.

McElroy, James Sr., 1838: My black man named **Tim**, set free. My black woman named **Violet** set free.

Meredith, Armistead, 1860: To wife, Elizabeth, my two blacks.

Mitchell, Willis Sr., 1840: To my wife, a black girl.

Moore, James W., 1863: To my wife, my four blacks.

Motley, Reubin, 1864: To my wife, all my black slaves.

Pitchford, Eli, 1836: To Daniel Pitchford, black girl named **Tabitha**. To Orange D. Pitchford, black woman named **Bob** and black girl named **Kitty**. To Sarah Pitchford, black girl named **Fanny**.

Poe, William, 1855: To wife Delana Poe, my black boys named **Reuben** and **Jacob** and one black girl named **Mary Ann**. To daughter, Feraruba Poe, one black boy named **Luke**.

Porter, Edward, 1841: William P. Neale and Kathrine S. Porter Neale, the black named **Teny**, **Fanny** and **Ellen**. son Luther Porter, three blacks named **Bill**, **George** and **Prica**. To son Uriah Porter, a **Tiny**. To my daughter Eliza A. Procter, two blacks worth $400 and **James Henry** worth $600. To my daughter, Zero?, two blacks, **Maria** worth $400 and **Allen** worth $500. To my daughter, Mary Frances Porter; two blacks **Lucy**, worth $400 and **William**, worth $400. To my wife Mary Porter, two blacks, **James** and **Charity**. To my son, George William Porter; my black, **Richard** worth $300.

Pulliam, William, 1851: To wife Mary G. Pulliam, blacks she inherited from her father, Jesse Curd. To my son, Henry C. Pulliam, a black boy worth $450. To my son, Benjamin Pulliam; a black boy worth $600. To my son William P. Pulliam, Ten black boys worth $600. To my son George Pulliam, a black boy worth $350

Ray, Baxter, 1838: I wish my black girl named **Nance** and children to be free of bondage. To have the place where I now live, gray mare, hogs, feather bed that I formerly lay on, with furniture. (a law suit was brought by Nancy, a woman of color, and her children; the court ordered the will recorded.)

Statin, Elijah J., 1860: To wife Celia G. Statin, my black woman named **Marinday**, my black boy named **Charles**, and small girl named **Patsy**.

Sears, Frances, 1833: To my son, Samuel Sears, my black man **James**.

Sears, Thomas, 1846: To daughter, Christiana Sears, my black named **Palmira**.

Sears, Thomas Sr., 1825: To the children of Elizabeth Sears, Deceased, black **Jimmy**, **Sucky**, and **Ellet**. To William Sears, black **Mary**, **Wilson** and **Jenny**.

Sears, William, 1859: To my daughter Elizabeth H. Claypool, a black named **John**. To my daughter, Sarah A. Mainer, a black named **Henry**. To my daughter, Lutitia W. Rector, a black named **Samuel**.

Wagoner, George, 1854: To wife Sally Wagoner, three blacks named **Esther**, **Lucy** and **Little Esther**. To daughter Agnes Wagoner, a black girl. To daughter Sally Dodd, a black girl. To daughter a black boy. To son William L. Wagoner, a black boy. To Fanny Guy's children, **Little Ester**.

Whitney, Emeline, 1865: To Sally P. Holder, my black woman **Matilda** and her children. To Herman Whitney, my husband, my black man and the girl named **Joe**. The latter I inherited from John Holder. To Margaret K. Austin, all my blacks I gave to my husband, at his death, goes to her.

Whitney, Simeon W., 1863: To wife Eliza Whitney to hire out one or more slaves.

Williams, Langston, 1840: To wife Ruth, a black man named **Lewis**.

Wright, Griffin, 1843: Children to be the only bidders for the slaves.

Chapter 9

Slaves Who Were Inherited

Inherited Slaves

The number of slaves per slave owner households in the south averaged between four and six. About 36 percent of southern households owned slaves. In Allen County, the number was about 25 percent. One tenth of southern slave owners were women who inherited the slaves from their father or husband.[1] Most southern plantation owners left their most valuable assets (the slaves) to their daughters and their land to their sons. Most of those slaves who went to the daughters were females, too. Widows traditionally received one third of an estate.[2]

Allen County's data were somewhat different, at least for the wills that specifically willed a slave to a person. Of the inheritors in the 36 wills that mentioned slaves, 32 (89%) were female and only 4 were male. The women received most of the slaves, but most of the land passed to male inheritors. The data were not sufficiently detailed to determine gender differences in the inherited slaves.

For the convenience of ancestral researchers, the information contained in Chapter 8 was resorted by the inheritor's name, that is to say, the new owner. Otherwise, the data on the following pages (Table 22) are the same as in Table 21 of Chapter 8.

---

[1] McDougall, Walter A. 2004. *Freedom just around the corner: a new American history, 1585-1828*. New York: HarperCollins Publishers.

[2] Berkin, Carol, and Eric Foner. 1999. *First generations*: women in colonial America. New York, NY: Hill and Wang.

Table 22

Slaves who were inherited in Allen County

Inherited slaves of Allen County are listed below sorted by the inheritor. Slave names are shown in bold print. List is alphabetical by inheritor's surname.

Inheritor Atwood, Nance: Inherited black people from father Jesse L. Hickman.

Inheritor Beheler, Isabella, 1868: Received from father black girl named **Angeline**.

Inheritor Beherler, Mary, 1853: Inherited from father Robert McClary a black girl.

Inheritor Brown, Martha, 1853: Inherited from father Robert McClary a black boy named **Henry**.

Inheritor Brown, Sarah, 1863: Inherited from A. C. Alexander a girl of color named **Pat Ann**.

Inheritor Brown, William F., 1853: Inherited from grandfather William Fitzpatrick his black boy **Lewis**.

Inheritor Buchanon, Peter, 1835: Inherited from Nancy Fish a black woman named **LoLa**.

Inheritor Claypool, Elizabeth H., 1859: Inherited a black named **John**.

Inheritor Davasher, Elizabeth, 1856: Wife of William Davasher inherited from her father, John Calvert, a black girl and two black boys.

Inheritor Davis, Susan, 1853: Inherited from father, Robert McClary, 3 blacks; **Mary, Matilda, and Lucinda**.

Inheritor Dry, Elizabeth, 1843: Inherited from father, Jesse L. Hickman some black people.

Inheritor Dry, Rebecca, 1843: Inherited from father, Jesse L. Hickman, some black people.

Inheritor Dodd, Frances, 1851: Inherited from father William Pulliam, a black, worth $400.

Inheritor Dodd, Sally, 1854: From father, G. Wagoner, a black girl.

Inheritor Duffer, Emily, 1853: Inherited from father, Robert McClary, a black named **Eliza**.

Inheritor Gatewood, Polly, 1856: Fletcher Gatewood's wife, inherited from father, John Calvert, a black woman and two black boys

Inheritor Glover, Jane, 1856: Inherited from father John Calvert, two black boys and a black girl.

Inheritor Guy, Fanny, 1854: Children from grandfather, G. Wagoner, a black girl named **Little Ester**.

Inheritor Haines, Malinda, 1851: Inherited from father, William Pulliam, two black girls worth $500.

Inheritor Heeter, Lucinda, 1851: Inherited from father, William Pulliam, a black worth $350.

Inheritor Holder, Sally P., 1865: From Emeline Whitney, inherited black woman, **Matilda** and her children, a black man, and the girl named **Joe.** The latter was inherited from John Holder.

Inheritor Kenady, Nancy, 1856: Wife of Andrew Kenady inherited from her father, John Calvert, a black woman and her two children.

Inheritor Lindsey, Rachel, 1846: To Ann M. the blacks inherited by her, will not be liable for debts of Richard S. at her death. Blacks descend to her Inheritors.

Inheritor Mainer, Sarah A., 1859: Inherited from William Sears, A black named **Henry**.

Inheritor Mayberry, Elizabeth, 1853: Inherited from father, Robert McClary, black boy, **Bur**, she swapped to Mr. Brown for a black woman.

Inheritor Montgomery, Polly, 1822: Received a black boy, named **James**, from her father.

Inheritor Napier, William F., 1853: Inherited from grandfather, William Fitzpatrick; his black boy, **Lewis**.

Inheritor Pitchford, William F., 1853: Inherited from William Fitzpatrick, his black boy, **Lewis**.

Inheritor Proctor, Rachel, 1834: Inherited from Samuel Downing, a black boy named **Thomas**.

Inheritor Railey, Eliza Ann, 1843: From father, Jessee L. Hickman, some black people.

Inheritor Read, Elizabeth, 1851: Inherited from her father, William Pulliam, two black girls worth $750.

Inheritor Read, Mary F., 1850: From father, a black woman.

Inheritor Rector, Lutitia W., 1859: Inherited from her father, William Sears, a black named **Samuel.**

Inheritor Smith, Elnora, 1863: A black boy named **Hugh Franklin**.

Inheritor Smith, Malina, 1863: A little girl named **Laura.**

Inheritor Williams, Elizabeth, 1854: Inherited from father a black girl.

Chapter 10

Slave Housing in Allen County, 1860

Slaves Provided Separate Houses in 1860

As the number of slaves grew, some slave owners built a separate house for them. One of those slave houses survives in Scottsville. That historic house (Figure 26) is located in the back yard of the house that is located on the southeast corner of West Main and South Dixon Streets.

Figure 26

Slave house built before 1860, probably by Sebastian Heeter

Sebastian Heeter was a son of a prominent merchant in Scottsville. The house was built sometime before 1860, when the US census recorded it. Sometime later, an addition was added to the back of the house to extend the original structure. The weatherboarding may have been added much later. Heeter had seven slaves who may have occupied the original house at that time. Of those slaves, there was a man over 55, a man between 36 and 55, a woman between 10 and 24, and four were children under 10: three boys and one girl.

The young girl in the 1860 census was Hannah Fishback, born in 1842, and living in the house when she was emancipated.[1] She was buried at the First Baptist Church's cemetery in Scottsville in 1923 (Figure 27).

The very earliest slave houses would likely have been log houses. Later ones would have resembled the Allen County one in Figure 26, except that it probably would not have had the porch when it was built. This one has had many modifications but the size is typical. Lofts were sometimes added as a sleeping area. Trundle beds were stowed beneath the regular bed during the day to save space. Beds were covered with straw ticks for warmth in winter.

Figure 27
Hannah Fishback's tombstone

In 1860, the US census counted

[1] Allen County Historical Society, 1985. *A pictorial history of Allen County, Kentucky*. Allen County Historical Society, Scottsville, Kentucky

slave houses as well as people. There were 210 slave houses in Allen County that year. These housed 1,138 slaves, about 75% of Allen County's slave population, averaging about 6 slaves per slave house. The typical slave house, like the one in Figure 26, was about 100 to 200 square feet with a dirt floor and a fireplace at one end for their cooking and heat.

Multiple Slave Houses

There were 38 Allen County slave owners who had multiple slave houses. In 1860, J. H. Page had the most slave houses. He provided eight houses for his 31 slaves and Uriah Porter had six houses for his 31 slaves. Jonathan Davis, C.C. Sears, and Samuel Sears each had five slave houses. Four other owners had four slave houses, 8 had three, and 21 had two.

Topographic maps of Allen County were published in 1926. The Scottsville Quadrangle of that series showed the Woodhall Ranch in northern Allen County, situated within a large meander loop of the Barren River. On a ridge just west of the Woodhall Ranch house, there is a row of five slave houses (indicated by small black squares) at the end of a road (marked by dashed lines). Those houses (Figure 28) were known locally as "The Row."[2] None of them exist now.

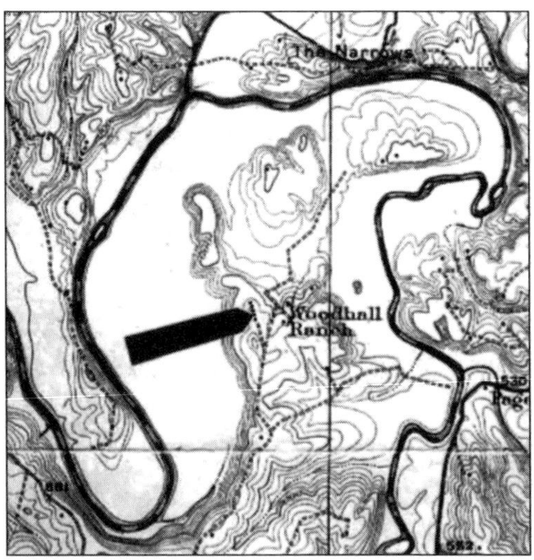

Figure 28
Slave houses at the Woodhall Ranch

[2] Verbal communication from Billie Hurt, 13 August 2009

Single Slave Houses

In Allen County there were 99 slave owners who provided a single house for their slaves in 1860. The number of occupants in these single houses varied from 1 to 66. The James Stark structure that housed his 66 slaves, the Uriah Porter structure that housed his 43 slaves, and the S. E. Carpenter structure with 29 slaves must have been significantly larger than most. In some states, large two-story structures with four rooms were used when there were large numbers of slaves to be housed.

Setting aside the Stark, Carpenter, and Porter anomalies, the other 97 single slave houses held 505 slaves. The average then was 5.0 slaves per house, about the same occupancy as in the owner's house.

One should remember that a slave house was not built as a home for a slave family. It was a structure to house the owner's collection of slaves, regardless of their familial relationships. Our view of crowded conditions is different from those in 1860. Large families were common among whites in an era before birth control. Families of ten to fourteen members of white families were not unusual.

Slaves Not Provided Separate Houses in 1860

Twenty-five percent of all slaves in Allen County, one out of every four, did not live in a separate slave house in 1860. These 373 slaves were the property of 145 owners. The notion that a slave owner would open his home to slaves is disconcerting and creates an urge to disbelieve and reject the data. Yet, the very large numbers insist that the data reflect actual occurrences.

Clearly, the early settlers on their trek to Kentucky shared the tent, lean-to, or puncheon camp structure (see page 3) with the slaves who accompanied them because there would not have been alternatives. At Fort Harrod, and presumably at other forts on the frontier, separate slave houses were not provided. One cannot imagine that the early settlers built two houses when they arrived, one for their family and another for one or two slaves.

The slaves in 1860 who were not provided a separate house would have lived in an attic, a loft, a basement, or a room in the owner's house. That arrangement becomes more understandable with the 77 slaves (21%) who were the only slave in the household.

There were 259 slaves who were in groups of from two to nine but not living in a slave house. They were almost evenly divided between males and females. Most of these were young, 33 percent were younger than 10, and only two were older than 55 (Figure 29).

Figure 29

Slaves by age group, who lived in groups of 2 to 9, but not in slave houses

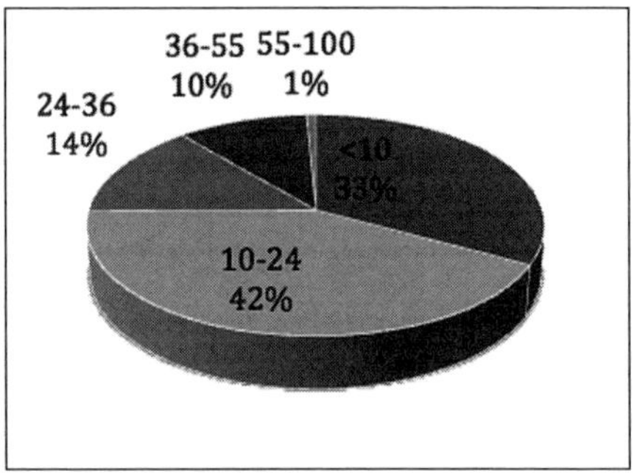

There were two anomalous groups, the eleven slaves of George Anthony and the twenty-six owned by J. W. Foster and six others. They had essentially the same age and gender attributes as the other groups. But, those numbers living in the slave owner's home seem unlikely. One possible explanation lies in the fact that slave owners sometimes placed their slaves up for hire. Nancy F. Parker had leased her slave boy named Mack for a period of about four months for the sum of $30 and "one good suit of winter clothing and shoes for winter and summer clothes suitable to be worn" (Figure 30). The payment was due on Christmas Day 1853.

Figure 30

Lease of slave named Mack for a period of about four months. Provided by Joyce Weaver.

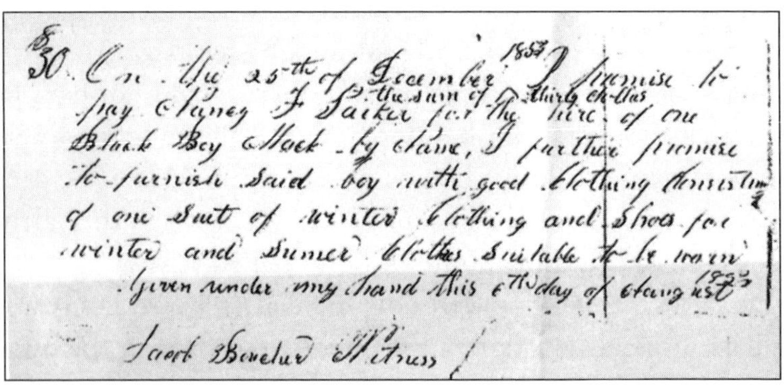
$30 On the 25th of December 1853 I promise to pay Nancy F Parker the sum of thirty dollars for the hire of one Black Boy Mack by name, I further promise to furnish said boy with good clothing consisting of one suit of winter clothing and shoes for winter and summer clothes suitable to be worn. Given under my hand this 6th day of August 1853

Witness

The following pages are data extracted from the 1860 US census for Allen County that enumerated the slave owners who did (Table 23) and did not (Table 24) provide separate houses for their slaves.

Table 23

Slave owners who provided separate slave houses in 1860

Slave Owner	**Enslaved Males**					**Enslaved Females**						
Alphabetical by Owner	*<10*	*10-24*	*24-36*	*36-55*	*55-100*	*<10*	*10-24*	*24-36*	*36-55*	*55-100*	*Slave Total*	*Houses*
Alexander, A. C.		1								1	2	4
Allen, Su			2				1		1	1	5	1
Anthony, J. G.	3	1				1	1	1			7	1
Anthony, W. H.	1				1	1		1			4	1
Austin, Eliza & 5 Others			3			1		1			5	1
Benedict, Mary				1					1		2	1
Bradley, Edward		1	2				1				4	1
Brown, Anny	2	1		1		1	1	1			7	1
Brown, Harrison						2		2			4	1
Brown, Henry		3	1			1			1		6	1
Brown, Robison	2	1				2	2	1			8	1
Burton, Adaline	6			1	1	2	2		2	1	15	3
Burton, Cuthbert			2			3	1	1		1	8	1
Burton, John	2	1	2			3		2			10	2
Burton, T. W.					1		1				2	1
Carpenter, Benjamin	4	1					2				7	1
Carpenter, J. D.	1			1		1		1	1		5	1
Carpenter, S. E.	6	6	1	2	1	6	2	4		1	29	1
Carpenter, Samuel		1					2		1		4	1
Carpenter, W. C.	1	1			1	1		1		1	6	1
Caruth, Thomas		2	1			2		1		1	7	2
Chaney, Washington	1	1			1	1	1	1			6	1
Claypool, S. D.							1				1	1
Collins, J. H.		1									1	1
Cook, Samuel		2				1	1		1		5	1
Corder, J. M.	1	3					1		1		6	1
Cushenberry, W.	1					2	1	1		1	6	1
Davasier, J. H.		1				1		1			3	1
Davis, Jonathan	3	6	3	1		6	1	4	1	1	26	5

Slave Owner	Enslaved Males					Enslaved Females						
Alphabetical by Owner	*<10*	*10-24*	*24-36*	*36-55*	*55-100*	*<10*	*10-24*	*24-36*	*36-55*	*55-100*	*Slave Total*	*Houses*
Dixon, T. R.	4	2				2	2	1	1		12	1
Dodson, J. S.	2					2		1			5	1
Downing, Benjamin	6	1	1	2		7	2	2		1	22	3
Downing, W. R.	2	1	1				1				5	1
Dunn, Margaret	5	1		2		3	1	1	1		14	1
Ellis, Robert F.	1					1		1			3	1
Eubank, C. T.	1	2					1	1			5	1
Ewing, J.	2						2				4	1
Fishback, Joseph	2	2				6	3	1			14	1
Fitzpatrick, J. N.									1		1	1
Fitzpatrick, William		1	1	3			1		2		8	2
Follis, George		1				1		1			3	1
Foster, B. A.	1	1				3	1	1			7	1
Francis, Addison	5	1	1	1		1	3		1		13	2
Gains, T. F. M.	3	1	1	1			2	1			9	1
Gains, T. H.	2		1			1	4				8	1
Garrison, E. D.	1	1					1			1	4	1
Gatewood, F.	2	3				2	2	1	1		11	1
Gibson, Randolph	5	1	1			4	1	1	1		14	1
Glasenflo, Sara		1							1		2	1
Godley, J. S.	2	5	1	1		3	2	2	1	1	18	2
Gosaney & Wollis		1				1					2	1
Haral, Rola				3			1			1	5	1
Harris, S. H.		1	1	1			1	1			5	1
Harston, Thomas	7	1	1	2		2	5	2			20	3
Harston, William	2	2	1			1	2	1			9	1
Heeter, Sebaston	3		1		1	1	1				7	1
Hinton, W. G.	5		1					1			7	1
Hobdy, M. C.	1					1		1			3	1
Holder, John	5	2	1		1	1	5	3		1	19	4
Horn, Thomas	3	6	2			3	3	1		1	19	2
Hudson, Huey	3	1				2			2		8	1
Hughes, Elizabeth	3					1	3		1	1	9	1
Hughes, T. R.	1		1	1		2	1	1			7	1
Hughs, A. P.	4							1			5	1
Ingram, J. A.	1			1		1	1				4	1
Jewel, G. W.			2						1		3	1
Jimerson, J. A.						2			1		3	1
Jimerson, M. D.	1						1				2	1

Slave Owner	Enslaved Males					Enslaved Females						
Alphabetical by Owner	*<10*	*10-24*	*24-36*	*36-55*	*55-100*	*<10*	*10-24*	*24-36*	*36-55*	*55-100*	*Slave Total*	*Houses*
Johnson, Mathew		1									1	1
Landers, Patsy	2	2	3			2	3			2	14	3
Lewis, William									1		1	1
Manion, Phenba		1	1	2			1	1			6	1
Manion, Tomtson	2	1		1		1		1			6	2
Marcrum, Peter									1		1	1
Milleken, J. H.		1		1		2					4	1
Moorhead, E. S.								1			1	1
Morgan, Jackson						1		1			2	1
Morgan, John M.						1					1	1
Motley, Joseph	1	3				1	3		1		9	3
Motley, Lynn	2							1			3	1
Motley, Narcissa	1							1			2	1
Mulligan, G. M.	1	1							1		3	1
Mulligan, J. C.	4	2				5	1	1		1	14	1
Neal, Benjamin	1					1	1	1			4	1
Oliver, William	2							1			3	1
Page, J. H.	9	4	5	1		4	4	2	2		31	8
Petty, James	2		1			8	1	2		1	15	2
Pinson, J. W.	2	5					3	1	1		12	2
Poe, Delany	1		1								2	1
Porter, E. W.	1		2			4	1				8	2
Porter, Luther	2	5	2			4	1	1	1		16	4
Porter, Uriah	3	5	2	2		8	5	4	2		31	6
Porter, Uriah	7	9	3	2	1	10	6	3	2		43	1
Porter, W. R.	1	3	1		1	2	1				9	1
Pulliam, Benjamin	1	1	1	1						1	5	1
Pulliam, J. C. C.	3	2	1			3	2	1	1		13	3
Pulliam, James P.		2					2				4	1
Pulliam, R. F.	1			1			1				3	1
Pulliam, W. P.		2				1	1		1		5	2
Read, S. J.	3		2			3	1	1	1		11	2
Richey, S. S.							6		1		7	1
Richey, Thomas						1	2				3	1
Richey, William		1				1	1				3	1
Roark, Henry	4							1	1		6	2
Robb, R. D.	2					2	2				6	1
Sears, Albert		2	1			1		1			5	1
Sears, C. C.	1							1			2	5

Slave Owner	Enslaved Males					Enslaved Females						
Alphabetical by Owner	*<10*	*10-24*	*24-36*	*36-55*	*55-100*	*<10*	*10-24*	*24-36*	*36-55*	*55-100*	*Slave Total*	*Houses*
Sears, Henry	2	3		2		3	3	1			14	4
Sears, Henry		3				3		1			7	2
Sears, Samuel	8	3	3	2		7	6	4	1	2	36	5
Seay, J. R.							1	1	1		3	1
Settle, T. J.				1		1	1				3	1
Smith, Sandford		2				1	1				4	1
Stark, Amanda	1	1	1			2	1	1	1		8	1
Stark, James	7	9	6	7	3	8	12	4	4	6	66	1
Stark, Lucy	4	1				3	2		2		12	2
Stark, Sally	2			3		2	4	2	1	1	15	2
Staton, E. J.	2	3	1			2	3		1		12	2
Stevens, William	2				1		2				5	1
Stone, John	1	2							1		4	1
Stovall, James	2	2	1	1		2	2				10	2
Stovall, Nancy	6	3		1		2		2	1	1	16	3
Sulser, Jefferson		1					1				2	1
Sydens, J. S.	2	3		1				1		1	8	1
Tabor, George	1						1				2	1
Thomas, Walter		2					2			1	5	1
Wagoner, W. S.		2							1		3	1
Walker, A. S.	2		1			4	5	1	1		14	2
Walker, William			1				1				2	1
Weaver, Elizabeth	1					1		1			3	1
Whitney, Herman	5	2	1	1	1	2	2	1	1		16	3
Whitney, Reaves	1	1			1	1	3			1	8	2
Whitney, S. W.		2					2		1		5	1
Willams, A. G.		3					1	1		1	6	2
Williams, J. R.	3		1			2	1	1			8	1
Williams, Nancy		2								1	3	1
Wright, Nancy V.		1		1					1		3	1
TOTAL	230	177	78	56	16	204	181	100	60	36	1138	210

Table 24

Slave owners who did not provide a separate slave house in 1860

Slave Owner	Enslaved Males					Enslaved Females					
Alphabetical by Owner	*<10*	*10-24*	*24-36*	*36-55*	*55-100*	*<10*	*10-24*	*24-36*	*36-55*	*55-100*	*Total*
Ackerman, Jacob							1	1			2
Alexander, C. H.							1				1
Allen, C. E.						1					1
Allen, E. S.						1					1
Allen, J. M.	1										1
Allen, Y. S.							1				1
Allen, W. G.		1									1
Anderson, J. A.							1				1
Anderson, J. J.	1					1			1		3
Anderson, Sampson								1			1
Anthony, B. F.	1										1
Anthony, George		3	1	1		1	4		1		11
Anthony, H. S.	2	3					1				6
Anthony, Joseph				1							1
Anthony, Lee	1					1	2	1			5
Anthony, R. D.		1									1
Anthony, W. T.	1		1			1	1				4
Asply, R. L.							1				1
Atwood, J. S.		1									1
Atwood, Jett									1		1
Atwood, Lemuel						3	1				4
Atwood, T. J.							1				1
Ayers, Elizabeth						1		1			2
Bailey, Catharine			1								1
Behuler, Samuel	1										1
Behuler, Susan					1						1
Blackburn, William		2				1			1		4
Booker, Freeman		2					1		1		4
Borger & Simpson		2									2
Bracken, Green		1				1	1	2	1		6
Bright, J. A.	2	2				1	1	1			7
Britt, W. A.							1				1
Brown & Mulligan				1							1
Brown, Alsy			1				1				2
Brown, Oliver							1				1
Burton, C.						1	1				2
Calvert, J. C.						2	1				3

Slave Owner	Enslaved Males					Enslaved Females					
Alphabetical by Owner	*<10*	*10-24*	*24-36*	*36-55*	*55-100*	*<10*	*10-24*	*24-36*	*36-55*	*55-100*	*Total*
Calvert, Jessee	1	2		1					1		5
Carpenter, Adaline			1								1
Chany, W. B.						1	1				2
Cockrill, J. H.							1				1
Collins, Henry				1							1
Cook, Green	1										1
Cook, Leonidus	1										1
Crow, Nancy		1									1
Dance, J. E.				1							1
Davis, Susan	2	1					2				5
Deane, Jr. N.			1								1
Dodds Estate		1					1				2
Dodson, Synatha	1			1		3		1			6
Downing, Benjamin Jr.		1									1
Dunn, John							1				1
Dye, Elizabeth									1		1
Dyre, Squire							1		1		2
Edmunds, R. W.	2	1				1					4
Ellis, James		1									1
Ellis, T. E.						1					1
Ellis, W. J.				1							1
Elllis, W.J. & W. Martin									1		1
Etherly, William							1				1
Fisher, Thomas	2	2				1		1			6
Follis, R. S.				1							1
Foster, A. S.	1					1					2
Foster, J. W. & six others	8	3	1	2		6	2	1	3		26
Francis, Joseph						1		1			2
Franklin, Samuel	2	4	1			1		1			9
Gibson, J. H.	1			1							2
Glover, Jane	1	1					1				3
Godley, John S.								1			1
Goodnight, Isaac	1	2	1			3	1		1		9
Goodnight, T. M. C.		1		1							2
Guy, William					1						1
Guy, William	1										1
Ham, M. F.				1							1
Ham, S. W.		1					1				2
Hammet, James										1	1
Harris, Amos		2				1		1			4

Slave Owner	Enslaved Males					Enslaved Females					
Alphabetical by Owner	*<10*	*10-24*	*24-36*	*36-55*	*55-100*	*<10*	*10-24*	*24-36*	*36-55*	*55-100*	*Total*
Harston, A. A.	1						1				2
Harston, Reca									1		1
Harston, Rot							1				1
Heeter, J. W.	2			1		1	1		1		6
Hill, Nancy		1					1				2
Horn, F. Estate									1		1
Howards Estate			1								1
Howards Estate		1									1
Hower, James	3							1			4
Hunt, C. D.			1				1				2
Jackson, Benjamin						1	2		1		4
Jackson, John										1	1
Jackson, John S.		1									1
Jewel, W. H.	1	2	1					1			5
Jimerson, Nancy	1	1				2		1			5
Johnson, Henderson									1		1
Johnson, Nancy									1		1
Johnson, W. V.	1	1			1		1				4
Kiger, C. C.		1									1
Long, G. P.	1	1	1			2	1	1			7
Mansfield, William									1		1
Martin, James W.		1							1		2
McElroy, Burnett		1									1
McFarland, J. B.							1				1
McLary, Daniel		1									1
Meridith, A.		1					1				2
Moore, E. C.										1	1
Moore, Joseph W.		1			1						2
Moore, Simpson		2		3				1			6
Moorhead, T. J.	2		1			1	1	1			6
Morrison, F. G.	1	1					1				3
Motley, John				1							1
Motley, Martha								1			1
Motley, Patsy	1	2				1	1	1			6
Napier, Thomas		1									1
Neikirk, William	1						1				2
Orr, William		1	1			1	1	1			5
Paris, G. P.						1					1
Paris, R. H. & M. Russle										1	1
Petty, James							1				1

Slave Owner	Enslaved Males					Enslaved Females					
Alphabetical by Owner	*<10*	*10-24*	*24-36*	*36-55*	*55-100*	*<10*	*10-24*	*24-36*	*36-55*	*55-100*	*Total*
Pitchford, Cyrus	1										1
Pitchford, J. F.	1										1
Pitchford, W. F.						1		1			2
Pope, N. K.		2	1	1		1		1			6
Pope, S. H.						1					1
Porter, Frank			1								1
Pruitt, Elijah		2					2				4
Read, G. D.						1	1				2
Richey, A. J.						1	1				2
Russell, George								1			1
Sarver, Wyett							1				1
Satterfield, Henry	2	1					1		1		5
Sears, William	2	1				1	3		1		8
Shaford, W. R.							1				1
Stark, C. D. J.		2	1				1				4
Stark, J. D.	1	1		4		1	1				8
Stephens, Mary		1									1
Stovall, Daniel		1				1	2	1	1		6
Street, C. J.						2		1			3
Sydens, James		1					1				2
Sydens, Sampson Estate	1										1
Tompson, Sally		1					1				2
Travelstead, John							1				1
Tucker, N. J.		1									1
Whitney, W. T.		1					1				2
Wilson, B. P.							1				1
Woodcock, G. B.			2				2	1			5
Worley, M. B.										1	1
TOTAL	58	78	20	24	4	56	74	28	26	5	373

Chapter 11

Birth States of African American in Allen County in 1870

1870 Census

The birthplaces of African Americans were not recorded in the US census until 1870, five years or so after those in Allen County were freed. That was twenty years after the census began to record the birth state for white Americans in 1850. Determination of where Allen County's slaves were born is not possible by direct evidence from the census during the years prior to 1870.

Another complicating factor is that about 75% of slaves in Kentucky were either freed or escaped to non-slave states during the war. Many others fled after all were freed in 1865. The 1860 slave schedule recorded 1,514 slaves in Allen County. The 1870 census recorded only 1,016 African Americans. Thus, the 1870 census recorded only those who stayed in or came back to Allen County — 498 others (33%) had departed when the opportunity arose to do so. The birth state of those who remained or came back can to some degree enlighten researchers who seek to extend their heritage beyond Allen County and Kentucky to their ancestral home (Table 25).

Table 25

Birth state by birth decade of African Americans living in Allen County in 1870

Birth Decade	KY	TN	NC	VA	SC	GA	MD
1770-1779			1	2			
1780-1889	3			2			
1790-1799	2		2	5			
1800-1809	7	1	3	6		1	1
1810-1819	16	5	3	5	1		
1820-1829	42	5	2	8		1	
1830-1839	76	12	3	4			
1840-1849	124	32	3	4			
1850-1859	225	30		1		2	
1860-1869	348	28		1			
TOTAL	843	113	17	38	1	4	1

There were two African American persons living in Allen County in 1870 who were centenarians. The oldest was Matt Clark who was born in Virginia in 1766 and was a farmer who owned property in the Allen Springs community. He was 104 years old. The other was Lempey Dosson who was born about 1770 in Virginia, twenty-two years before Kentucky became a state. She was 100 years old and living in the household of John and Millie Horn, who also were African Americans and who owned a farm in the Butlersville community. Dollie Carpenter was 99 years old, a native of North Carolina who lived in Scottsville. It was unusual for anyone to reach these ages in 1870, even more so for people who had been enslaved for most of their lives.

In 1870, the oldest African American who was born in Kentucky was Archie Bahela who was 80 years old. He was living in the household of Ned and Hannor[1] Bradley, also African Americans, in Scottsville. He was born in 1790, two years before Kentucky became a state. There were seventeen others who were born in Kentucky before Allen County was formed in 1815.

[1] Probably the phonetically spelled name Hannah as that name would have been pronounced in those days

There were thirty-six African Americans in the 1870 census who were more than sixty years old, that is to say that they were born before 1810 (Table 25). Sixty-seven percent of them were born in states other than Kentucky. This tells us that these ex-slaves accompanied their owners on their journey to Kentucky. Forty percent of them were born in Virginia and seventeen percent were from North Carolina (Figure 31), the two primary sources of white immigration into Allen County. Those two states' emigration was not a significant contributor to the population after 1850.

Figure 31

Birth state of African Americans older than sixty living in Allen County in 1870

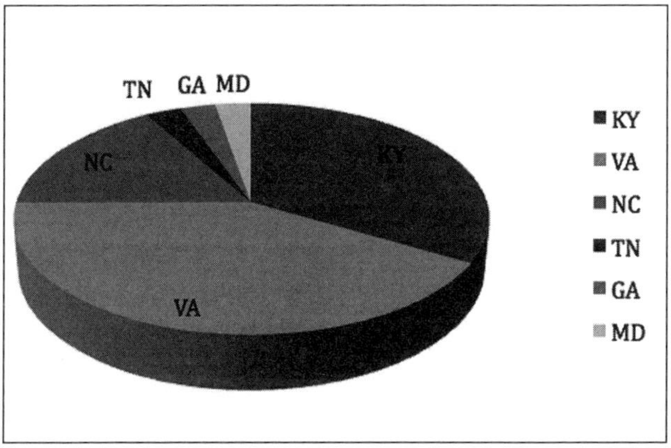

From the data, one may conclude that many of the earliest slave immigrants shown in Table 25 had died before the 1870 census.

Most of the 170 African Americans who were between thirty and sixty years old in 1870 were born in Kentucky. Even so, there were still a enough survivors to maintain Virginia in second place as a birth state while Tennessee had increased to third (Figure 32).

Figure 32

Birth state of African Americans between thirty and sixty living in Allen County in 1870

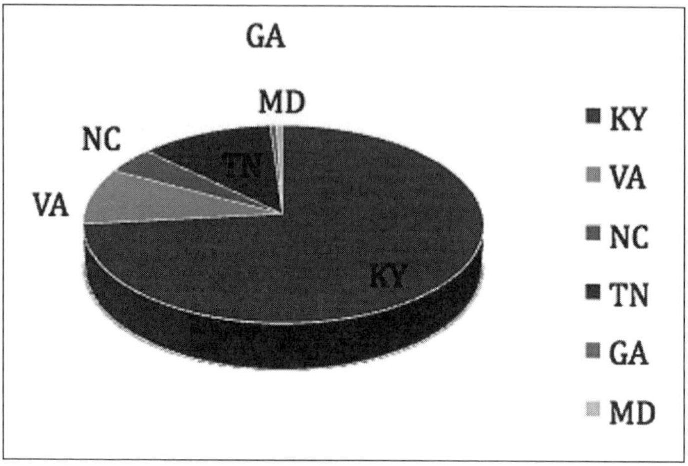

Increasingly, Kentucky dominated the other birth states through the younger than thirty African Americans. Tennessee was in second place but its number remained about the same during each of the three decades. Virginia, the source of the earliest immigration, and the other states had negligible numbers (Figure 33).

Figure 33

Birth state of African Americans younger than thirty living in Allen County in 1870

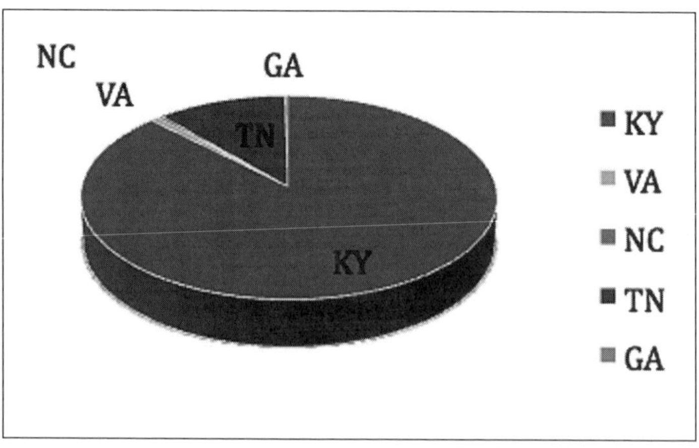

The numbers of African Americans born in Tennessee tells a different story from those born in the other states. There were small numbers of emigrations from Tennessee according to the numbers in Table 25 prior to 1830, indicating that few slaves and owners emigrated together from that state. The larger numbers that show up in each of the last four decades in Figure 34 appear to be the result of slave trading, the importation of slaves purchased from Tennessee. That importation began in 1833 and continued until slavery ended.

Figure 34

Comparison of Tennessee, North Carolina, and Virginia as birth states

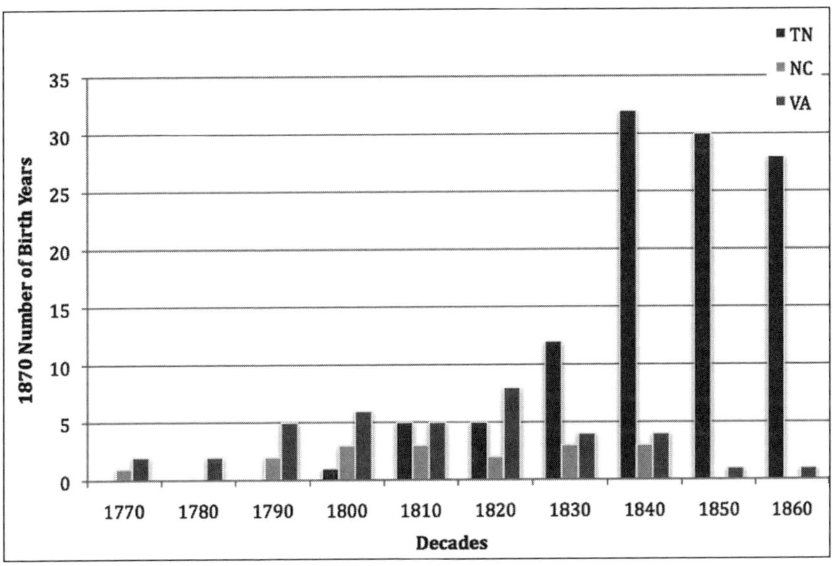

Information about the African Americans from the 1870 census were extracted and are listed on the following pages of this chapter. The extraction was done using tools available through Ancestry.com. Names are spelled as they occurred in that extraction. Some of the extraction errors stem from interpretation of the handwritten originals. For example, the letter S is sometimes mistaken for the letter L as in Leares for Seares. Then there are the phonetic spellings of names by the original writer as in Seares for Sears. If you are searching for a particular, expect these kinds of misspellings.

The birth state information is in two tables, one for those born outside Kentucky (Table 26) and the other for those born inside Kentucky (Table 27). Both tables are sorted alphabetically by surname.

Table 26

African Americans in 1870 who were born outside of Kentucky

1870 Census					
Name	**Location**	**Approximate Birth Year**	**Birth State**	**Color**	**Sex**
Arnold, Wiley	Precinct 2	1853	TN	B	M
Ashford, James	District 6	1840	TN	M	M
Ashford, Mariah	District 6	1850	TN	B	F
Benedick, Eda	Precinct 4	1825	NC	B	F
Black, John	Precinct 6	1810	VA	B	M
Black, Easton	District 6	1830	TN	M	M
Black, Malakiah	District 6	1855	TN	B	M
Black, Lucy N.	District 6	1857	TN	B	M
Black, Fish	District 6	1859	TN	B	M
Black, Delila	District 6	1861	TN	B	F
Black, Manerva	District 6	1865	TN	B	F
Bracken, Sarah	Precinct 6	1849	VA	M	F
Bracken, Milton	District 6	1848	TN	M	M
Bracken, Benjamin	District 6	1846	TN	M	M
Bracken, Chaney	District 6	1849	TN	M	F
Bracken, William A.	District 6	1868	TN	M	M
Bracken, Nancy	District 6	1869	TN	M	F
Bracken, Matthew	New Roe	1856	TN	B	M
Brackin, Dock	District 6	1849	TN	M	M
Brackin, Jane	District 6	1850	TN	B	F
Brackin, Allice	District 6	1867	TN	B	F
Brackin, Abagal	District 6	1869	TN	B	F
Brackin, Dock	District 6	1849	TN	M	M
Brackin, Tucker	District 6	1847	TN	B	M
Bratten, Sarrah	District 7	1850	TN	M	F
Brisentine, Frances	New Roe	1822	VA	B	F
Brisentine, Eligah	District 6	1847	TN	B	M
Brisentine, Ruth	New Roe	1853	TN	B	F
Brisentine, Moses	New Roe	1855	TN	B	M
Brocket, Henry	Precinct 1	1861	TN	B	M

Name	Location	Approximate Birth Year	Birth State	Color	Sex
Brocket, James	Precinct 1	1863	TN	B	M
Brocket, Ann	District 6	1837	TN	B	F
Brockett, Mary	Precinct 1	1856	TN	B	F
Brown, Lucinda	Precinct 1	1840	VA	B	F
Brown, Mary A.	Precinct 2	1845	NC	B	F
Brown, Dianner	Precinct 1	1835	TN	B	F
Burton, Millie	Precinct 3	1795	VA	B	F
Butt, Richard	District 6	1847	TN	B	M
Carpenter, Dollie	Precinct 1	1771	NC	B	F
Carpenter, Merry	District 6	1796	NC	B	F
Carpenter, Robert	Precinct 1	1844	TN	B	M
Clark, Matt	Precinct 3	1766	VA	B	M
Clark, Lenor	Precinct 3	1810	NC	B	F
Clark, Lenor	Precinct 3	1860	TN	B	F
Colbert, John	Scottsville	1820	VA	B	M
Colbert, M.	Scottsville	1825	VA	B	F
Colvert, Phoba	Precinct 1	1810	VA	B	F
Davis, Nancy	Scottsville	1855	TN	B	F
Dening, Samantha	Precinct 3	1865	TN	B	F
Denning, Joseph	Precinct 3	1832	NC	B	M
Denning, Sarah	Precinct 3	1848	TN	B	F
Denning, Mark	Precinct 3	1855	TN	B	M
Denning, Bird	Precinct 3	1863	TN	B	M
Dodson, Edmon	Precinct 1	1822	VA	B	M
Dosson, Lempey	Precinct 2	1770	VA	B	F
Downing, George	Precinct 7	1790	VA	B	M
Duvall, John	Precinct 2	1835	TN	B	M
Dye, Nancy A.	Precinct 2	1805	VA	B	F
Fitzpatrick, John	Precinct 1	1800	VA	B	M
Fitzpatrick, Mary	Precinct 1	1830	VA	B	F
Fitzpatrick, Eda	Precinct 1	1800	VA	B	F
Gaines, Elisabeth	Precinct 6	1820	VA	B	F
Gains, Rachel	New Roe	1820	GA	B	F
Gains, Isabella	New Roe	1852	GA	B	F
Gains, George H.	New Roe	1854	GA	B	M
Heeter, Jerry	Precinct 1	1800	MD	B	F
Henretta, Matilda	Precinct 2	1790	VA	B	F
Herald, Calvin	District 6	1850	TN	B	M

Name	Location	Approximate Birth Year	Birth State	Color	Sex
Hill, George	Precinct 1	1844	TN	B	M
Hill, Dishann	Precinct 1	1845	TN	B	F
Hill, Jane	Precinct 1	1861	TN	B	F
Hobson, Jerry	Precinct 3	1800	NC	B	M
Holder, Susan A.	Precinct 1	1833	VA	B	F
Horn, John	Precinct 2	1815	TN	B	M
House, Amy	District 6	1818	TN	M	F
House, William	District 6	1846	TN	M	M
House, Judeth	District 6	1856	TN	M	F
House, Joseph A.	District 6	1858	TN	M	M
House, Agness H.	District 6	1861	TN	M	F
House, Mary	District 6	1866	TN	M	F
House, Wesley R.	District 6	1840	TN	M	M
House, James	Scottsville	1853	TN	B	M
House, Amy	District 6	1818	TN	M	F
House, William	District 6	1846	TN	M	M
House, Judeth	District 6	1856	TN	M	F
House, Joseph A.	District 6	1858	TN	M	M
House, Agness H.	District 6	1861	TN	M	F
House, Mary	District 6	1866	TN	M	F
House, Wesley R.	District 6	1840	TN	M	M
House, Reuben	New Roe	1825	TN	B	M
House, Ellen	New Roe	1865	TN	B	F
Huddleston, Martin G.	Precinct 4	1837	TN	M	M
Huddleston, Maggie	Precinct 4	1847	TN	M	F
Huddleston, Martin	Precinct 4	1837	TN	M	M
Hughes, Eary A.	Precinct 7	1804	VA	M	F
Jackson, Martha	Precinct 2	1845	NC	B	F
Jewell, Henry	Precinct 3	1835	NC	B	M
King, Hampton	District 6	1804	TN	B	M
King, Lucy	District 6	1818	TN	B	F
Lenkins, John	Precinct 1	1840	TN	B	M
Levi, Cretty	Precinct 1	1810	VA	B	F
Lyles, Margret	Precinct 1	1799	VA	B	F
Manion, Ann	Precinct 1	1835	VA	B	F
Manion, Dick	Precinct 1	1817	TN	B	M
Mansfield, Rebecca	Scottsville,	1810	SC	B	F
Martin, William	Precinct 4	1840	TN	B	M

Name	Location	Approximate Birth Year	Birth State	Color	Sex
Mayhan, Isaac	Precinct 2	1839	TN	B	M
McHenry, George	Precinct 2	1853	TN	B	M
Millegan, Edward	Precinct 1	1833	TN	B	M
Millegan, Ruther J.	Precinct 1	1831	TN	B	F
Moore, Jennie	Precinct 2	1800	GA	B	F
Motley, Kissiah	Precinct 3	1810	NC	B	F
Motley, Beck	Precinct 3	1808	NC	B	F
Mulligan, John	Precinct 1	1855	TN	B	M
Petty, Eliza	Precinct 3	1807	VA	B	F
Petty, Ned	Precinct 3	1829	VA	B	M
Pharis, Adline	Precinct 3	1849	TN	B	F
Piland, Bruce	Scottsville	1864	TN	B	M
Pope, Alexander	Precinct 2	1808	NC	B	M
Porter, America	Precinct 1	1820	VA	B	F
Read, Liller	District 1	1834	TN	B	F
Robinson, Charles H.	District 5	1845	TN	M	M
Sarver, Martha	District 6	1842	TN	M	F
Sarver, James L.	District 6	1839	TN	B	M
Sarver, Martha	District 6	1842	TN	M	F
Sarver, Isaac	District 6	1824	TN	B	M
Sarver, Hanna	District 6	1844	TN	B	F
Sarver, Daniel	District 6	1853	TN	B	M
Sarver, Adline	District 6	1864	TN	B	F
Sarver, John	District 6	1866	TN	B	M
Sarver, Jane	District 6	1868	TN	B	F
Sarver, Ardella	District 6	1860	TN	B	F
Sarver, Roda	District 6	1822	TN	B	F
Sarver, Joseph	District 6	1850	TN	B	M
Sarver, Mary	District 6	1853	TN	B	F
Sarver, George A.	District 6	1855	TN	B	F
Sarver, Diller	District 6	1861	TN	B	F
Sarver, Eliza	District 6	1853	TN	B	F
Sarver, Samuel	District 6	1863	TN	B	M
Sarver, Sarah	District 6	1866	TN	B	F
Sarver, Fish	New Roe	1849	TN	B	F
Searer, Salina	Precinct 4	1795	VA	B	F
Searer, Rabeca	Precinct 4	1840	NC	B	F
Sears, Charlott	Precinct 4	1823	NC	B	F

Name	Location	Approximate Birth Year	Birth State	Color	Sex
Siddens, Mather	District 7	1813	NC	B	F
Siddens, Let	District 7	1836	NC	M	F
Stark, Hettie	Precinct 3	1780	VA	B	F
Stark, Sallie	Precinct 3	1806	VA	M	F
Stark, Fannie	Precinct 3	1788	VA	B	F
Stark, Cassander	Precinct 4	1790	NC	B	F
Steward, Armsted	Precinct 4	1846	TN	B	M
Steward, Peter	New Roe	1838	TN	B	M
Steward, Sarah	New Roe	1845	TN	B	F
Steward, Calvin	New Roe	1858	TN	B	M
Steward, Emaline	New Roe	1860	TN	B	F
Steward, Margaret	New Roe	1862	TN	B	F
Steward, Vista	New Roe	1864	TN	B	F
Taylor, Alexander	Precinct 2	1857	TN	B	M
Thomas, Betsey	District 7	1854	TN	M	F
Trail, Hagar	Precinct 2	1825	VA	B	F
Trail, Caroline	Precinct 2	1858	VA	B	F
Umbles, Leroy	Precinct 2	1812	VA	B	M
Umbles, Samuel H.	Precinct 2	1848	VA	B	M
Umbles, Charles W.	Precinct 2	1846	VA	B	M
Umbles, Rachel	Precinct 2	1825	TN	B	F
Walker, Dinah	Scottsville	1815	VA	B	F
Wallace, Benjamin	Precinct 2	1849	TN	B	M
Webb, Henny	Precinct 4	1853	TN	B	M
Williams, Delsa	Precinct 1	1860	VA	B	F
Williams, Sarah	Precinct 3	1830	VA	B	F
Woodcock, George	Precinct 1	1827	TN	B	M

Table 27

African Americans in 1870 who were born in Kentucky

1870 Census					
Name	Location	Approximate Birth Year	Birth State	Color	Sex
Absher, America	District 6	1820	KY	M	F
Alexander, Susan	Precinct 1	1862	KY	B	F
Anderson, Asenath	Scottsville	1857	KY	B	F
Anthony, David	New Roe	1835	KY	M	M
Anthony, Adaline	New Roe	1840	KY	B	F
Anthony, James	Precinct 3	1845	KY	B	M
Anthony, Aleagail	New Roe	1851	KY	M	M
Anthony, Burd	New Roe	1858	KY	M	M
Anthony, Samuel	New Roe	1860	KY	M	M
Anthony, Harrison	New Roe	1864	KY	M	M
Anthony, George	New Roe	1866	KY	M	M
Anthony, Mary	New Roe	1870	KY	M	F
Ashford, Bell	District 6	1857	KY	B	F
Ashford, Eliza	District 6	1866	KY	M	F
Aynes, Anderson	Precinct 2	1845	KY	B	M
Aynes, Mary H.	Precinct 2	1847	KY	M	F
Aynes, Drury B.	Precinct 2	1869	KY	M	M
Aynes, William F.	Precinct 2	1870	KY	M	M
Bahela, Archie	District 5	1780	KY	B	M
Bahela, Abraham	District 5	1834	KY	B	M
Baley, Reuben	Precinct 1	1835	KY	B	M
Benedick, Burell	Precinct 4	1819	KY	B	M
Benedick, Jennie	Precinct 4	1855	KY	B	F
Benedick, Ellis	Precinct 4	1858	KY	B	M
Benedick, Charles	Precinct 4	1860	KY	B	M
Benedick, Grant	Precinct 4	1863	KY	B	M
Benedick, George A.	Precinct 4	1865	KY	B	M
Bergam, Edward	Precinct 1	1852	KY	M	M
Boren, Ann	District 6	1847	KY	B	F
Boren, Frances	District 6	1866	KY	B	F
Boren, Jinnie	District 6	1870	KY	B	F
Boyd, Ralph	Precinct 1	1827	KY	M	M
Boyd, Mariah	Precinct 1	1843	KY	M	F
Boyd, Asa	Precinct 1	1854	KY	M	M

Name	Location	Approximate Birth Year	Birth State	Color	Sex
Boyd, Frances	Precinct 1	1856	KY	M	F
Boyd, Mollie	Precinct 1	1859	KY	M	F
Boyd, Edward	Precinct 1	1862	KY	M	M
Boyd, Margret	Precinct 1	1868	KY	M	F
Boyd, Sallie B.	Precinct 1	1870	KY	M	F
Bracken, Manda E.	District 6	1868	KY	M	F
Bradley, Ned	District 5	1829	KY	B	M
Bradley, Hannes	District 5	1832	KY	B	F
Brashiers, Betty L.	District 6	1867	KY	B	F
Bratten, Souson M.	District 7	1870	KY	M	F
Bright, Ceilah	Precinct 1	1848	KY	B	F
Bright, Zackriah T.	Precinct 1	1849	KY	B	M
Bright, Siman	Precinct 1	1857	KY	B	M
Brisentine, Zack	New Roe	1870	KY	M	M
Brocket, John	District 6	1866	KY	B	M
Brow, Doney	Precinct 1	1835	KY	B	F
Brow, Joseph L.	Precinct 1	1860	KY	B	M
Brow, Sidney W.	Precinct 1	1862	KY	B	M
Brown, America J.	Precinct 1	1869	KY	B	F
Brown, David	Precinct 1	1820	KY	B	M
Brown, Catharine	District 7	1820	KY	B	F
Brown, Mary	Precinct 1	1840	KY	B	F
Brown, Charles	Precinct 1	1843	KY	B	M
Brown, Phillis	Precinct 1	1845	KY	B	F
Brown, Mima	Precinct 1	1845	KY	B	F
Brown, Kitty	Precinct 1	1847	KY	B	F
Brown, Agnus	Precinct 1	1848	KY	B	F
Brown, John	Precinct 1	1850	KY	B	M
Brown, George	Precinct 1	1853	KY	B	M
Brown, Less A.	District 7	1853	KY	B	F
Brown, Sarah	Precinct 1	1858	KY	B	F
Brown, Deannah	Precinct 1	1858	KY	B	F
Brown, Bruce	Precinct 1	1861	KY	B	M
Brown, Vina	Precinct 1	1861	KY	B	F
Brown, Amanda	Precinct 1	1862	KY	B	F
Brown, Robert	Precinct 1	1863	KY	B	M
Brown, Harriett	Precinct 1	1864	KY	B	F
Brown, Alleck	Precinct 1	1864	KY	B	M

Name	Location	Approximate Birth Year	Birth State	Color	Sex
Brown, William	Precinct 1	1865	KY	B	M
Brown, Arena J.	Precinct 1	1865	KY	B	F
Brown, Edna	Precinct 1	1866	KY	B	F
Brown, William M.	Precinct 1	1866	KY	B	M
Brown, George	Precinct 1	1866	KY	B	M
Brown, Lugenia	Precinct 1	1869	KY	B	F
Bruce, George A.	District 6	1860	KY	B	F
Burness, Patsy	Precinct 2	1818	KY	B	F
Burness, Harry	Precinct 2	1840	KY	B	M
Burness, Theadore	Precinct 2	1865	KY	B	M
Burness, Martha	Precinct 2	1867	KY	M	F
Burness, Mary	Precinct 2	1869	KY	M	F
Burton, Richard	Precinct 1	1797	KY	B	M
Burton, Walker	Precinct 1	1812	KY	B	M
Burton, Cintha	Precinct 3	1830	KY	M	F
Burton, Jackson	Precinct 4	1831	KY	B	M
Burton, Robert	Precinct 4	1832	KY	B	M
Burton, Mariah	Precinct 3	1835	KY	B	F
Burton, Masey J.	Precinct 4	1835	KY	B	F
Burton, Martha	Precinct 4	1839	KY	B	F
Burton, Edney	Precinct 4	1852	KY	B	F
Burton, Alfred	Precinct 4	1853	KY	B	M
Burton, Matilda	Precinct 4	1856	KY	B	F
Burton, Elman	Precinct 3	1856	KY	M	M
Burton, George A.	Precinct 4	1858	KY	B	M
Burton, John	Precinct 3	1858	KY	M	M
Burton, Elmon	Precinct 4	1860	KY	B	M
Burton, Hanner	Precinct 3	1860	KY	M	F
Burton, James C.	Precinct 4	1862	KY	B	M
Burton, Rousean	Precinct 3	1863	KY	M	M
Burton, Martha E.	Precinct 4	1867	KY	B	F
Burton, Lucinda	Precinct 4	1869	KY	B	F
Burton, Eugene C.	Precinct 4	1869	KY	B	M
Burton, William H.	Precinct 3	1869	KY	M	M
Calruent, Price	Precinct 1	1853	KY	B	M
Calver, Charlie	Scottsville	1858	KY	B	M
Calvert, Steven	District 7	1823	KY	B	M
Calvert, Mary E.	District 7	1839	KY	B	F

Name	Location	Approximate Birth Year	Birth State	Color	Sex
Calvert, Robbert E.	District 7	1844	KY	B	M
Calvert, Angeline	Precinct 1	1857	KY	B	F
Calvert, July A.	District 7	1861	KY	B	F
Calvert, William H.	District 7	1863	KY	B	M
Cammel, Adline	District 7	1848	KY	M	F
Cammel, Thomas	District 7	1850	KY	M	M
Carpenter, Isaac	District 6	1812	KY	B	M
Carpenter, David	Precinct 1	1815	KY	B	M
Carpenter, Carline	District 6	1826	KY	M	F
Carpenter, Phillis	Precinct 1	1830	KY	B	F
Carpenter, Dilly	Precinct 1	1830	KY	B	F
Carpenter, Fannie	Precinct 1	1835	KY	B	F
Carpenter, Luther	Precinct 1	1840	KY	B	M
Carpenter, Anaca	Precinct 1	1842	KY	M	F
Carpenter, Richard	Precinct 1	1847	KY	B	M
Carpenter, Betsy A.	Precinct 1	1848	KY	B	F
Carpenter, Lulie A.	Precinct 1	1851	KY	M	F
Carpenter, George W.	District 7	1855	KY	M	M
Carpenter, Allice	District 6	1856	KY	M	M
Carpenter, Matılda	Precinct 1	1857	KY	B	F
Carpenter, Camila	Precinct 1	1858	KY	B	F
Carpenter, Henry	Precinct 1	1859	KY	B	M
Carpenter, George W.	District 7	1859	KY	M	M
Carpenter, Drury	Precinct 1	1860	KY	B	M
Carpenter, Henry C.	District 7	1860	KY	M	M
Carpenter, Lucinda	Precinct 1	1861	KY	B	F
Carpenter, Bell	Precinct 1	1862	KY	B	F
Carpenter, Washington	Precinct 1	1863	KY	B	M
Carpenter, Sarah	District 6	1863	KY	B	F
Carpenter, Mary F.	Precinct 1	1864	KY	B	F
Carpenter, Carline	Precinct 1	1864	KY	B	F
Carpenter, Nellie E.	District 6	1865	KY	B	F
Carpenter, Fielding	Precinct 1	1866	KY	B	M
Carpenter, Bell	Precinct 1	1866	KY	B	F
Carpenter, Johnson	Precinct 1	1866	KY	B	M
Carpenter, Henry	Precinct 1	1866	KY	B	M
Carpenter, William	District 6	1866	KY	M	M
Carpenter, Edward	Precinct 1	1867	KY	B	M

Name	Location	Approximate Birth Year	Birth State	Color	Sex
Carpenter, Allice	Precinct 1	1867	KY	B	F
Carpenter, Gilbert	Precinct 1	1868	KY	B	M
Carpenter, Samuel	Precinct 1	1868	KY	B	M
Carpenter, Peter	Precinct 1	1868	KY	B	M
Carpenter, Dollie C.	District 6	1868	KY	B	F
Carpenter, Lucinda	Precinct 1	1869	KY	B	F
Carpenter, Louisa	Precinct 1	1869	KY	B	F
Carpenter, Johnnie	Precinct 1	1870	KY	B	M
Carpinter, Malinda	Precinct 1	1844	KY	B	F
Caruth, Daniel	District 7	1826	KY	M	M
Caruth, Mariah	District 7	1833	KY	B	F
Caruth, Seaske	District 7	1847	KY	B	M
Caruth, Seley J.	District 7	1854	KY	B	F
Caruth, Barton	District 7	1859	KY	M	M
Caruth, Mary E.	District 7	1862	KY	M	F
Caruth, Sarrah	District 7	1863	KY	M	F
Caruth, Sodenia A.	District 7	1866	KY	M	F
Caruth, Frances M.	District 7	1867	KY	M	M
Caruth, Alisa S.	District 7	1868	KY	M	F
Caruth, Charles C.	District 7	1869	KY	M	M
Claypool, Calvan	Precinct 4	1830	KY	B	M
Claypool, Angeline	Precinct 4	1850	KY	B	F
Claypool, Dink	Precinct 3	1859	KY	B	M
Claypool, Jackson	Precinct 4	1863	KY	B	M
Claypool, William	Precinct 4	1866	KY	B	F
Colbert, J.	Scottsville	1861	KY	B	M
Colbert, J.	Scottsville	1868	KY		
Collins, Fielding	Precinct 1	1814	KY	B	M
Collins, Lilas	Scottsville	1846	KY	B	M
Collins, James	Precinct 1	1863	KY	B	M
Cook, Licenia S.	Precinct 1	1858	KY	B	F
Cose, Byron	Precinct 2	1843	KY	B	F
Cowden, Fannie	Precinct 1	1810	KY	B	F
Cowden, Sedney	Precinct 1	1841	KY	B	M
Cowden, Hariett	Precinct 1	1851	KY	M	F
Cowden, James	Precinct 1	1854	KY	B	M
Dadson, John	Precinct 2	1850	KY	B	M
Darasher, Clark	District 7	1849	KY	B	M

Name	Location	Approximate Birth Year	Birth State	Color	Sex
Darasher, Rasa	District 7	1849	KY	B	F
Darasher, Cara	District 7	1870	KY	B	F
Daves, Robert	Precinct 2	1852	KY	B	M
Davis, Charles	Precinct 2	1849	KY	B	M
Davis, Virginie	Precinct 2	1850	KY	B	F
Davis, Eliza	Precinct 2	1850	KY	B	F
Davis, Harriett	Precinct 2	1858	KY	B	F
Davis, William	Precinct 2	1860	KY	M	M
Davis, Ellen	Precinct 2	1869	KY	B	F
Deal, Zephaniah	Precinct 1	1860	KY	B	M
Dening, Matthew	Precinct 3	1869	KY	B	F
Dixon, James	Scottsville	1849	KY	B	M
Dodd, Elsy	Precinct 1	1848	KY	B	M
Dodd, Henietta	Precinct 1	1851	KY	M	F
Dodson, Hagoner Ester	Precinct 1	1800	KY	B	F
Dodson, Mariah	Precinct 1	1826	KY	B	F
Dodson, Henry W.	Precinct 1	1863	KY	B	M
Dodson, Hester A.	Precinct 1	1865	KY	B	F
Dodson, Mariah F.	Precinct 1	1869	KY	B	F
Downing, Wesley	District 5	1833	KY	B	M
Downing, Margret	District 7	1834	KY	M	F
Downing, Carlin	District 7	1836	KY	M	F
Downing, Mary J.	District 7	1837	KY	B	F
Downing, Frances	District 5	1840	KY	B	F
Downing, Smith	District 7	1840	KY	B	M
Downing, Grandville	District 7	1841	KY	B	M
Downing, Silvester	District 7	1847	KY	B	M
Downing, Roza	District 7	1848	KY	B	F
Downing, Angeline	District 5	1854	KY	B	F
Downing, Malissey A.	District 7	1854	KY	M	F
Downing, Rebecca A.	District 7	1856	KY	B	F
Downing, Mayar	District 5	1858	KY	B	M
Downing, George W.	District 7	1859	KY	B	M
Downing, Levi	District 5	1860	KY	B	M
Downing, Jacob	District 7	1860	KY	B	M
Downing, Rusaw	District 5	1862	KY	B	M
Downing, Amanda	District 7	1862	KY	B	F
Downing, Henry E.	District 5	1864	KY	B	M

Name	Location	Approximate Birth Year	Birth State	Color	Sex
Downing, James P.	District 7	1866	KY	B	M
Downing, Malissey	District 7	1867	KY	B	F
Downing, Harvy A.	District 7	1867	KY	B	M
Downing, John W.	District 7	1868	KY	B	M
Downing, Mary	District 5	1869	KY	B	F
Downing, James	District 5	1870	KY	B	M
Dunn, Jack	District 7	1847	KY	B	M
Dunn, Kittey	District 7	1852	KY	B	F
Dunn, William	District 7	1869	KY	B	M
Edmonds, Perrene	Precinct 3	1830	KY	B	F
Edmonds, James T.	Precinct 1	1857	KY	B	M
Edmonds, Laura	Precinct 1	1859	KY	B	F
Ewing, Robert	Precinct 4	1854	KY	M	M
Fergurson, Jasper	Precinct 1	1848	KY	B	M
Fishback, Hannes	Precinct 1	1842	KY	B	F
Fishback, George E.	Precinct 1	1860	KY	B	F
Fitzpatrick, Pleasant	Precinct 1	1823	KY	B	F
Fitzpatrick, Lewis	Precinct 1	1843	KY	B	M
Fitzpatrick, Amanda	Precinct 1	1847	KY	B	F
Fitzpatrick, Dolly S.	Precinct 1	1852	KY	B	F
Fitzpatrick, Martha	Precinct 1	1854	KY	B	F
Fitzpatrick, Titus I.	Precinct 1	1857	KY	B	M
Fitzpatrick, Louwisa	Precinct 1	1861	KY	B	F
Fitzpatrick, Catharine	Precinct 1	1863	KY	B	F
Fitzpatrick, John	Precinct 1	1865	KY	B	M
Fitzpatrick, Betsy J.	Precinct 1	1865	KY	B	F
Fitzpatrick, Sidney W.	Precinct 1	1867	KY	B	M
Fitzpatrick, Enoch N.	Precinct 1	1867	KY	B	M
Fitzpatrick, James T.	Precinct 1	1868	KY	B	M
Follis, Alfred	Scottsville	1820	KY	B	M
Follis, Elizabeth	Scottsville	1853	KY	B	F
Follis, John A.	Scottsville	1861	KY	M	M
Foster, Phillip	Precinct 1	1848	KY	B	M
Foster, Cata	District 6	1852	KY	B	F
Foster, John	District 6	1861	KY	B	M
Frame, Joseph	Precinct 1	1852	KY	B	M
Frame, Fountain	Precinct 1	1859	KY	B	M
Francis, Margret	Precinct 4	1854	KY	B	F

Name	Location	Approximate Birth Year	Birth State	Color	Sex
Francis, Berry	Precinct 1	1855	KY	B	M
Francis, Anthony	Precinct 4	1859	KY	B	M
Francis, John	Precinct 4	1865	KY	B	M
Franklin, Jane A.	District 7	1836	KY	M	F
Franklin, James D.	District 7	1856	KY	B	M
Franklin, William H.	District 7	1858	KY	M	M
Franklin, Larra B.	District 7	1861	KY	M	F
Fulcher, James	Precinct 1	1855	KY	B	M
Gaines, Julie A.	District 6	1819	KY	B	F
Gaines, Mariah	District 6	1850	KY	B	F
Gaines, Isan	District 6	1855	KY	B	M
Gaines, Albert	District 6	1859	KY	B	M
Gaines, Elnora	District 6	1863	KY	B	M
Gaines, Francis B.	District 6	1864	KY	B	F
Gaines, Ida	District 6	1866	KY	B	F
Gains, Joe	New Roe	1860	KY	B	F
Gains, Agnis	New Roe	1862	KY	B	F
Godley, Dolly	Precinct 4	1820	KY	B	F
Godley, Sallie	Precinct 1	1845	KY	B	F
Godley, Alfred	Precinct 4	1846	KY	B	M
Godley, Cephus	Precinct 4	1846	KY	M	M
Godley, Henretta	Precinct 4	1852	KY	B	F
Godley, William P.	Precinct 4	1854	KY	M	M
Godley, Malissa	Precinct 3	1855	KY	B	F
Harston, Henry	Precinct 4	1822	KY	B	M
Harston, Eliza	Precinct 4	1825	KY	B	F
Harston, Riley	Precinct 4	1842	KY	B	M
Harston, Ellen	Precinct 4	1845	KY	B	F
Harston, Ama M.	Precinct 4	1855	KY	B	F
Harston, William	Precinct 4	1858	KY	B	M
Harston, Franklin	Precinct 4	1864	KY	B	M
Harston, Henry	Precinct 4	1866	KY	B	M
Harston, Lucy	Precinct 4	1867	KY	B	F
Harston, Mollie	Precinct 4	1869	KY	B	F
Hayes, Silas	Precinct 4	1805	KY	B	M
Hayes, Sarah	Precinct 4	1835	KY	B	F
Hayes, Elizabeth	Precinct 4	1857	KY	B	F
Hayes, Lafayette A. D.	Precinct 4	1858	KY	B	M

Name	Location	Approximate Birth Year	Birth State	Color	Sex
Hayes, Hannerd	Precinct 4	1861	KY	B	F
Hayes, Lucy	Precinct 4	1862	KY	B	F
Hayes, Lilas	Precinct 4	1864	KY	B	M
Hayes, Lennie	Precinct 4	1868	KY	B	F
Hayes, Charles D.	Precinct 4	1869	KY	B	M
Hays, Aleseander	Precinct 3	1817	KY	B	M
Hays, Hanner	Precinct 3	1834	KY	B	F
Hays, Ceiley	Precinct 3	1854	KY	B	F
Hays, William T.	Precinct 3	1856	KY	B	M
Heeter, William	Precinct 1	1856	KY	B	M
Heeter, Jacob	Precinct 1	1858	KY	B	M
Henretta, No Name	Precinct 2	1864	KY	B	F
Herald, Samuel	District 6	1852	KY	B	M
Hester, Louis	Precinct 1	1833	KY	B	M
Hester, Lane	Precinct 1	1847	KY	M	F
Hester, Charles	Precinct 1	1863	KY	M	M
Hester, Cezan	Precinct 1	1867	KY	M	M
Hester, David	Precinct 1	1869	KY	B	M
Hill, William A. C.	Precinct 1	1866	KY	B	M
Hill, Lula	Precinct 1	1869	KY	B	F
Holder, Mariah	Precinct 1	1785	KY	B	F
Holder, Mary R.	Precinct 1	1846	KY	M	F
Holder, Sidney	Precinct 1	1848	KY	M	M
Holder, Lucinda	Precinct 1	1848	KY	M	F
Holder, Joseph	Precinct 1	1849	KY	M	M
Holder, Edney	Precinct 1	1859	KY	M	F
Holder, Anggietine	Precinct 1	1863	KY	M	F
Holder, Bell	Precinct 1	1865	KY	M	F
Holder, Phillis	Precinct 1	1867	KY	M	F
Holder, Mariah	Precinct 1	1869	KY	M	F
Horn, Millie	Precinct 2	1840	KY	B	F
House, Melvina	New Roe	1835	KY	B	F
House, William V.	New Roe	1854	KY	B	M
House, Eliza E.	New Roe	1856	KY	B	F
House, Leanda E.	New Roe	1858	KY	B	F
House, Joseph F.	New Roe	1860	KY	B	M
House, Newton	New Roe	1866	KY	B	M
Howell, Joseph	Precinct 1	1857	KY	B	M

Name	Location	Approximate Birth Year	Birth State	Color	Sex
Hughes, Louis	District 7	1849	KY	M	M
Hughes, Nelley	District 7	1852	KY	M	F
Hughes, John W.	District 5	1870	KY	M	F
Hurston, Edmon	Precinct 4	1837	KY	B	M
Hurston, Kana	Precinct 4	1848	KY	B	F
Hurston, Aleck	Precinct 4	1864	KY	B	M
Hurston, Julie A.	Precinct 4	1867	KY	B	F
Hurston, Charles	Precinct 4	1869	KY	B	M
Jackson, Adline	Precinct 2	1852	KY	B	F
Jackson, Mahala	Precinct 2	1866	KY	B	F
Jewell, Canolene	Precinct 3	1835	KY	B	F
Jewell, James H.	Precinct 4	1851	KY	M	M
Jewell, Milton	Precinct 3	1857	KY	B	M
Jewell, John	Precinct 3	1858	KY	B	M
Jewell, Daniel	Precinct 3	1861	KY	B	M
Jewell, Henry	Precinct 3	1862	KY	B	M
Jewell, Nannie	Precinct 3	1863	KY	B	F
Jewell, George	Precinct 3	1867	KY	B	M
Jewell, William	Precinct 3	1869	KY	B	M
Johnson, Tempy	District 5	1790	KY	B	F
Johnson, Isam	District 7	1821	KY	B	M
Johnson, Midan	District 5	1842	KY	B	F
Johnson, Richard	District 5	1843	KY	B	M
Johnson, Margret	Precinct 1	1860	KY	B	F
Kowell, George	Precinct 2	1856	KY	B	M
Kowell, Allen	Precinct 2	1860	KY	B	M
Landers, Rebecca	Precinct 3	1827	KY	B	F
Landers, Jerry	Precinct 3	1828	KY	B	M
Landers, Lessie L.	Precinct 4	1857	KY	M	M
Landers, William	Precinct 3	1858	KY	B	M
Landers, Alfred	Precinct 3	1860	KY	B	M
Landers, Cintta C.	Precinct 3	1863	KY	B	F
Landrum, Rose	Precinct 1	1820	KY	B	F
Leares, Alfred	Precinct 4	1825	KY	B	M
Leares, Mariah	Precinct 4	1830	KY	B	F
Leares, Jennie	Precinct 4	1835	KY	B	F
Leares, Delsa	Precinct 4	1845	KY	B	F
Leares, Henry	Precinct 4	1846	KY	B	M

Name	Location	Approximate Birth Year	Birth State	Color	Sex
Leares, John	Precinct 4	1852	KY	B	M
Leares, Mary	Precinct 4	1853	KY	B	F
Leares, James W.	Precinct 4	1853	KY	B	M
Leares, Elijah	Precinct 4	1856	KY	B	M
Leares, Sidney M.	Precinct 4	1856	KY	B	M
Leares, Mary E.	Precinct 4	1857	KY	B	F
Leares, Margret	Precinct 4	1857	KY	B	F
Leares, Lucinda	Precinct 4	1860	KY	B	F
Leares, Lon S.	Precinct 4	1860	KY	B	F
Leares, Scott	Precinct 4	1861	KY	M	M
Leares, James	Precinct 4	1862	KY	B	M
Leares, Mary	Precinct 4	1862	KY	B	F
Leares, William R.	Precinct 4	1862	KY	B	M
Leares, Coatney	Precinct 4	1864	KY	B	F
Leares, William H.	Precinct 4	1866	KY	B	M
Leares, William	Precinct 4	1866	KY	B	M
Lears, Daniel	Precinct 2	1835	KY	B	M
Lenkins, Mary	Precinct 1	1840	KY	M	F
Lenkins, Buckner	Precinct 1	1862	KY	M	M
Lenkins, Martha	Precinct 1	1864	KY	M	F
Levelle, Tempy	Precinct 4	1816	KY	B	F
Lightfoot, William C.	Precinct 2	1822	KY	B	M
Lightfoot, Lucy A.	Precinct 2	1835	KY	B	F
Lightfoot, Mary H.	Precinct 2	1854	KY	B	F
Lightfoot, Margret J.	Precinct 2	1859	KY	B	F
Lightfoot, George A.	Precinct 2	1862	KY	B	F
Lightfoot, John B.	Precinct 2	1867	KY	B	M
Lightfoot, Mordaica	Precinct 2	1869	KY	B	M
Limmerson, Mary	Precinct 4	1834	KY	M	F
Limmerson, Dallas	Precinct 4	1858	KY	M	F
Limmerson, Ann E.	Precinct 4	1863	KY	M	F
Limmerson, Harrlett A.	Precinct 4	1864	KY	M	F
Limmerson, Scott A.	Precinct 4	1866	KY	M	F
Limmerson, Henry	Precinct 4	1869	KY	M	M
Linck, Melvina	Precinct 2	1848	KY	B	F
Linck, Nathan	Precinct 2	1853	KY	B	M
Manion, Sines	District 5	1830	KY	B	F
Manion, Shelby	District 5	1835	KY	B	M

Name	Location	Approximate Birth Year	Birth State	Color	Sex
Manion, Berny	Precinct 1	1848	KY	B	M
Manion, Samuel	Precinct 1	1852	KY	B	M
Manion, Richard	District 5	1853	KY	B	M
Manion, Mary W.	District 5	1854	KY	B	F
Manion, Martha	Precinct 1	1856	KY	B	F
Manion, James H.	District 5	1857	KY	B	M
Manion, Simon	Precinct 1	1859	KY	B	M
Manion, Manda C.	District 5	1859	KY	B	F
Manion, Matilda	District 5	1859	KY	B	F
Manion, Amanda	Precinct 1	1863	KY	B	F
Manion, Sreline	Precinct 1	1864	KY	B	M
Manion, James W.	District 5	1866	KY	B	M
Martin, James	Precinct 4	1843	KY	B	M
Martin, Dica	Precinct 4	1850	KY	B	F
Martin, Willia	Precinct 4	1851	KY	B	M
Martin, Albert	Precinct 4	1865	KY	B	M
Martin, Edmond	Precinct 4	1869	KY	B	M
Mason, William	Scottsville	1844	KY	B	M
Mason, Louisa	Scottsville	1853	KY	M	F
McGoodnight, Peter	Precinct 3	1839	KY	B	M
McGoodnight, Penny	Precinct 3	1839	KY	B	F
McGoodnight, James A.	Precinct 3	1861	KY	B	M
McGoodnight, Tarda W.	Precinct 3	1865	KY	B	M
McGoodright, Dicy	Precinct 3	1815	KY	B	F
Merideth, Angeline	Precinct 2	1848	KY	B	F
Millegan, Mary J.	Precinct 1	1861	KY	B	F
Mitchell, Buckaman	Precinct 1	1857	KY	B	M
Mitchell, Samuel	Precinct 1	1864	KY	B	M
Moor, Joseph	Precinct 3	1860	KY	B	M
Moor, Melvina	Precinct 3	1862	KY	B	F
Moor, Newton	Precinct 3	1864	KY	B	M
Motley, Moses	Precinct 3	1801	KY	B	M
Motley, Ninnie	Precinct 3	1830	KY	B	F
Motley, Tamer	Precinct 3	1847	KY	B	F
Motley, Samuel	Precinct 3	1852	KY	B	M
Motley, Press	Precinct 3	1852	KY	B	M
Motley, William E.	Precinct 3	1860	KY	B	M

Name	Location	Approximate Birth Year	Birth State	Color	Sex
Motley, Cristiden	Precinct 3	1864	KY	B	F
Motley, Susan	Precinct 3	1867	KY	B	F
Muldagon, Scott	Precinct 1	1866	KY	B	M
Muldagon, Rohoda	Precinct 1	1869	KY	B	F
Neal, Washington	Precinct 4	1850	KY	B	M
Page, Aaron	Precinct 4	1826	KY	B	M
Petty, Luthena	Precinct 3	1827	KY	B	F
Petty, Henry	Precinct 3	1855	KY	B	M
Petty, Asberry	Precinct 3	1858	KY	B	M
Petty, Harriett	Precinct 3	1861	KY	B	F
Petty, Calvan	Precinct 3	1863	KY	B	M
Petty, John	Precinct 3	1866	KY	B	M
Petty, Eliza	Precinct 3	1869	KY	B	F
Pharis, Willia	Precinct 3	1866	KY	B	M
Pharis, Elden	Precinct 3	1869	KY	B	F
Pope, Gabreal	Precinct 2	1822	KY	B	M
Pope, Fannie A.	Precinct 2	1832	KY	B	F
Pope, Lennette A.	Precinct 2	1856	KY	B	F
Pope, Joseph A.	Precinct 2	1858	KY	B	M
Pope, James E.	Precinct 2	1862	KY	B	M
Pope, Eliza A. C.	Precinct 2	1863	KY	B	F
Pope, Marion G.	Precinct 2	1867	KY	B	M
Porter, Palmina	Precinct 2	1832	KY	M	F
Porter, Ella	Precinct 1	1849	KY	B	F
Porter, William E.	Precinct 2	1852	KY	M	M
Porter, Charles	Precinct 3	1855	KY	B	M
Porter, Catharine	Precinct 4	1856	KY	B	F
Porter, Annie E.	Precinct 2	1857	KY	M	F
Porter, Samuel	Precinct 2	1860	KY	M	M
Porter, Sarah J.	Precinct 2	1862	KY	M	F
Porter, Shelby	Precinct 2	1864	KY	M	M
Porter, George	Precinct 1	1867	KY	B	M
Potts, Nancy	New Roe	1850	KY	B	F
Prewett, Henry	Precinct 2	1849	KY	B	M
Prewitt, Josiah	Precinct 2	1846	KY	M	M
Prewitt, Martha J.	Precinct 2	1854	KY	B	F
Price, Millie	Precinct 2	1815	KY	B	F
Price, Dempy	Precinct 2	1859	KY	B	M

Name	Location	Approximate Birth Year	Birth State	Color	Sex
Pulliam, Thomas	Precinct 1	1822	KY	B	M
Pulliam, Perciller	Precinct 1	1835	KY	B	F
Pulliam, Dianna	Precinct 1	1843	KY	B	F
Pulliam, Susan	Precinct 1	1844	KY	B	F
Pulliam, Thomas	Precinct 1	1846	KY	B	M
Pulliam, Susan	Precinct 1	1852	KY	B	F
Pulliam, Maranda	Precinct 4	1852	KY	B	F
Pulliam, John	Precinct 4	1855	KY	B	M
Pulliam, Emly J.	Precinct 4	1857	KY	B	F
Pulliam, Daniel	Precinct 1	1858	KY	B	M
Pulliam, Amanda	Precinct 1	1859	KY	B	F
Pulliam, Anna	Precinct 1	1860	KY	B	F
Pulliam, Rennie	Precinct 1	1860	KY	B	F
Pulliam, Dick	Precinct 4	1861	KY	B	M
Pulliam, Wallace	Precinct 1	1862	KY	B	M
Pulliam, George	Precinct 1	1863	KY	B	M
Pulliam, Evaline	Precinct 1	1865	KY	B	F
Pulliam, William	Precinct 1	1866	KY	B	M
Pulliam, Edney	Precinct 1	1867	KY	B	F
Pulliam, Belle	Precinct 1	1868	KY	B	F
Pulliam, Mary M.	Precinct 1	1869	KY	B	F
Pulliam, Edward	Precinct 1	1870	KY	B	M
Read, Amos	Precinct 1	1829	KY	B	M
Read, Hester	Precinct 2	1842	KY	B	F
Read, Rufus	Precinct 1	1856	KY	B	M
Read, Eller	Precinct 1	1857	KY	B	F
Read, Jacob	Precinct 1	1863	KY	B	M
Read, Lucy	Precinct 1	1865	KY	B	F
Read, Benjamin F.	Precinct 2	1867	KY	B	M
Reaves, Emily F.	District 6	1842	KY	M	F
Rhodes, Eliza J.	Precinct 1	1858	KY	B	F
Richey, Dianner	Precinct 3	1820	KY	B	F
Richey, Amanda H.	Precinct 3	1851	KY	B	F
Rickey, Adam	Precinct 3	1825	KY	B	M
Rickey, Hester	Precinct 3	1828	KY	B	F
Rickey, Sarah A.	Precinct 3	1849	KY	M	F
Rickey, Hayden	Precinct 3	1852	KY	B	M
Rickey, John L.	Precinct 3	1855	KY	B	M

Name	Location	Approximate Birth Year	Birth State	Color	Sex
Rickey, Mitt W.	Precinct 3	1860	KY	B	M
Rickey, Emmer D.	Precinct 3	1868	KY	B	F
Rickey, Bell T.	Precinct 3	1870	KY	M	F
Rigsby, Luther T.	Precinct 3	1870	KY	B	M
Ritcherson, Ann	District 7	1824	KY	M	F
Ritcherson, Carline	District 7	1863	KY	M	F
Ritcherson, Margret	District 7	1866	KY	M	F
Rogers, Aaron	Precinct 4	1832	KY	B	M
Rogers, Ellen	Precinct 4	1848	KY	B	F
Rogers, Charles	Precinct 4	1854	KY	B	M
Rogers, Emmer	Precinct 4	1856	KY	B	F
Roork, George	Precinct 1	1856	KY	B	M
Roork, Watt	Precinct 1	1858	KY	B	M
Roork, Lane	Precinct 1	1861	KY	B	M
Roork, Bettie	Precinct 1	1863	KY	B	F
Roork, Critenders	Precinct 1	1865	KY	M	F
Rountree, Julie	District 6	1845	KY	B	F
Rountree, Henry C.	District 6	1852	KY	B	M
Rowntree, Anderson	Precinct 2	1857	KY	B	M
Sarver, Eliza H.	District 6	1863	KY	M	F
Sarver, Sarah	District 6	1868	KY	M	F
Sarver, William	District 6	1869	KY	B	M
Satterfield, Rachel	Precinct 1	1820	KY	B	F
Satterfield, Bettie	Precinct 1	1848	KY	B	F
Satterfield, Haywood	Precinct 1	1849	KY	B	M
Satterfield, Albert	Precinct 1	1858	KY	B	M
Satterfield, Bell	Precinct 1	1866	KY	B	F
Satterfield, Lane	Precinct 1	1868	KY	B	F
Sayles, Matilda	Precinct 4	1861	KY	B	F
Searer, Fredrick	Precinct 4	1823	KY	B	M
Searer, Evaline	Precinct 4	1840	KY	B	F
Searer, Wesley	Precinct 4	1848	KY	B	M
Searer, Harriett	Precinct 4	1852	KY	B	F
Searer, Charles	Precinct 4	1860	KY	B	M
Searer, James H.	Precinct 4	1860	KY	B	M
Searer, Shed	Precinct 3	1861	KY	B	M
Searer, Joseph F.	Precinct 4	1863	KY	B	M
Searer, Randel	Precinct 4	1865	KY	B	M

Name	Location	Approximate Birth Year	Birth State	Color	Sex
Searer, Charles R.	Precinct 4	1866	KY	B	F
Searer, Mariah J.	Precinct 4	1867	KY	B	F
Searer, Joshuah	Precinct 4	1868	KY	B	M
Searer, Benjamin F.	Precinct 4	1868	KY	B	M
Searer, Mary A.	Precinct 4	1868	KY	B	F
Searer, Sarah A.	Precinct 4	1868	KY	B	F
Searer, William H.	Precinct 4	1869	KY	B	M
Sears, Isaac	Precinct 4	1820	KY	M	M
Sears, Edmon	Precinct 3	1824	KY	B	M
Sears, Mariah	Precinct 3	1830	KY	B	F
Sears, George	District 7	1855	KY	B	M
Sears, Margret	Precinct 3	1856	KY	B	F
Sears, Millie	Precinct 3	1859	KY	B	F
Sears, William	Precinct 3	1862	KY	B	M
Seay, Deley	District 7	1846	KY	B	F
Setterfield, Adlnee	Precinct 1	1851	KY	B	F
Shipley, Phillip	Precinct 1	1803	KY	M	M
Shipley, Matilda	Precinct 1	1815	KY	M	F
Shipley, Toliver	Precinct 1	1852	KY	M	M
Shipley, John E.	Precinct 1	1854	KY	M	M
Shipley, Matilda F.	Precinct 1	1857	KY	M	F
Shipley, William W. S.	Precinct 1	1861	KY	M	M
Siddens, Sarrah	District 5	1830	KY	B	F
Siddens, Jane	District 7	1838	KY	M	F
Siddens, James	District 5	1839	KY	M	M
Siddens, Angenine C.	District 5	1844	KY	M	F
Siddens, Matha	District 5	1852	KY	B	F
Siddens, Hanna	District 7	1854	KY	M	F
Siddens, Henry	District 7	1858	KY	M	M
Siddens, Spencer F.	District 7	1860	KY	M	M
Siddens, Thomas C.	District 5	1861	KY	M	M
Siddens, John A.	District 7	1864	KY	M	M
Smith, Reece	Precinct 3	1848	KY	B	M
Smith, Mary F.	Precinct 3	1853	KY	B	F
Smith, Ann	Precinct 3	1870	KY	B	F
Stark, Mahala	Precinct 3	1812	KY	B	F
Stark, Calap	Precinct 3	1820	KY	B	M
Stark, Moses	Precinct 3	1825	KY	B	M

Name	Location	Approximate Birth Year	Birth State	Color	Sex
Stark, Willice	Precinct 4	1829	KY	M	M
Stark, George	Precinct 3	1833	KY	M	M
Stark, Virginie	Precinct 3	1835	KY	B	F
Stark, Martha W.	Precinct 4	1835	KY	B	F
Stark, John W.	Precinct 3	1835	KY	M	M
Stark, Mary	Precinct 4	1837	KY	M	F
Stark, Jessee	Precinct 3	1838	KY	B	M
Stark, Jemima	Precinct 3	1840	KY	M	F
Stark, Isham	Precinct 3	1844	KY	M	M
Stark, Georges A.	Precinct 3	1845	KY	M	F
Stark, John	Precinct 3	1846	KY	B	M
Stark, Amanda	Precinct 4	1846	KY	B	F
Stark, Julie	Precinct 3	1848	KY	B	F
Stark, Limima	Precinct 3	1849	KY	B	F
Stark, Thomas	Precinct 4	1849	KY	B	M
Stark, James W.	Precinct 4	1850	KY	B	M
Stark, Grace	Precinct 3	1850	KY	M	F
Stark, James E.	Precinct 3	1851	KY	B	M
Stark, Samuel	Precinct 3	1852	KY	B	M
Stark, Frances	Precinct 3	1852	KY	M	F
Stark, Mary F.	Precinct 3	1854	KY	B	F
Stark, Eldorado	Precinct 4	1854	KY	M	M
Stark, Doctor B.	Precinct 3	1855	KY	B	M
Stark, Witherspoon	Precinct 4	1855	KY	B	M
Stark, Sarah	Precinct 4	1855	KY	M	F
Stark, Elizabeth	Precinct 3	1858	KY	B	F
Stark, Lennie	Precinct 4	1858	KY	M	F
Stark, Angeline	Precinct 3	1861	KY	B	F
Stark, Eller D.	Precinct 4	1861	KY	M	F
Stark, Lucy	Precinct 4	1862	KY	B	F
Stark, Elliott	Precinct 3	1862	KY	M	M
Stark, Washington	Precinct 4	1864	KY	B	M
Stark, Festus	Precinct 3	1864	KY	M	M
Stark, Fannie	Precinct 4	1864	KY	M	F
Stark, Mary E.	Precinct 3	1866	KY	M	F
Stark, Thomas L.	Precinct 3	1867	KY	M	M
Stark, Leonora	Precinct 4	1867	KY	M	F
Stark, Charles E.	Precinct 3	1868	KY	M	M

Name	Location	Approximate Birth Year	Birth State	Color	Sex
Stark, Hettie J.	Precinct 3	1869	KY	M	F
Stark, Levie T.	Precinct 3	1869	KY	M	F
Stark, James H.A.	Precinct 4	1869	KY	M	M
Stark, George B.	Precinct 3	1870	KY	M	M
Startt, Lucy J.	Precinct 4	1837	KY	M	F
Startt, Mary E.	Precinct 4	1857	KY	M	F
Startt, Charles	Precinct 4	1860	KY	M	M
Startt, Isaac C.	Precinct 4	1863	KY	M	M
Startt, Martha B.	Precinct 4	1866	KY	M	F
Startt, Anna B.	Precinct 4	1868	KY	M	F
Steward, Robert	New Roe	1866	KY	B	M
Steward, Fannie	New Roe	1868	KY	B	F
Steward, William	New Roe	1870	KY	B	M
Stone, Rachel	Precinct 4	1834	KY	B	F
Stone, Henry W.	Precinct 4	1841	KY	B	M
Stone, Samuel	Precinct 4	1852	KY	B	M
Stone, Henry	Precinct 4	1854	KY	B	M
Stone, Franklin	Precinct 4	1856	KY	B	M
Stone, Lafayette	Precinct 4	1858	KY	B	M
Stone, Jessee	Precinct 4	1862	KY	B	M
Stone, Bell T.	Precinct 4	1870	KY	B	F
Stovall, Dicy	Precinct 3	1805	KY	B	F
Stovall, Cuped	Precinct 4	1829	KY	B	M
Stovall, Judah F.	Precinct 3	1835	KY	B	F
Stovall, James	Precinct 3	1838	KY	B	M
Stovall, Harriett	Precinct 4	1838	KY	B	F
Stovall, Price	Precinct 3	1840	KY	B	M
Stovall, Matilda	Precinct 3	1840	KY	B	F
Stovall, John W.	Precinct 3	1841	KY	B	M
Stovall, Sarah E.	Precinct 3	1843	KY	B	F
Stovall, John	Precinct 4	1850	KY	B	M
Stovall, Angeline R.	Precinct 4	1856	KY	B	F
Stovall, Mary E.	Precinct 3	1857	KY	B	F
Stovall, Dica A.	Precinct 4	1857	KY	B	F
Stovall, Eliza	Precinct 3	1860	KY	B	F
Stovall, James A.	Precinct 3	1861	KY	B	F
Stovall, Calvan	Precinct 3	1862	KY	B	M
Stovall, Thomas B.	Precinct 3	1863	KY	B	M

Name	Location	Approximate Birth Year	Birth State	Color	Sex
Stovall, Lewis E.	Precinct 3	1865	KY	B	M
Stovall, Fannie S.	Precinct 3	1866	KY	B	F
Stovall, Freley D.	Precinct 3	1866	KY	B	M
Stovall, John C.	Precinct 3	1869	KY	B	M
Stovall, Frances	Precinct 3	1870	KY	B	F
Street, Laine	District 5	1835	KY	B	F
Street, Hannah	District 5	1853	KY	B	F
Street, Steven A.	District 5	1857	KY	B	M
Sweat, Sousen	District 7	1857	KY	B	F
Tabor, Angeline	Scottsville	1835	KY	B	F
Tabor, Scott	Precinct 4	1860	KY	B	M
Tabor, Elmer	Scottsville	1864	KY	B	M
Tabor, Lou	Scottsville	1868	KY	B	F
Tabor, Unnamed	Scottsville	1870	KY	B	M
Thomas, Benjamin	Scottsville	1835	KY	B	M
Thomas, Mary	Scottsville	1842	KY	B	F
Thomas, Annie	Scottsville	1855	KY	B	F
Thomas, Eliza	Precinct 2	1855	KY	B	F
Thomas, Mary	Precinct 1	1857	KY	B	F
Thomas, Laura	Scottsville	1860	KY	B	F
Tope, William	Precinct 2	1830	KY	B	M
Tope, Mary A.	Precinct 2	1836	KY	B	F
Tope, Robert P.	Precinct 2	1842	KY	B	M
Tope, Sarah	Precinct 2	1847	KY	B	F
Tope, Julie H.	Precinct 2	1851	KY	B	F
Tope, David F.	Precinct 2	1856	KY	B	M
Tope, Lucinda F.	Precinct 2	1859	KY	B	F
Tope, Margret A.	Precinct 2	1861	KY	B	F
Tope, James H.	Precinct 2	1864	KY	B	M
Tope, Josiah	Precinct 2	1869	KY	B	M
Tope, Harriett E.	Precinct 2	1870	KY	B	F
Travelstead, John	District 6	1811	KY	M	M
Umbles, Lee A.	Precinct 2	1850	KY	B	M
Umbles, Frances E.	Precinct 2	1850	KY	B	F
Umbles, Thomas J.	Precinct 2	1855	KY	B	M
Umbles, Mallssa J.	Precinct 2	1857	KY	B	F
Umbles, Joseph W.	Precinct 2	1861	KY	B	M
Umbles, Mary A.	Precinct 2	1863	KY	B	F

Name	Location	Approximate Birth Year	Birth State	Color	Sex
Umbles, Emly F.	Precinct 2	1865	KY	B	F
Vance, Franklin	Precinct 4	1856	KY	B	F
Wagoner, William L.	Precinct 1	1825	KY	M	M
Wagoner, Lurvisa J.	Precinct 1	1838	KY	M	F
Walker, Mariah	Scottsville	1805	KY	B	F
Walker, Robert H.	District 6	1829	KY	B	M
Walker, Amy M.	Scottsville	1830	KY	B	F
Walker, Hannor	Precinct 2	1830	KY	B	F
Walker, Lucinda	District 6	1834	KY	B	F
Walker, Taylor	Precinct 2	1853	KY	B	M
Walker, Caroline B.	Scottsville	1855	KY	B	F
Walker, Green B.	District 6	1858	KY	B	M
Walker, Lillie	Scottsville	1858	KY	M	F
Walker, Robert G.	District 6	1867	KY	B	M
Walker, Matilda J.	District 6	1869	KY	B	F
Wheeler, Harriet	District 6	1820	KY	B	F
Wheeler, Sarilda	Precinct 4	1846	KY	B	F
Wheeler, Allen	Precinct 4	1847	KY	B	M
Wheeler, Thompson	District 6	1858	KY	B	M
Whitney, Peter	Precinct 1	1807	KY	M	M
Whitney, Lottie	Precinct 1	1820	KY	B	F
Whitney, Joseph	Precinct 1	1825	KY	B	M
Whitney, Ambrose	Precinct 1	1830	KY	M	M
Whitney, Lucinda	Precinct 1	1830	KY	M	F
Whitney, Phillis P.	Precinct 1	1832	KY	B	F
Whitney, Mariah	Precinct 1	1834	KY	M	F
Whitney, Thomas	Precinct 1	1835	KY	B	M
Whitney, Sarah	Precinct 1	1840	KY	B	F
Whitney, James	Precinct 1	1840	KY	M	M
Whitney, Elick	Precinct 1	1841	KY	B	M
Whitney, Aleck	Precinct 1	1841	KY	B	M
Whitney, Phillip	Precinct 1	1842	KY	M	M
Whitney, Dennis	Precinct 1	1843	KY	B	M
Whitney, Lucinda	Precinct 1	1843	KY	B	F
Whitney, Emily	Precinct 1	1844	KY	B	F
Whitney, Diannan	Precinct 1	1844	KY	B	F
Whitney, Lallie	Precinct 1	1845	KY	B	F
Whitney, Joseph	Precinct 1	1845	KY	B	M

Name	Location	Approximate Birth Year	Birth State	Color	Sex
Whitney, Sarah	Precinct 1	1845	KY	B	F
Whitney, Daniel	Precinct 1	1845	KY	B	M
Whitney, Henry	Precinct 3	1845	KY	B	M
Whitney, Charles	Precinct 3	1847	KY	B	M
Whitney, Fredrick	Precinct 1	1848	KY	B	M
Whitney, Nelson	Precinct 1	1849	KY	B	M
Whitney, Emely	Precinct 3	1849	KY	B	F
Whitney, Sallie A.	Precinct 1	1850	KY	B	F
Whitney, Fannie	Precinct 1	1850	KY	B	F
Whitney, Wesley M.	Precinct 1	1850	KY	M	M
Whitney, Ann	Precinct 1	1852	KY	B	F
Whitney, Olive	Precinct 1	1853	KY	M	F
Whitney, Turner	Precinct 1	1854	KY	B	M
Whitney, Haden	Precinct 1	1855	KY	B	M
Whitney, Harriett	Precinct 1	1855	KY	B	F
Whitney, Narcisser T.	Precinct 1	1856	KY	B	F
Whitney, Susan	Precinct 1	1858	KY	B	F
Whitney, Elbridge	Precinct 1	1858	KY	B	M
Whitney, Mary A.	Precinct 1	1859	KY	B	F
Whitney, Matilda	Precinct 1	1860	KY	B	F
Whitney, Perry G.	Precinct 1	1860	KY	M	M
Whitney, Edmond	Precinct 1	1861	KY	B	M
Whitney, Mariah	Precinct 1	1861	KY	B	F
Whitney, William	Precinct 3	1861	KY	B	M
Whitney, John E.	Precinct 1	1861	KY	M	M
Whitney, Scott	Precinct 1	1862	KY	B	M
Whitney, Willey	Precinct 1	1862	KY	B	M
Whitney, Ann E.	Precinct 1	1862	KY	M	F
Whitney, Samuel	Precinct 1	1863	KY	B	M
Whitney, Eliza	Precinct 1	1863	KY	B	F
Whitney, George A.	Precinct 1	1863	KY	B	F
Whitney, Paradine	Precinct 1	1863	KY	B	F
Whitney, Angelina	Precinct 1	1863	KY	B	F
Whitney, James W.	Precinct 1	1863	KY	B	M
Whitney, Grant	Precinct 1	1864	KY	B	M
Whitney, Sallie	Precinct 1	1864	KY	B	F
Whitney, Matilda	Precinct 1	1864	KY	M	F
Whitney, Mary O.	Precinct 1	1865	KY	B	F
Whitney, Fannie	Precinct 1	1865	KY	B	F

Name	Location	Approximate Birth Year	Birth State	Color	Sex
Whitney, Eliza	Precinct 1	1865	KY	B	M
Whitney, Lulie A.	Precinct 1	1865	KY	B	F
Whitney, Oma	Precinct 1	1865	KY	M	F
Whitney, Litus	Precinct 1	1866	KY	B	M
Whitney, Henrietta	Precinct 1	1866	KY	B	F
Whitney, Lucy A.	Precinct 1	1867	KY	B	F
Whitney, Susan F.	Precinct 1	1867	KY	B	F
Whitney, Rosco	Precinct 1	1867	KY	B	M
Whitney, Marcellus	Precinct 1	1867	KY	B	M
Whitney, Malissa	Precinct 3	1867	KY	B	F
Whitney, Olive	Precinct 1	1867	KY	M	F
Whitney, Robert E. L.	Precinct 1	1867	KY	M	M
Whitney, George	Precinct 1	1868	KY	B	M
Whitney, Loueller	Precinct 1	1868	KY	B	F
Whitney, Anthony	Precinct 1	1868	KY	B	M
Whitney, Eller F.	Precinct 1	1868	KY	M	F
Whitney, James H.	Precinct 3	1869	KY	B	M
Whitney, Giddie	Precinct 1	1869	KY	M	F
Whitney, Malisa	Precinct 1	1870	KY	B	F
Whitney, Laura J.	Precinct 1	1870	KY	B	F
Whitney, Samuel	Precinct 1	1870	KY	B	M
Whitney, Matilda E.	Precinct 1	1870	KY	B	F
Whitney, Phillis	Precinct 1	1870	KY	M	F
Williams, Simon	Precinct 1	1789	KY	B	M
Williams, Stephen	Precinct 1	1842	KY	B	M
Williams, Martha	Precinct 1	1846	KY	B	F
Williams, Dolly A.	Precinct 3	1852	KY	B	F
Williams, Judson	Precinct 3	1854	KY	B	F
Williams, Henry	Precinct 3	1856	KY	B	M
Williams, Peter	Precinct 1	1858	KY	B	M
Williams, Benjamin F.	Precinct 3	1858	KY	B	M
Williams, Deanner	Precinct 3	1860	KY	B	F
Williams, Elza E.	Precinct 3	1863	KY	B	F
Williams, Levi	Precinct 1	1866	KY	B	M
Willson, Delpha	District 6	1830	KY	B	F
Woodcock, Dick	Precinct 4	1836	KY	B	M
Woodcock, Patsy	Precinct 4	1850	KY	B	F
Woodcock, George	Precinct 1	1854	KY	B	M

Name	Location	Approximate Birth Year	Birth State	Color	Sex
Woodcock, Robert	Precinct 1	1855	KY	B	M
Woodcock, Ellin	Precinct 1	1861	KY	B	F
Woodcock, John	Precinct 4	1868	KY	B	M
Woodcock, Robert	Precinct 4	1870	KY	B	M
Wright, David	Precinct 2	1812	KY	B	M
Wright, Julie A.	Precinct 2	1830	KY	B	F
Wright, Rachel J.	Precinct 2	1836	KY	B	F
Wright, James W.	Precinct 2	1843	KY	B	M
Wright, Sarah J.	Precinct 2	1858	KY	B	F
Wright, Joseph L.	Precinct 2	1868	KY	B	M

Chapter 12

Patrollers in Allen County

Background

Slavery was involuntary servitude and, as such, had to be enforced. Otherwise, it would not have persisted. Kentucky had a variety of state and local laws designed to assure that persistence. For example, Bowling Green in 1825 ordered ten stripes [lashes with a whip] for a slave found away from home after 10:00 p.m.[1] The Allen County Court in 1828 ordered that stocks and a whipping post be erected on the grounds at the jail.[2] Punishments were not recorded.

The Emancipation Proclamation by Abraham Lincoln freed the slaves in states that had seceded. Because Kentucky had not seceded, the Emancipation Proclamation did not free Kentucky's slaves. In response to the Proclamation, the Kentucky Legislature approved an act on 2 March 1863 that prohibited any slaves freed by the Proclamation from entering Kentucky. If any of these freed slaves were caught in Kentucky, they were to be sent back into slavery. It required that an attempt be made to locate the owner of a captured runaway slave by advertising in the newspaper. If no one laid claim to the runaway, the slave was required to be sold to the highest bidder at the courthouse door. So it was that Henry, a runaway slave, was captured in Allen County and held in jail. The County Court ordered that his capture be advertized for 20 days at eight different locations.[3] That action did not identify an owner. The Allen County Court then ordered that he be sold to the highest bidder and his sale was concluded.[4]

On another occasion, the Allen County Court ordered the sheriff to advertize that Lazarus, a jailed runaway slave, would

[1] Minutes of the Trustees for the City of Bowling Green, 7 June 1825

[2] Allen County Court Orders, January 1828

[3] Allen County Court Order Book, December 1826

[4] Allen County Court Order Book, 1858-1860

be offered for hire for a period of four months for the best price offered. That was not an isolated instance because, three years later, a jailed runaway slave named Mourning was offered for hire for a period of six months.[5]

Kentucky, like other slave states, used slave patrols to apprehend runaways, disperse slaves who assembled, and search slave quarters, acts that inspired fear among slaves. In most slave states, service as a patroller was directed by the county courts but such service was purely voluntary in Kentucky.[6] The Allen County Court approved rather than appointed white men as patrollers, and assigned a specific area that they were to patrol. The term for the early approvals was not defined but by the 1850s it was defined as for twelve months. For each patrol area, one of these men was approved as Captain and three or four others were approved as his assistants. These patrollers typically worked at night on irregular schedules. Slaves called them "pattyrollers." The patrollers in Kentucky effectively enforced the laws. In 1860, only 119 of 225,483 slaves were recorded as runaways, about one half of one percent.[7]

Surnames of Some Patrollers

A list of the patrollers approved by the Allen County Court for service from 1826 through 1855 was prepared. There appears to be data missing for the years 1837 through 1850. The reason is unclear but the list is almost certainly incomplete. There was no attempt to find the names of the patrollers after 1855 because the intent of the research was to determine who they were in general rather than in specific terms. The ninety names of the list are sufficient for that intent.

Among the surnames of the patrollers are many family names of slave owners, including some slave owners themselves. That doesn't seem to be unusual because there would not be much motivation for men who were neutral about or opposed to slavery to accept an appointment as a patroller. The patrollers from 1826 to 1855 are in Table 28.

[5] Allen County Court Order Book, October 1859

[6] Sally E. Hadden, 2001. *Slave Patrols: Law and Violence in Virginia and the Carolinas*. Harvard University Press, Cambridge, MA

[7] Statistical View of the United States, 65: Statistics of the United States in 1860, page 338

Table 28

Patrollers in Allen County 1826 to 1855

Allen County Day Book, 1826-1838						
Month	**Year**	**Captain**	**Assistant**	**Assistant**	**Assistant**	**Assistant**
June	1826	Holder, William	Hatler, Michael	Pitchford, Daniel Jr.	Brown, William K.	
June	1826	Burton, John	Porter, Denton	Read, Dillard	Burton, Richard	Porter, William
June	1827	Edmonds, Richard	Cayton, George W.	Stephens, Elisha	Gennins, Will	
Dec.	1827	Williams, Henry	Read, Dillard	Pulliam, Henry	Wade, John	Fishback, John
June	1828	Hagan, Levi	Hagan, Jesse	Ragland, Joseph	Dodd, Josiah	
April	1830	Burton, Drewry	Neale, Thomas	Drane, Anthony	Tutt, Richard	
June	1830	Coleman, Will	Agee, Samuel	Poe, Amos*	Allen, John	
June	1830	Sears, Will	Doores, James	Finney, Henry	Jamesin, Achilles	
Sep.	1830	Hagan, Will	Murphy, John H.	Herrington, James		
Sep.	1832	Woodsin, Anderson	Austin, Willis	Manion, Ambrose	Austin, Williamson	
April	1833	Stark, Jeremiah	Finney, Henry	Thomas, James	Strait, Wright	Young, Branch
June	1835	Wagoner, Samuel	Reeves, William	Johnson, Benjamin	Dalton, Thomas	
Dec.	1836	Mulligan, James C.	Mulligan, John C.	Cobb, Lebreus	Hammett, Willis	
Dec.	1836	Reeves, William	Dalton, Daniel	Waggoner, Williamson	Harris, Henry	
Nov.	1851	Ritchey, Samuel	Patton, Benjamin	Patton, John	Williams, Thomas A.	
Feb.	1852	Hagan, John J.	Thompson, John C.	Boyers, William G.		
June	1852	Holland, Y. H.	Thompson, William	Johnson, William		
June	1852	Davis, Jonathan	Venable, Joseph	Guy, William		
Dec.	1852	Burnett, Alfred	Dohery, J. M.	Hickman, I. S.		
July	1854	Godley, John S.	Stark, C. D. J.	Jameson, J. A.	Read, J. W.	

Month	Year	Captain	Assistant	Assistant	Assistant	Assistant
Nov.	1854	Frances, Joseph	Austin, Williamson	Johnson, W. V.		
March	1855	Stark, C. D. J.	Sears, Albert	Stovall, Joseph	Jameson, M. D.	Patten, Benjamin
Oct.	1855	Dana, D. B.	Kenady, Lockhart	Ragsdale, Thomas		
Oct..	1855	Benedict, James	Bennett, A.	Bennett, T. G.	Walker, William H.	

**Alva Jackson replaced Amos Poe September 1830*

Chapter 13

Freedmen in Allen County, 1815-1865

Freedmen 1815-1865

The power to enslave includes the power to set free. We can speculate about what motivates a person to enslave another or to free another but we all can agree that freedom is the preferred condition. However, the quote, "Give me liberty or give me death," was spoken by a slave owner named Patrick Henry. Clearly, he would not have approved of such a statement from one of his slaves. Yet he recognized and wrote about that dichotomy.

> *Is it not amazing that, at a time when the rights of humanity are defined and understood with precision, in a country above all others fond of liberty, in such an age, we find men, professing a religion the most humane, mild, meek, gentle, and generous, adopting a principle as repugnant to humanity as it is inconsistent with the Bible and destructive to liberty? Would any one believe that I am master of slaves of my own purchase?*[1]

The aspiration of slaves for eventual freedom must have been universal. Few ever achieved that status. Indeed, very few of the slaves in Allen County were granted freedom. Even fewer were able to buy their own freedom. Those who gained freedom were called Freedmen. Some Freedmen from Virginia and other eastern states came to Kentucky but most moved on to states in which they would be truly free.

Emancipation and Manumission

There are two terms that were related to the freedom of slaves. Manumitted appears in the census. Manumission freed the individual from slavery but did not provide other rights. Emancipation freed the slave and granted civil rights too. However,

[1] Tyler, Moses Coit. 1898. Patrick Henry. Boston: Houghton, Mifflin.

freedom was not totally unrestricted.

The freedom granted to Freedmen was not the same as that which white Kentuckians enjoyed. There were many restrictions placed on their activities. For example, patrollers could still enter and search the Freedmen's homes at will.

Kentucky passed a law in 1798 to allow Freedmen to possess just one gun. Slaves on the other hand, could only have guns under a license from a Justice of the Peace.[2] Freedmen who harbored a runaway slave were fined $15 and given twenty lashes with a whip. Freedmen could not legally sell alcohol, could be arrested for "loitering," and could get thirty lashes for attacking a white person. Marriage to another Freedman was illegal until 1825, a strange law even for that era.[3]

The first priority of a slave who had acquired money was to purchase his own freedom. The next priority was to purchase the freedom of his wife to preclude their future children from being born as slaves. Freedmen were only allowed to buy slaves who were closely related to them.

An example of these priorities occurred in January 1851. The Allen County Court recorded that "Will, a freeman of color" appeared in person before the Court to emancipate a 45- year-old woman who he described as "Cynthia, his servant and wife."[4] Note that Will did not have a surname. That would have to wait until after the 13th Amendment gave equal rights to all Freedmen. Also note that the word the Court used was "emancipate," not manumit.

Edward Holder was the owner of 15 slaves when he brought one of them with him to the Allen County Court. There in open Court he declared that he emancipated the "negro man named Phil or Phillip" who stood beside him. The Court ordered that the emancipation be recorded and then described this newly freed man. Phil was about 43 yeas old, a mulatto man who was yellow in color and who stood about five foot ten inches tall. His right hand had been maimed by a gunshot and the third finger had been taken

[2] Farman, Henry W. and Clive Day, 2000. *Chapters in the history of social legislation in the United States to 1860.* Lawbook Exchange, Union NJ

[3] Lucas, Marion Brunson. 2003. *A history of Blacks in Kentucky: from slavery to segregation, 1760-1891.* [Frankfort]: Kentucky Historical Society.

[4] Allen County Court Order Book, January 1851

off.[5] Such detailed descriptions were necessary so that Freedmen could prove that they had been legally freed when stopped by the patrollers. They could stop them on the roads, could search their homes, and could demand positive identification. See Chapter 12 for more details about the Patrollers.

Lucy Stark on 13 May 1850 appeared before the Court to emancipate Lewis, one of her five slaves. He was about 34 years old, a light mulatto color, five foot six or seven, straight brown hair, with three scars; one on his forehead, one immediately above his nose, and one running up near his hair.[6]

Freedmen in 1820

The 1820 census did not record Freedmen's names. Only the white Heads of Household name was recorded with the Freedmen tabulated by gender and age group. In 1820, all nine of the Freedmen in Allen County lived in Scottsville, five with Wilson Bass and four with Nancy Walker (Table 29).

Table 29

Freedmen in Allen County in 1820

	Males by Age				Females by Age				
Head of Household	<14	14-26	26-45	>45	<14	14-26	26-45	>45	Total Freed
Bass, Wilson		1	1		3				5
Walker, Nancy	3					1			4
TOTAL	3	1	1		3	1			9

Freedmen in 1830

The first Freedman in Allen County who was listed as Head of Household was Samuel Pope who was listed as being less than ten years old in the 1830 census. The female living in his household was between 36 and 55 years old, likely his mother. The other three

[5] Allen County Court Order Book, May 1850

[6] Ibid

Freedmen were in white households, one living with Hugh Brown, two living with James Clark, and two living with Fredrick Heeter. None of them were living in Scottsville. There were about the same number of Freedmen of Allen County in 1830 (Table 30) as there had been in 1820.

Table 30

Freedmen in Allen County in 1830

	Males by Age						**Females by Age**						
Head of Household	<10	10-24	24-36	36-55	55-100	>100	<10	10-24	24-36	36-55	55-100	>100	Total Freed
Brown, Hugh				1									1
Clark, James				1						1			2
Heeter, Fredrick	1	1											2
Pope, Samuel	1									1			2
Total	2	1		2						2			7

Freedmen in 1840

The numbers of Freedmen had increased to nineteen in the 1840 census. The names of the Freedmen were not recorded. As before, the name of the "free white" head of household was recorded with the gender and age of the Freedmen listed in the "Free Colored" section (Table 31). Note that none of the Freedmen who were in the 1830 census remained in Allen County for the 1840 one.

Table 31

Freedmen in Allen County 1840

	Males by Age						Females by Age						
Head of Household	*<10*	*10-24*	*24-36*	*36-55*	*55-100*	*>100*	*<10*	*10-24*	*24-36*	*36-55*	*55-100*	*>100*	*Total Freed*
Absher, Nancy	1							1					2
Allen, Luke P.												1	1
Bass, Jerimiah					1								1
Colbert, Elijah				1			2	1					4
Garmon,				1									1
Jackson, William							1						1
Logan, Young	3	1					2	1					7
Martin, Joseph		1											1
TOTAL	4	2		2	1		6	3				1	19

Freedmen in 1850

There was a dramatic increase of Freedmen during the decade ending in 1850 census to 44 individuals. Although the increase had more than doubled their numbers during the previous decade, their number was still was just 3.3 percent of the total number of slaves in Allen County. Although small, that percentage was higher than the 1.0 percent for Kentucky as a whole.

Exactly half of the Freedmen in 1850 were male. Of them, only six were 24 years old or older. Of the females, eight were older than 24. One of those eight females was Elisha Boon, a centenarian, who resided in Samuel Harston's household.

The birth states and birth years show that the original pattern of immigration into Kentucky had ended. Six Freedmen were born in Virginia and one from North Carolina, all were older than 32. Two Freedmen were born in Tennessee, and both were under 20 years old.

There was one Freedman who was listed in the Slave Schedule of the census as a 34-year-old man who had been emancipated and was living in the household of Lucy Stark. He was the same Lewis mentioned above and was added to the list of Freedmen presented in Table 32. Mariah Walker was the only one of the Freedmen who was listed as a resident of Scottsville.

Table 32

Freedmen in Allen County 1850

Freedman	Head of Household	Birth	Color	State
Absher, M.	Absher, M.	1820	M	KY
Barlow, Phibe	Barlow, J. J.	1830	B	TN
Boon, Elisha	Harston, Samuel	1750	B	VA
Carpenter, Free Dick	Carpenter, Free Dick	1789	B	NC
Colvert, J. W.	Colvert, Ann	1838	M	KY
Colvert, S.	Colvert, Ann	1837	M	KY
Colvert, S. E.	Colvert, Ann	1844	M	KY
Colvert, S. M.	Colvert, Ann	1846	M	KY
Colvert, Shepen	Colvert, Ann	1831	M	KY
Colvert, V. V.	Colvert, Ann	1841	M	KY
Crary, Europe	Shanks, Juliet A.	1836	M	KY
Cross, J.W.	Hinton, E.	1843	M	KY
Gibbs, Sarah S.	McElroy, S.	1845	M	KY
Glover, J. G.	Duncan, A.	1836	M	KY
Glover, K.	Anderson, R. G.	1805	M	KY
Glover, R.	Duncan, A.	1837	M	KY
Goodman, Katharine	Jackson, N.	1836	M	KY
Graham, Clary	Graham, Clary	1815	B	VA
Graham, J. F.	Graham, Clary	1830	B	KY
Graham, M. A.	Graham, Clary	1838	B	KY
Graham, R. J.	Graham, Clary	1836	B	KY
Graham, William C.	Graham, Clary	1840	B	KY
Graham, E. F.	Graham, Clary	1833	B	KY
Hatler, Sally	Thompson, J. C.	1782	B	VA
Humble, C. W.	Humble, Leroy	1850	B	KY
Humble, James E.	Humble, Leroy	1843	B	KY
Humble, Leander	Humble, Leroy	1850	M	KY
Humble, Leroy	Humble, Leroy	1818	B	VA
Humble, M. A.	Humble, Leroy	1827	M	KY
Humble, S. H.	Humble, Leroy	1847	B	KY
Lee, Rachael	Lee, Solomon	1798	B	MA
Lee, Solomon	Lee, Solomon	1797	B	KY
Pope, Gabriel R.	Follis, G.	1822	B	KY
Ray, Ellis	Ray, Nancy	1829	B	KY
Ray, Fanny	Ray, Nancy	1828	B	KY
Ray, George	Ray, Nancy	1836	B	KY

Freedman	Head of Household	Birth	Color	State
Ray, Nancy	Ray, Nancy	1796	B	VA
Ray, Pensing	Ray, Nancy	1847	B	KY
Ray, Susan	Ray, Nancy	1834	B	KY
Ray, Temperance	Ray, Nancy	1840	B	KY
Richardson, Wyley	Brown, John H.	1800	M	VA
Stark, Lewis	Stark, Lucy	1816	M	KY
Walker, Mariah	Griggs, William	1802	B	KY
Williams, John	Minyard, John	1843	M	TN

Surnames of Freedmen

The traditional assumption is that Freedmen adopted the surname of their last owner. One analysis of the slaves from Alabama and Louisiana revealed that 71 percent used the surname of the last owner but only 17 percent of those from South Carolina did so.[7] Of the 22 Freedmen living in a white household in Allen County in 1850, only nine shared the same surname as the white head of household. The traditional view seems not to apply to Allen County.

The selection of a surname required a perception of the purpose of a surname as viewed by white people, particularly the relation of surname to the male lineage of a family and to marriage. For many generations, surnames for slaves had not existed. Therefore, their ancestral heritage and oral histories could use only first names. The lack of a surname precluded a change of the woman's name when she married. So, there was no urge nor perceived need for a surname after so many generations without one.

The universal freedom granted by the 13th Amendment created another complicating factor. Would the newly freed woman take the surname of her last owner, her husband's new name, the name of her husband's last owner, her father's new name, the name of some previous owner, or some other name. She could determine the surname of her children but who did that for her children who had been sold away from her?[8] Slavery had not allowed the permanency of family that the use of surnames requires.

[7] Miller, Randall M., and John David Smith. 1997. *Dictionary of Afro-American slavery*. Westport, Conn: Praeger.

[8] Regosin, Elizabeth Ann. 2002. *Freedom's promise: ex-slave families and citizenship in the Age of Emancipation*. Charlottesville: University Press of Virginia.

An ex-slave may not have fully understood that they, and they alone, could choose their surname. County or state officials may have written the last owner's name on an official form that thereafter became the de facto official name.

Freedmen in 1860

Times were changing in 1860 as the specter of secession and war became increasingly likely. Less than a year after the census of 1860 was completed, the war would begin. The decision that Freedmen made to remain in Allen County, and incur the risk of being re-enslaved if the Confederacy won, is not easily understood. Perhaps fear of the unknown, abject poverty, or unwillingness to leave their parents or children were the reasons. Some may have left before the war began and returned after the war was over but before the next census was taken, but that can't be verified. Whatever the reason, 37 Freedmen were in Allen County in 1860, seven less than in the previous census.

The reduction in the number of Freedmen between 1850 and 1860 was consistent with a similar reduction throughout Kentucky. The National Fugitive Law of 1850 is thought to be the cause since it allowed any suspected slave to be taken into custody and returned to an alleged owner. Many free blacks were conscripted back into slavery as they had no rights in court and could not defend themselves against accusations.

Tim McElroy, at age 88, was the oldest of the Allen County Freedmen in 1860 (Table 33). The next oldest Freedman was Mariah Walker of Scottsville, who was just 56. She was one of nine Freedmen in the Scottsville enumeration district.

Table 33

Freedmen in Allen County in 1860

Freedman Name	Location	Age	Approx. Birth Year	Color	Born In
Absher, America	New Roe	31	1829	M	KY
Brown, Preston	Scottsville	25	1835	B	KY
Center, Anthony	Scottsville	1	1859	B	KY
Center, J. E.	Butlersville	6	1854	M	KY
Duncan, Rubin	Scottsville	22	1838	B	KY
Gibbs, Elizabeth	Butlersville	23	1837	M	KY
Glover, Julus	Scottsville	27	1833	B	KY
Goodman, Kate	Scottsville	24	1836	M	KY
Graham, R. J.	Butlersville	22	1838	B	KY
Graham, R. M.	Butlersville	2/12	1860	B	KY
Graham, S. J.	Butlersville	2	1858	B	KY
Lindsey, S. E.	Scottsville	9	1851	M	KY
Lindsey, Sally	Scottsville	50	1810	B	VA
Lynn, Emily	Scottsville	16	1844	M	KY
McElroy, Tim	Butlersville	88	1772	B	SC
Pope, Eliza	New Roe	28	1832	B	KY
Pope, G. A.	New Roe	5	1855	B	KY
Pope, Gabriel	New Roe	38	1822	B	KY
Pope, J. A.	New Roe	3	1857	B	KY
Pope, T. S.	New Roe	1/12	1860	B	KY
Ray, B. M.	Butlersville	2/12	1860	B	KY
Ray, George	Butlersville	20	1840	B	KY
Ray, L. F.	Butlersville	9	1851	B	KY
Ray, M. J.	Butlersville	3	1857	B	KY
Ray, Nancy	Butlersville	50	1810	B	VA
Ray, Penny	Butlersville	12	1848	B	KY
Ray, Susan	Butlersville	24	1836	B	KY
Ray, Tompy	Butlersville	17	1843	B	KY
Umbles, C. W.	Butlersville	14	1846	B	KY
Umbles, Jack	Butlersville	8	1852	B	KY
Umbles, L.	Butlersville	10	1850	B	KY
Umbles, Leroy	Butlersville	48	1812	B	VA
Umbles, M. A.	Butlersville	33	1827	M	KY
Umbles, M. J.	Butlersville	3	1857	B	KY
Umbles, S. H.	Butlersville	12	1848	B	KY
Umbles, T. J.	Butlersville	5	1855	B	KY
Walker, Mariah	Scottsville	56	1804	B	VA

A comparison of the 1850 and 1860 Freedmen reveals that some Freedmen had left Allen County, and there were some new Freedmen on the 1860 list. Of the 1850 Freedmen, 57 percent were not in the County in 1860. Four of the older ones (Elisha Boon, Dick Carpenter, Sally Hatler, and Solomon Lee) likely died in the interim. Of the other fifteen, one must assume that most if not all had moved away.

There were 19 Freedmen who were listed in both the 1850 and 1860 census. The family of Nancy Ray from the Butlersville area accounted for seven of those who stayed in Allen County. She was born in Virginia, but the other family members were Kentuckians. Gabriel Pope was a 38-year old man who lived with his wife and three children in the New Roe area.

There were 18 new Freedmen in the 1860 census, new at least in the listing. Whether they were newly freed in Allen County or emigrated from elsewhere after being freed could not be determined. Of these 18, eight were in the Leroy Umbles family. He was born in Virginia, but all the other family members were born in Kentucky. In the 1850 census, the census taker spelled his name "Humbles."

Chapter 14

Slaves Born in Allen County Who Joined the Union Army 1863-1866

Background

The white population of Kentucky did not approve of presidential candidate Abraham Lincoln's association with the anti-slavery movement. There were 146,216 Kentuckians (all white and all male, of course) who voted in the election of 1860. Of that number, only 1,364 voted for Lincoln, 99.1 percent of Kentuckians voted against him. About 40-45 % of Allen Countians voted for John Bell, the Constitutional Union candidate. His slogan was "The Union as it is, the constitution as it is." On the other hand, Lincoln's election brought great hope among slaves that freedom was coming to them. Indeed it was coming, just not as quickly as they expected.

At first, no slaves were permitted to join the Union Army because they were property, not citizens, according to the Dred Scott decision. Freedmen were not allowed to enlist either. Those positions changed as the need for soldiers increased and the enlistment by whites declined. President Lincoln authorized the induction of freedmen and slaves, but exempted Kentucky from that provision to pacify the supporters of continued legal slavery. Undaunted, slaves fled from Kentucky to free states and enlisted there. By the end of the war, over 186,000 African Americans were in the Union Army, about 10 percent of the total number of troops.

Enlistment of Slaves into the Union Army

In early 1863, after the Emancipation Proclamation, enlistment of slaves in Kentucky began after the President removed the enlistment restriction. To partially assuage the objections by slave owners to losing their slaves without recompense, the enlistment bounty (bonus) was to be paid to the slave's owner. No Allen County slave enlisted during the period of that rule.

The enlistment of slaves infuriated Kentucky's legislature. They approved a resolution that protested "...the enlistment of negroes as soldiers into the armies of the United States..." and their enlistment "...within the State of Kentucky." The resolution requested President Lincoln to remove all "...camps for negro (sic) soldiers by which our slaves are enticed to leave the service of their owners."[1] Antagonism is evident in that resolution and was an indicator of the atmosphere that was prevalent at the time.

The opposition to enlistment of slaves did not weaken when, in July 1864, the law was changed to provide the bounty to the enlisted slave volunteer instead of to his owner. Recruitment centers were established at eight locations in Kentucky, one of which was in Bowling Green. Within a month, that office had enlisted 300 slave volunteers. Those volunteers came from Warren and the surrounding counties. Enlistments rose rapidly. By the end of the war about a year later, 23,703 Kentucky slaves had joined the United States Army. That number was more than 59% of the 40,285 male slaves between the enlistment ages of 18 and 45, according to the 1860 census. That compares to the 44% of the 180,580 Kentucky white men between those ages who joined the Union Army.[2] Only Louisiana contributed more African Americans to the Union army. Ultimately, thirteen out of every one hundred Union soldiers were African American. There is a memorial in Frankfort, Kentucky in the Greenhill Cemetery to honor the nearly 25,000 African American Kentuckians in the Union Army. Nearer home, the memorial in the National Cemetery in Nashville (Figure 35) was erected in recognition of their service.[3]

Thirty-eight slaves enlisted who had been born in Allen County. Most of them enlisted in Bowling Green. In most cases, those enlistees living in Allen County would have had to runaway from their owners; avoid being captured, whipped, and returned to them by the patrollers; and find their way to the army camp there.

---

[1] Kentucky General Assembly, resolution number 49, approved 22 February 1864

[2] Speed, Thomas, 1907. *The Union cause in Kentucky 1860-1865.* G. P. Putnam's Sons, New York

[3] Lucas, Marion Brunson. 2003. *A history of Blacks in Kentucky: from slavery to segregation, 1760-1891.* [Frankfort]: Kentucky Historical Society.

The act of enlistment was a courageous one, a preview of the valor they later showed in battle.

Figure 35

Memorial to the U.S. Colored Troops, National Cemetery, Nashville, Tennessee

Motivation for Enlistment

Each slave had some motivation behind his enlistment, but there is no record of what prompted him. There were three enlistees who had been born slaves in Allen County who joined the army from free states: from Chicago, Illinois; Hillsboro, Ohio; and Cincinnati, Ohio. How did they get to be in those cities and, because slavery was illegal in those states, why would they want to join the Union army? The urge to be free no doubt explains their getting to those places. The urge to help eradicate slavery no doubt was a strong motivation for their enlistment.

One problem that ex-slaves faced arose from the fugitive slave law passed in 1850, something new that had not been law previously. It required United States governmental officials to help recapture runaway slaves and made it legal for slave owners to reclaim them. One ex-slave affected by that law was George Brown, who was living as a free African American man and working as a barber in Cincinnati in September 1850. Under the fugitive slave law, he was accused of being a runaway slave. He had to appear before a judge to defend himself from those charges brought by a slave catcher. The judge determined that there was insufficient proof that he was a runaway and he was released.[4] Remaining free was a strong motivation for joining the Union army.

An Allen County born slave named George Brown enlisted in the Union army fourteen years later in Hillsboro, Ohio just sixty miles east of Cincinnati. No relationship could be established beyond doubt with the George Brown just described.

Year of Enlistment

There were only three years of enlistment data, 1863, 1864, and 1865, that reported Allen County-born enlistees. There were eight enlistees in 1863, the first year that slaves were accepted. None of those enlisted in Kentucky, seven joined the army in Gallatin, Tennessee. The other enlisted in Cincinnati, Ohio.

These 1864 enlistments showed the effect of the opening of an enlistment camp at Bowling Green. Eighteen of the 23 enlistments that year were made there. The other four were made in Hillsboro, OH, Chattanooga, TN, Clarksville, TN, and Nashville, TN.

Lee surrendered in April 1865 and the war was soon over. There were seven enlistees that year. Five enlisted in Bowling Green and the other two in Louisville.

Draftees and Substitution

The United States Army soldiers in the Civil War were white volunteers, until the number of volunteers decreased after two years of war. So much so that the size of the army could not be sustained. On 3 March 1863, the United States Congress passed a law authorizing conscription of men into the army.[5] The Confederacy had instituted a draft a year earlier, but it applied only to white men.[6] The new draft law had a provision that allowed draftees to purchase an exemption for $300 or to provide a substitute. Enrollment of draftees or substitutes began on 25 May 1863.[7] When a slave was drafted in Kentucky or from the other three slave states that did

---

[4] "George Brown," Ohio History Central, December 5, 2008, http://www.ohiohistorycentral.org/entry.php?rec=3375

[5] Sheehan-Dean, Aaron, 2007. *Struggle for a vast future.* Osprey Publishing, Oxford, United Kingdom

[6] Ransom, Roger L. 1989. *Conflict and compromise: the political economy of slavery, emancipation, and the American Civil War*. Cambridge [England]: Cambridge University Press.

[7] Weigley, Russell Frank. 2000. A great Civil War: a military and political history, 1861-1865. Bloomington: Indiana University Press.

not secede, his owner was not permitted to procure a substitute for him nor withhold him from enrollment. There were strenuous protests by slave owners.[8] If the drafted slave preferred to continue in slavery rather than to enroll in the army, the slave himself could make that choice by paying the $300 or providing a substitute.

Two of Allen County's slaves were drafted and both were enrolled on the same day. One was Sam Pulliam, who was enrolled 23 September 1864 in Bowling Green. He served in Company I of the 6th U.S. Colored Cavalry. The other draftee was Ed Sears, who was enrolled 23 September 1863 in Company I of the same unit. They had chosen the army and freedom over remaining in slavery.[9]

Ages of Enlistees

One might expect that the younger slaves would be the ones most eager to join the Union Army. The data show that there were 15 enlistees under 21 years old, 12 between 21 and 30, 9 between 31 and 40, and 2 older than 40 (Figure 36).

Figure 36

Allen County-born enlistees 1863-1865 by age at enlistment

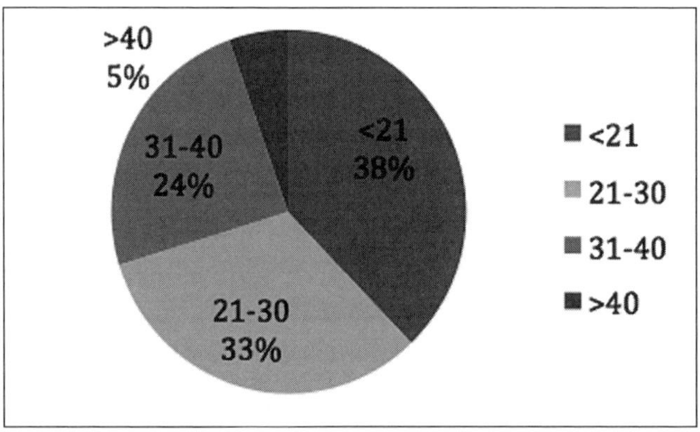

[8] Berlin, Ira and Joseph P. Reidy, and Leslie S. Rowland, 1998. *Freedom's Soldiers: The Black Military Experience in the Civil War.* Edited by Cambridge, England: Cambridge University Press

[9] United States Government, Robert N. Scott, H. M. Lazelle, George B. Davis, Leslie J. Perry, Joseph W. Kirkley, Fred C. Ainsworth, John S. Moodey, and Calvin D. Cowles. 1880. The War of the Rebellion: a compilation of the official records of the Union and Confederate armies. Washington: Govt. Print. Off.

The youngest was Isaac Godley, who was sixteen when he enlisted at Bowling Green on 4 August 1864. He was assigned to Company B, 6th US Colored Cavalry. He was a slave who was owned by Jesse Godley, presumed to be the J. S. Godley who owned 18 slaves in 1860. Private Godley was mustered out with the 6th US Colored Cavalry at De Vall Bluff, Arkansas in 1866.

The second youngest was Cuba Stovall, a seventeen year-old farmer, who was also the last to enlist. He enlisted in Bowling Green on 31 May 1865 for a three year tour just as the Civil War was ending.

The older of the two men who were over forty was Anthony Hatfield who was 43 when he enlisted for a three years term in Company C of the 14th US Colored Infantry in Gallatin, Tennessee. He was mustered out of the service on 26 March 1866 in Nashville.

The second oldest was George Page, who was 41 when he enlisted in Louisville in Company E of the 13th US Colored Heavy Artillery on 27 March 1865. He was a blacksmith in civilian life before becoming an "atificer" (skilled craftsman) in this unit.

Regiments with Allen County-Born Slave Enlistees

It was army policy to fill regiments with slave enlistees except for the leadership positions. White officers and non-commissioned officers were assigned to provide the leadership of those units. That action appears to be prejudicial but it really was not as much so as it seems. The leadership qualifications included the ability to read and write. The owners, the County, and the State had not educated the slaves. Few were fluent in reading and writing. It was expedient to identify literate leadership from the larger pool of literate whites. As a result, all slave enlistees born in Allen County held the rank of Private except for Sergeant Isham T. Stark, Sergeant Bird Follas, and Corporal Willis W. Williams. They were promoted to their ranks after enlistment, an exceptional achievement that no doubt recognized some special leadership abilities.

The word "colored" was used by the Army, and is used herein, because there were units with the same unit number that were all white. For example, there were the 6th U.S. Colored Cavalry and the 6th U.S. Cavalry. The latter was all white.

The following paragraphs identify the regiments known to have had African Americans soldiers who were born in Allen County. There may have been others, but records only indicate the place of birth of the slaves, not their residence at the time of enlistment. There were 67 enlistees who were born in Barren County, 15 born in Monroe County, and 114 born in Warren County. Some of those could have been slaves in Allen County when they enlisted.

2nd U.S. Colored Light Infantry

There was one Allen County born soldier in the 2nd U.S. Colored Light Infantry. He was Stanford Williams, who was about 21 years old when he enlisted in Nashville, Tennessee. He may have been sold previously to someone in Tennessee. He enlisted on 2 April 1864, went into the hospital shortly afterward and died 30 July 1864 in the hospital in Nashville.

5th U.S. Colored Infantry

The first enlistment of an ex-slave who was born in Allen County was by John Baker who was born there in 1844. He enlisted in Cincinnati, Ohio on 14 July 1863. He had brown eyes, dark hair, and a yellow complexion. He was a five foot eight and a half inches tall farmer who was born in Scottsville nineteen years earlier. His enlistment in Cincinnati probably means that he was already a free man when he joined the 5th U.S. Colored Infantry. Unfortunately, he died from the measles in a hospital in Delaware, Ohio on 12 October 1863.

6th U.S. Colored Cavalry

The 6th Kentucky Colored Cavalry had sixteen members who were born in Allen County (See Table 34 at the end of this chapter for their names). These Allen Countians enlisted in Bowling Green between 31 July and 23 September 1864. The unit was organized at Camp Nelson, near Nicholasville, with the understanding that they could confiscate horses for the army's use.

With no more than six weeks of training, they participated in the battle at Saltville, Virgina on 2 October 1864. The morning after that battle, black and white soldiers were executed as they lay wounded on the battlefield by the Confederates who were angry that black soldiers had been allowed on the battlefield. Some ranked the brutality as equal to a similar racial massacre at Fort Pillow, Tennessee.[10]

They participated in Stoneman's Raid into southwestern Virginia 10-29 December 1864: the capture and destruction of lead mines and a battle on 17-18 December near Marion, and in the second Saltville battle 20-21 December. During 1865, they served at LaGrange, Tennessee and at Paducah, Wild Cat, Danville, New Haven, Catlettsburg, Covington, and Louisville, Kentucky. Their last assignment was as an occupying force in Helena and De Vall, Arkansas. They were mustered out 15 April 1866 in De Vall.

6th U.S. Colored Heavy Artillery

Private Nelson Brown was born in Allen County about 1837 enlisted in the 6th US Colored Heavy Artillery on 15 January 1864 in Natchez, Mississippi. No information was found about how he came to be in Natchez, but it seems likely that he had been "sold down the river" earlier. The unit was involved in the action to protect the steamer "Clara Bell" in July 1864, and participated in skirmishes, one at Vidalia, one at Buck's Ferry, and two at Black River. It also participated in four expeditions within Louisiana and one to Mississippi. The unit was mustered out on 18 May 1866 at Natchez, Mississippi.

12th U.S. Colored Heavy Artillery

The 12th Colored Heavy Artillery had three Allen Countians who were slaves when they enlisted. They were Farrew[11] Pulliam who enlisted in 10 September 1864, Daniel Whitney who enlisted on 28 March 1865 and Willis W. Williams who enlisted on 5 April 1865 in Bowling Green. Before their enlistment, the unit was in the battles at Munfordville and Glasgow. The unit moved from Bowling Green to Columbus in the fall of 1865, and then to Paducah before being mustered out on 24 April 1866.

---

[10] Smith, John David. 2002. *Black soldiers in blue: African American troops in the Civil War era.* Chapel Hill: University of North Carolina Press.

[11] This may be a phonetic spelling of Pharoah

13th U.S. Colored Heavy Artillery

Six Allen County born slaves joined the 13th US Colored Heavy Artillery in Bowling Green between October 1864 and May 1865. See Table 34 at the end of the chapter for their names. The unit was attached to 2nd Brigade, 1st Division at Camp Nelson in Jessamine County and performed garrison duty until it was mustered out on 24 April 1866. Camp Nelson was the third largest in the nation, and was a major recruitment center for colored troops.

14th U.S. Colored Infantry

Three of the Allen County soldiers from the 14th U.S. Colored Infantry are buried on a knoll in the National Cemetery at Chattanooga, Tennessee. The graves of Privates Peter Gibson, Isaac Hughes, and Nelson Behela[12] are within forty feet of each other.

Figure 37

Grave markers for Privates Gibson, Hughes, and Behela.

Nine Allen Countians (Table 34) enlisted into the 14th Colored Infantry between October 1863 and January 1864 at Gallatin, Tennessee. They were in garrison duty at Chattanooga until November 1864. They moved to Dalton, Georgia and were in action there on 14-15 August. They were part of the siege of Decatur, Alabama 27-30 October, the battle of Nashville Tennessee on 15-16 December, Overton's Hill on 16 December, and the pursuit of General Hood to the Tennessee River 17-28 December, before

[12] The surname should be Behela, an apparent clerical error

returning to duty at Chattanooga. These battle-tested soldiers were mustered out on 16 March 1866 in Greenville, Tennessee.

15th U.S. Colored Infantry

Private Richard Parish was born in Allen County about 1824. He was enlisted into Company D of the 15th Colored Infantry at Clarksville, Tennessee on 6 May 1864. He was 40 years old at that time. The unit was attached to the 5th Corps de Afrique Engineers during the previous February. Private Parish was a hostler [horse and mule handler] in the unit. He was discharged by doctor's orders while in the hospital in Nashville in March 1865.

27th U.S. Colored Infantry

George Brown was the only native of Allen County in the 27th Colored Infantry. He was 27 when he enlisted at Hillsborough, Ohio on 12 August 1864. He was described as five foot eleven farmer with dark complexion with black hair. He joined the unit for the siege of Petersburg and Richmond, Virginia up to 7 December 1864. The unit moved to Fort Fisher, North Carolina and was part of the assault and its capture on 15 January 1865 and of Wilmington on 22 February. The unit was advancing on Raleigh, North Carolina when the war ended. It occupied Raleigh and was present when General Johnston surrendered his Confederate army there. Private Brown was mustered out on 21 September 1865 at the end of his enlistment period in New Bern, North Carolina.

29th U.S. Colored Infantry

The only Allen County born enlistee in the 29th Colored Infantry was Levi Bryson. He was a 25 year-old laborer and free when he enlisted on 23 January 1864 in Chicago. He became a member of the 29th Colored Infantry when it was organized in Quincy, Illinois in April. By June, the unit was part of the forces that laid siege to Petersburg and Richmond, Virginia and participated in the famous battle following the explosion in the mine dug under the confederate line on 30 July 1864. The unit also was in the Appomattox campaign in late March of 1865, until the surrender on 9 April that ended the war. The unit eventually moved for duty along the Rio Grande River where he stayed until he mustered out on 6 November 1865 in Brownsville, Texas.

The regiment lost 3 officers and 43 enlisted men killed or mortally wounded and 188 enlisted men by disease, a total loss of 234 men from the unit. Private Bryson was one of the survivors.

Mortality Among the Enlistees

Thirty-eight slaves born in Allen County enlisted in the Army of the United States. The mortality rate among them was high, two were killed in action and ten died while in the service of their country. The mortality rates were also high among the African American troops in the Union army during the Civil War. About 20.5% of them died. That rate was considerably higher than the white troops' 15.2 % mortality rate.

Non-Combat Deaths

Most slaves who joined the army were healthy. The 10 percent rejection rate for them was fewer than among white soldiers. The slaves who passed the physical for enlistment were described as muscular and fit.[13]

The need for sanitation was not understood and the lack of it contributed to the spread of disease. Vaccines, antibiotics, and most medicines were not yet available to the army physicians. Great advancements in knowledge about what caused disease, how to stop it from spreading, and how to treat it, would not come until after the war was over.

Almost all of Allen County's slaves lived in rural areas and in areas of low population density. In contrast, the army personnel lived in crowded and often unsanitary conditions both in garrison and in the field. The result was that soldiers were exposed to diseases that they had avoided as children. Outbreaks of measles, mumps, chickenpox, whooping cough, and other such illnesses affected many of them. Rural white enlistees were similarly affected.

One estimate was that one of every thirteen soldiers in the Civil War died of disease.[14] Whether or not that statistic is true, the rate among the African American soldiers from Allen County was much higher. In fact, 10 of 38 of them died of disease. For

[13] Lucas, Marion Brunson. 2003. *A history of Blacks in Kentucky: from slavery to segregation, 1760-1891*. [Frankfort]: Kentucky Historical Society.

[14] Beecher, Henry Ward. 1888. Patriotic addresses in America and England, 1850-1885, on slavery, the Civil War, and the development of civil liberty in the United States. New York: Fords, Howard & Hulbert.

example, John Baker and Henry Jewell were hospitalized with measles. Contagion of measles was common as was the deaths that resulted, Baker died in Ohio and Jewell died in Kentucky.

Pneumonia, pleurisy, tuberculosis, and other respiratory illnesses were common among the troops. Exposure to the elements was common, especially during winter's wet and cold. The exposure was worsened by the lack of proper clothing, which was a strong contributing factor in these diseases. Nelson Behela, John B. Griswold and James Hughes were among those who died of lung diseases.

Private James Hughes was buried at Section K site 13293 (Figure 38) in the National Cemetery in Nashville. He was one of 1,447 colored troops (U.S.C.T.) who are buried there along with 10,300 white soldiers who died during the Civil War. There are 429 unknown Colored Troops and 3,098 unknown white soldiers buried there too.

Figure 38
Grave Marker of James Hughes, National Cemetery, Nashville, Tennessee.

Lack of proper sanitation, contamination of water, and general lack of cleanliness produced the conditions that led to dysentery, diarrhea, typhoid fever, and erysipelas, all of which were common. Dysentery was fatal to James S. Sears and Stanford Williams succumbed to diarrhea.

Others were disabled by disease, non-combat related health problem, or non-combat injuries. Farrew Pulliam, whose wife Eliza waited for him in Gainesville, was hospitalized and eventually discharged because of a severe hernia. Others, who were discharged because of disabilities that developed during their service, were Richard Parish and Robert H. Walker.

Killed In Action

Two of the Allen County born soldiers of the 6th U.S. Colored Cavalry were killed in action, but in different battles. Six slaves named Sears (Ed, Isham, John, Orphy, and two named James) joined the army in Bowling Green on 6 September 1864. Their relationship with each other is unknown. All six of them of them were assigned to Company F, 6th U.S. Colored Cavalry. Two of these Sears men, James and John, were killed in action.

James Sears

James Sears, had been a slave owned by Henry Sears. He enlisted on 6 September 1864 in Bowling Green and was sent to Camp Nelson, Kentucky, the largest training depot in the nation for African Americans. Two weeks later, on 20 September, he deployed from Mount Sterling, Kentucky with a force of about 4,000 men to attack Saltville, Virginia. The objective was to destroy the salt production there. Salt was a necessity to preserve meat for the Confederate soldiers. James Sears was killed in the Saltville action on 1 October, about 25 days after he enlisted, (Figure 39) in a skirmish during the approach to Saltville.

The battle continued into the next day. The African American troops in his unit dismounted because their rifles could not be reloaded from horseback. They charged and penetrated through the first line of defense, but heavy losses prompted the order to withdraw. Their withdrawal left 114 black soldiers and four of their white officers dead or wounded on the battlefield. The next morning, Confederate troops and guerillas killed those that lay wounded, one of the worst atrocities of the war.

Figure 39

Casualty sheet for James Sears, killed in action at Saltville, Virginia

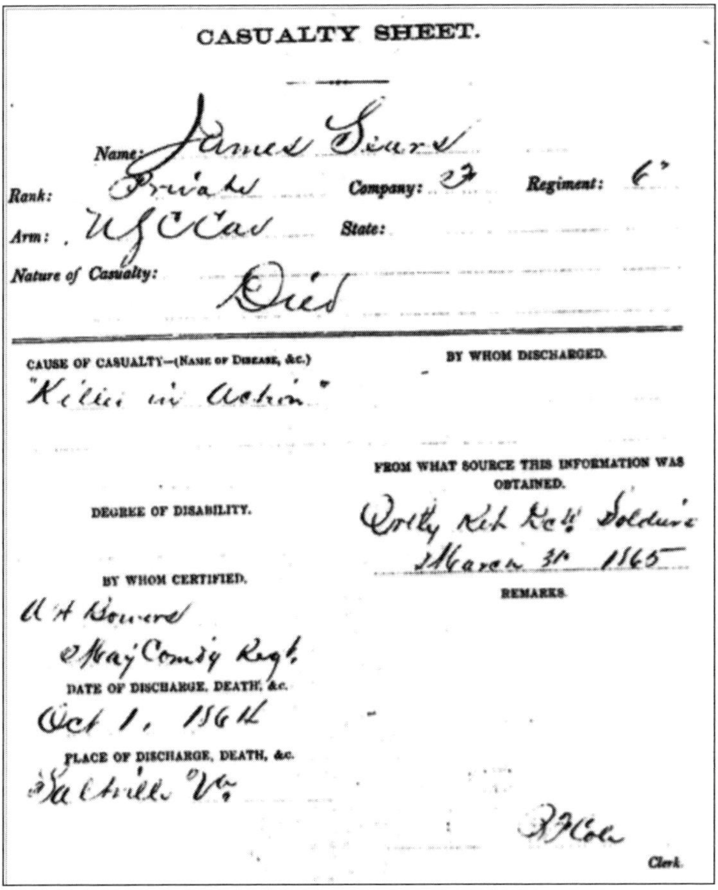

CASUALTY SHEET.

Name: James Sears

Rank: Private Company: 27 Regiment: 6

Arm: U S C Cav State:

Nature of Casualty: Died

CAUSE OF CASUALTY—(Name of Disease, &c.)

"Killed in Action"

BY WHOM DISCHARGED.

FROM WHAT SOURCE THIS INFORMATION WAS OBTAINED.

March 31 1865

DEGREE OF DISABILITY.

BY WHOM CERTIFIED.

DATE OF DISCHARGE, DEATH, &c.

Oct 1, 1864

PLACE OF DISCHARGE, DEATH, &c.

Saltville Va

REMARKS.

Clerk.

John Sears

John Sears was a slave owned by Samuel Sears before he enlisted on 6 September 1864 in Bowling Green. As a member of Company F of the 6th U.S. Colored Cavalry, he would have been present at the battle at Saltville when James Sears was killed. For sure, he would have known about the atrocity that occurred after that battle. In December 1864, another expedition, led by Major General Stoneman, brought about 4,000 men through Cumberland Gap back to the same area of Virginia to destroy the lead and salt works. During the battle at Marion, Virginia that ended on 18

December 1864, the African Americans of the 6th Colored Cavalry attacked about 350 men of the Confederate cavalry, charged under fire over open ground, held their fire until they were within thirty yards of the Confederate, and drove the Confederates back about a half mile.[15] Sometime during the battle for Marion, John Sears was killed in action. Details of his death are unknown (Figure 40).

Figure 40

Casualty sheet for John Sears, killed in action at Marion, Virginia

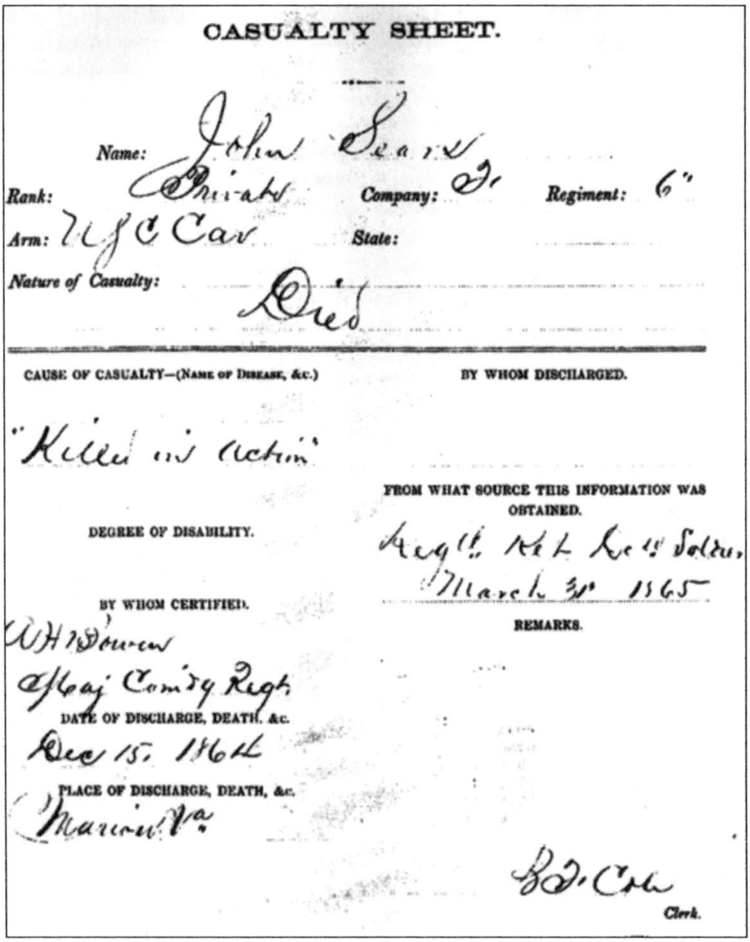

CASUALTY SHEET.

Name: John Sears

Rank: Private Company: D Regiment: 6th

Arm: U S C Cav State:

Nature of Casualty: Died

CAUSE OF CASUALTY—(NAME OF DISEASE, &c.)

"Killed in action"

DEGREE OF DISABILITY.

BY WHOM CERTIFIED.

W H Bowen

Maj Comdg Regt

DATE OF DISCHARGE, DEATH, &c.

Dec 15, 1864

PLACE OF DISCHARGE, DEATH, &c.

Marion Va

BY WHOM DISCHARGED.

FROM WHAT SOURCE THIS INFORMATION WAS OBTAINED.

March 30 1865

REMARKS.

Clerk.

---

[15] Beecher, Henry Ward. 1888. Patriotic addresses in America and England, 1850-1885, on slavery, the Civil War, and the development of civil liberty in the United States. New York: Fords, Howard & Hulbert.

Spellings of Soldiers' Surnames

The war records of the former slaves were replete with variant spellings of surnames. Some of those surname variants were:

Hatfield:	Halfield
Heater:	Heeter, Heter
Harston:	Hurston, Herston
Jewell:	Jewett
Landers:	Landis
Pulliam:	Pullam, Pullum, Pulum, Pattam
Sears:	Sayers

All of the African American soldiers born in Allen County used an X instead of a signature on their enlistment papers. That indicates that they probably could not write, not a surprise because no formal education had been given to them. The variant spellings of surnames then were the result of a phonetic spelling of the surnames as the writer heard them. The old pronunciation of the name Harston sounded as it were spelled Hurston or Herston. The Sayers variant seems to have been a drawled pronunciation of Sears.

The transcription of handwritten war records may have contributed to the variant spellings. Although the penmanship was often beautiful, it was and is very difficult to read. Shapes of the letters changed through the years as well as the styles of penmanship. As documents were transcribed to typed print, errors were sometimes induced by those changes.

List of Slaves Who were Born in Allen County and Joined the Union Army

Table 34 presents the thirty-eight Allen County born slaves who joined the Union Army during the Civil War. The data were extracted from service records available through Ancestry. Com. Several records were incomplete. Those soldiers who were killed in action are shown in bold type, the ones who died in service from other causes are in italics.

Lists of slaves, who were born in Barren County (Table 35),

Monroe County (Table 36), and Warren County (Table 37) and joined the Union Army, are at the end of this chapter. Some of these soldiers may have lived in Allen County at the time of enlistment. These lists are included here as a genealogical aid.

Table 34

Allen County born slaves who joined the Union Army

Bold = Killed in Action *Italics = Non-combat Deaths*

Name	Born	Enlisted At	Colored Regiment	Discharged At	Owner
Allen, John	*1846, Allen Co.*	*Louisville KY, 03/29/65*	*Co E, 13th Hvy. Arty.*	*Louisville KY, 8/15/65*	
Anthony, James	1828, Allen Co.	Gallatin TN, 10/15/63	Co D, 14th Inf.	Nashville TN, 07/26/66	
Baker, John	*1841, Scottsville*	*Cincinnati OH, 07/14/63*	*Co H, 5th Inf.*	*Camp Delaware OH, 10/12/63*	
Behela, Nelson	*1846, Allen Co.*	*Chattanooga TN, 12/01/64*	*Co H, 14th Inf.*	*Chattanooga TN, 04/15/64*	
Brown, George	1837, Allen Co.	Hillsborough OH, 08/12/64	Co A, 27th Inf.	New Bern NC, 09/09/65	
Brown, Nelson	1837, Allen Co.	Natchez MS, 01/15/64	Co L, 6th Hvy. Arty.	Natchez MS, 05/13/66	Ceculs Plantation
Bryson, Levi	1828, Allen Co.	Chicago IL, 01/23/64	Co B, 29th Inf.	Brownsville TX, 11/05/65	
Flippin, Adam	1837, Allen Co.	Gallatin TN, 01/15/64	Co K, 14th Inf.	Gallatin TN, 01/16/64	Hugh Flippin
Follas, Bird	1845, Allen Co.	Bowling Green KY, 09/18/64	Co F, 6th Cav.	De Valls AR, 04/15/66	Joseph Hill
Gibson, Peter	*1829, Allen Co*	*Gallatin TN, 10/01/63*	*Co C, 14th Inf.*	*Chattanooga TN, 03/24/64*	
Godley, Isaac	1848, Allen Co.	Bowling Green KY, 08/04/64	Co B, 6th Cav.	De Valls AR, 04/15/66	Jesse Godley
Griswold, John B.	*1844, Allen Co.*	*Bowling Green KY, 08/01/64*	*Co M, 6th Cav.*	*Camp Nelson KY, 05/23/64*	*Thomas B Griswold*
Hatfield, Anthony	1820, Allen Co.	Gallatin TN, 10/15/63	Co C, 14th Inf.	Nashville TN, 03/26/66	
Heater, Lewis	1833, Allen Co.	Bowling Green KY, 05/27/65	Co C, 13th Hvy. Arty.	Louisville KY, 11/18/65	Sebastian Heater
Hughes, Isaac	*1841, Allen Co.*	*Gallatin TN, 11/01/63*	*Co C, 14th Inf.*	*Chattanooga TN, 04/21/64*	

Name	Born	Enlisted At	Colored Regiment	Discharged At	Owner
Hughes, James	*1845, Allen Co.*	*Gallatin TN, 11/15/63*	*Co G, 14th Inf.*	*Nashville TN, 12/29/64*	
Hurston, Robert	1847, Allen Co.	Bowling Green KY, 03/30/65	Co B, 13th Hyv. Arty.	Louisville KY, 11/18/65	William Harston
Jewell, Henry	*1846, Allen Co.*	*Bowling Green KY, 10/24/64*	*Co A, 13th Hvy. Arty.*	*Smithland KY, 01/11/65*	*Thomas Jewell*
Landers, Jerry	1828, Allen Co.	Bowling Green KY, 08/11/64	Co B, 6th Cav.	De Valls AR, 04/15/66	Patsy Landers
Page, George	1824, Allen Co	Louisville KY, 03/27/65	Co E, 13th Hvy. Arty.	Louisville KY, 11/18/65	
Paris, John	1842, Scottsville	Gallatin TN, 10/01/63	Co A, 14th Inf.	Gallatin TN, 07/18/64	
Parish, Richard	1824, Allen Co.	Clarksville TN, 05/06/64	Co D, 15th Inf.	Nashville TN, 06/03/65	
Porter, Thomas	1846, Allen Co.	Bowling Green KY, 7/31/64	Co B, 6th Cav.	Bowling Green KY, 09/01/64	
Pulliam, Farrew	1829, Allen Co.	Bowling Green KY, 09/10/64	Co A, 12th Hvy. Arty.	Louisville KY, 05/24/66	
Pulliam, Sam	1838, Allen Co.	Bowling Green KY, 09/23/64	Co I, 6th Cav.	Lexington KY, 10/19/65	
Sears, Ed	*1824, Allen Co.*	*Bowling Green KY, 09/23/64*	*Co I, 6th Cav.*	*Camp Nelson KY, 06/26/65*	
Sears, Isham	1841, Allen Co.	Bowling Green KY, 09/06/64	Co F, 6th Cav.	De Valls AR, 04/15/66	Samuel Sears
Sears, James	**1843, Allen Co.**	**Bowling Green KY, 09/06/64**	**Co F, 6th Cav.**	**Saltville VA, 10/01/64**	**Henry Sears**
Sears, James	*1843, Allen Co.*	*Bowling Green KY, 09/06/64*	*Co F, 6th Cav.*	*De Valls AR, 02/24/66*	*William Taylor*
Sears, John	**1844, Allen Co.**	**Bowling Green KY, 09/06/64**	**Co F, 6th Cav.**	**Marion VA,**	**Samuel Sears**
Sears, Orphy	1845, Allen Co.	Bowling Green KY, 09/06/64	Co F, 6th Cav.	De Valls AR, 04/15/66	Samuel Sears

Name	Born	Enlisted At	Colored Regiment	Discharged At	Owner
Stark, Isham T.	1846, Allen Co.	Bowling Green KY, 08/04/64	Co B, 6th Cav.	De Valls AR, 04/15/66	Grandeson Stark
Stoval, Cuba	1847, Allen Co.	Bowling Green KY, 05/31/65	13th Hvy. Arty.	Louisville KY, 11/18/65	James Stovall
Walker, Robert H.	1848, Allen Co.	Gallatin TN, 10/15/63	Co C, 14th Inf.	Nashville TN, 05/02/65	
White, Pleasant	1849, Allen Co.	Bowling Green KY, 08/08/64	Co B, 6th Cav.	De Valls AR, 04/15/66	Uriah Porter
Whitney, Daniel	1850, Allen Co.	Bowling Green KY, 03/28/65	Co A, 12th Heavy Arty.	Louisville KY, 04/24/66	William Whitney
Williams, Stanford	*1851, Allen Co.*	*Nashville TN, 04/02/64*	*Co A, 2nd Heavy Arty.*	*Nashville TN, 07/30/64*	
Williams, Willis W.	*1852, Allen Co.*	*Bowling Green KY, 04/05/65*	*Co M, 12th Hvy Arty.*	*Louisville KY, 04/24/66*	*Edmund Williams*

Table 35

Barren County born slaves who joined the Union Army

Name	Born	Enlisted On	Enlisted At	Colored Regiment
Anderson, Joseph	1846	2 Aug 1864	Bowling Green, KY	6th U.S. Cavalry
Armstrong, Henry	1843	15 Feb 1865	Memphis TN	3rd U.S. Cavalry
Baker, Jordan	1837	26 Sep 1864	Drafted	6th U.S. Cavalry
Barton, Lowe	1840	18 May 1864	Clarksville TN	17th U.S. Infantry
Boyd, Jeremiah	1842	27 Jan 1864	Nashville TN	2nd U.S. Light Arty.
Clark, Booker	1835	30 Mar 1865	Bowling Green, KY	12th U.S. Heavy Arty.
Cole, William	1841	26 Sep 1864	Bowling Green, KY	6th U.S. Cavalry
Davidson, Albert	1843	23 Jan 1865	Bowling Green, KY	12th U.S. Heavy Arty.
Davis, Charles	1845	14 Oct 1864	Knoxville TN	1st U.S. Heavy Arty.
Davis, Clay	1844	11 Oct 1864	Knoxville TN	1st U.S. Heavy Arty.

Name	Born	Enlisted On	Enlisted At	Colored Regiment
Davis, George W.	1832	26 Sep 1864	Bowling Green, KY	13th U.S. Heavy Arty.
Davis, Lewis	1846	21 Dec 1864	Bowling Green, KY	12th U.S. Heavy Arty.
Dishman, John	1839	3 Feb 1865	Bowling Green, KY	12th U.S. Heavy Arty.
Dodd, George	1843	5 Sep 1864	Bowling Green, KY	6th U.S. Cavalry
Drain, Willlliam	1844	7 Mar 1865	Bowling Green, KY	12th U.S. Heavy Arty.
Duff, William Henry	1836	26 Sep 1864	Bowling Green, KY	6th U.S. Cavalry
Ennis, Abram	1841	15 Aug 1864	Bowling Green, KY	6th U.S. Cavalry
Essex, King	1846	9 Feb 1865	Louisville KY	13th U.S. Heavy Arty.
Evans, James L	1846	6 Dec 1864	Louisville KY	13th U.S. Heavy Arty.
Flippin, Charles	1845	13 Apr 1864	Chattanooga TN	14th U.S. Infantry
Forrest, James	1842	1 Sep 1863	Nachez MS	6th U.S. Heavy Arty.
Franklin, Hayden	1842	26 Sep 1864	Bowling Green, KY	6th U.S. Cavalry
Garnett, Robert	1844	13 Apr 1865	Bowling Green, KY	12th U.S. Heavy Arty.
Garvin, Nelson	1843	20 Mar 1865	Bowling Green, KY	12th U.S. Heavy Arty.
Gassaway, John	1831	26 Sep 1864	Bowling Green, KY	6th U.S. Cavalry
Gill, John S.	1847	26 Apr 1865	Glasgow KY	12th U.S. Heavy Arty.
Harvey, James	1845	1 Nov 1863	Gallatin TN	14th U.S. Infantry
Helen, James	1841	17 Sep 1864	Bowling Green, KY	6th U.S. Cavalry
Hill, Dick	1838	4 Sep 1864	Bowling Green, KY	6th U.S. Cavalry
Hill, Hayden	1829	20 Sep 1864	Bowling Green, KY	13th U.S. Heavy Arty.
Jewell, Joseph	1834	29 Jun 1864	Bowling Green, KY	5th U.S. Cavalry
Jones, Major Moffit	1845	1 Aug 1863	Vicksburg MS	5th U.S. Heavy Arty.

Name	Born	Enlisted On	Enlisted At	Colored Regiment
Lewis, Levi	1824	24 Jan 1864	Knoxville TN	1st U.S. Heavy Arty.
Lewis, Lewis	1842	26 Sep 1864	Bowling Green, KY	13th U.S. Heavy Arty.
Lewis, Richard	1836	26 Sep 1864	Bowling Green, KY	14th U.S. Infantry
Logan, Albert	1837	14 Nov 1863	Providence RI	11th U.S. Heavy Arty.
Mathew, Benjamin	1838	25 Jun 1864	Bowling Green, KY	5th U.S. Cavalry
Modley, Anderson		1863	Nashville TN	12th US Infantry
Mumford, Samuel	1840	1 Nov 1863	Gallatin TN	14th U.S. Infantry
Nance, Sterlring	1832	2 Apr 1864	Knoxville TN	1st U.S. Heavy Arty.
Newland, Henry C.	1839	26 Sep 1864	Bowling Green, KY	13th U.S. Heavy Arty.
Norris, Richard	1847	28 Mar 1865	Bowling Green, KY	12th U.S. Heavy Arty.
Page, Amberson		1863	Nashville TN	12th US Infantry
Parish, Benjamin	1846	28 Jun 1864	Bowling Green, KY	5th U.S. Cavalry
Parish, Henry	1840	25 Jul 1864	Bowling Green, KY	6th U.S. Cavalry
Parrish, Edward	1834	26 Sep 1864	Bowling Green, KY	6th U.S. Cavalry
Penson, David	1843	22 May 1865	Bowling Green, KY	13th U.S. Heavy Arty.
Pool, Jno	1832	25 Apr 1865	Bowling Green, KY	12th U.S. Heavy Arty.
Poole, John E.	1832	25 Apr 1865	Bowling Green, KY	12th U.S. Heavy Arty.
Scrievener, George	1820	26 Sep 1864	Bowling Green, KY	6th U.S. Cavalry
Snyder, James	1826	8 Dec 1863	Natchez MS	6th U.S. Heavy Arty.
Trabue, Ed	1842	24 Sep 1864	Bowling Green, KY	6th U.S. Cavalry
Trabue, Wesley	1841	26 Sep 1864	Bowling Green, KY	6th U.S. Cavalry
Trigg, Washington	1840	24 Sep 1864	Bowling Green, KY	6th U.S. Cavalry

Name	Born	Enlisted On	Enlisted At	Colored Regiment
Tutt, Solomon	1847	26 Aug 1864	St Louisiana	18th U.S. Infantry
Vaugh, George		1863	Nashville TN	12th US Infantry
Walker, Virgil	1824	24 Sep 1864	Bowling Green, KY	6th U.S. Cavalry
Wallace, Harrison	1821	29 Nov 1864	Henderson KY	13th U.S. Heavy Arty.
Watt, Joseph	1847	17 Jul 1864	Bowling Green, KY	6th U.S. Cavalry
Wood, Benjamin	1821	7 Jan 1864	Shelbyville KY	15th U.S. Infantry
Wood, Joseph	1821	27 Mar 1865	Louisville KY	13th U.S. Heavy Arty.
Wood, Ralph	1848	19 Jul 1864	Bowling Green mKY	6th U.S. Cavalry

Table 36

Monroe County born slaves who joined the Union Army

Name	Born In	Born	Enlisted on
Adams, Jerry Henry	Monroe Co.	1838	29 Aug 1864
Barlow, George W.	Monroe Co.		1863
Biggerstaff, George	Monroe Co.	1844	22 Jul 1864
Black, George	Monroe Co.	1839	3 Apr 1865
Brown, Henry	Monroe Co.	1838	1 Mar 1864
Duncan, Richmond	Monroe Co.	1844	28 May 1865
Harris, Nathaniel	Monroe Co.	1843	1 Aug 1863
Martin, Albert	Monroe Co.		1864
Martin, Samuel	Monroe Co.	1836	27 Mar 1865
McCarver, Charles A.	Monroe Co.	1839	1 Nov 1863
McNary, William H.	Martinsburg	1827	28 May 1864
Taylor, Charles	Monroe Co.	1845	19 May 1865
Wade, John	Monroe Co.		1863
Wélls, Levi	Monroe Co.	1824	11 Dec 1863
Wickliffe, Charles	Monroe Co.		1864

Table 37

Warren County born slaves who joined the Union Army

Name	Born At	Enlisted On	Enlisted At	Regiment
Adams, Jack, James	Warren County, 1849	15 May 1865	Bowling Green KY	13th U.S. Colored Heavy Arty.
Anderson, Reuben	Warren County, 1847	1 Apr 1865	Louisville KY	6th U.S. Colored Cavalry
Barclay, Isaac	Warren County, 1844	3 Apr 1865	Bowling Green KY	12th U.S. Colored Heavy Arty.
Barnett II, Isaac	Bowling Green, 1840	5 Jun 1864	Paducah KY	8th U.S. Colored Heavy Arty.
Barrett, Frank	Warren County, 1827	29 Aug 1863	Natchez MS	6th U.S. Colored Heavy Arty.
Blackburn, Henry C.	Warren County, 1844	1 Feb 1864	Gallatin TN	14th U.S. Colored Infantry
Boots, Warren	Warren County, 1828	28 Feb 1865	Leavenworth KS	Ind. Bat. U.S. Colored Light Arty.
Butts, William	Warren County, 1844	7 Sep 1864	Bowling Green KY	6th U.S. Colored Cavalry
Caldwell, Edward	Warren County	1863	Hamilton, OH	5th US Colored Infantry
Carter, John	Warren County, 1842	1 Oct 1863	Gallatin TN	14th U.S. Colored Infantry
Carventer, Joseph	Warren County	1865	Terre Haute IN	28th U.S. Colored Infantry
Chastain, Samuel E.	Bowling Green, 1838	24 Oct 1864	Camp Nelson KY	6th U.S. Colored Cavalry
Chaypool, Peter	Warren County, 1840	1 Jan 1864	Gallatin TN	14th U.S. Colored Infantry
Chesnutt, James	Warren County, 1829	22 Feb 1865	Columbus OH	5th U.S. Colored Heavy Arty.
Cook, Albert	Warren County, 1837	1 Apr 1865	Bowling Green KY	12th U.S. Colored Heavy Arty.
Cook, Benjamin	Bowling Green	1864	Indianapolis VA	28th U.S. Colored Infantry
Cook, Thomas	Warren County, 1840	19 Sep 1864	Bowling Green KY	6th U.S. Colored Cavalry
Cook, Thomas	Bowling Green, 1848	15 Nov 1863	Gallatin TN	14th U.S. Colored Infantry
Cooke, Albert	Warren County, 1837	1 Apr 1865	Bowling Green KY	12th U.S. Colored Heavy Arty.
Covington, Archie	Bowling Green, 1836	6 Mar 1865	Louisville KY	13th U.S. Colored Heavy Arty.
Covington, Joseph	Warren County	1865	Terre Haute IN	28th U.S. Colored Infantry
Cox, James	Bowling Green, 1848	18 May 1865	Bowling Green KY	13th U.S. Colored Heavy Arty.

Name	Born At	Enlisted On	Enlisted At	Regiment
Curd, Zachariah	Warren County, 1839	25 Apr 1864	Fort Donelson TN	8th U.S. Colored Heavy Arty.
Daggers, Wesley	Warren County, 1846	15 Jan 1864	Gallatin TN	14th U.S. Colored Infantry
Daniel, Francis O.	Warren County, 1845	22 May 1865	Lebanon KY	13th U.S. Colored Heavy Arty.
De Gustus, Charles H.	Bowling Green, 1844	8 Dec 1863	Clarksville TN	16th U.S. Colored Infantry
Dial, Alexander	Warren County, 1824	3 Apr 1865	Bowling Green KY	12th U.S. Colored Heavy Arty.
Duke, Jerry	Warren County, 1846	24 May 1864	Paducah KY	8th U.S. Colored Heavy Arty.
Duncan, Dennis	Warren County, 1840	23 Jan 1865	Bowling Green KY	12th U.S. Colored Heavy Arty.
Dunn, John	Warren County, 1837	1 May 1864	Vicksburg MS	3rd U.S. Colored Cavalry
Edmonson, Peter	Warren County, 1841	25 May 1865	Bowling Green KY	13th U.S. Colored Heavy Arty.
Faunt, Absalom	Warren County, 1845	15 Nov 1863	Gallatin TN	14th U.S. Colored Infantry
Ford, Alexander	Warren County, 1848	12 Apr 1865	Bowling Green KY	12th U.S. Colored Heavy Arty.
Ford, Henry	Warren County, 1842	3 Mar 1865	Bowling Green KY	12th U.S. Colored Heavy Arty.
Gaines, Peter	Warren County, 1842	1 Oct 1863	Gallatin TN	14th U.S. Colored Infantry
Gladdish, Thomas	Warren County	1864	Greene, OH	27th U.S. Colored Infantry
Goodnight, Jacob	Warren County, 1821	1 Jan 1864	Gallatin TN	14th U.S. Colored Infantry
Grider, Charles	Warren County, 1846	25 Jan 1864	Bowling Green KY	5th U.S. Colored Cavalry
Grider,William	Warren County, 1842	5 Apr 1865	Bowling Green KY	12th U.S. Colored Heavy Arty.
Hafford, Robert	Warren County, 1845	26 Jun 1864	Knoxville TN	1st U.S. Colored Heavy Arty.
Halford, Robert	Warren County, 1801	26-Jun	Knoxville TN	1st U.S. Colored Heavy Arty.
Hampton, George	Warren County, 1831	16 Feb 1864	Clarksville TN	16th U.S. Colored Infantry
Hampton, Hezekiah	Warren County, 1845	29 Oct 1864	Bowling Green KY	13th U.S. Colored Heavy Arty.
Harrison, George	Warren County, 1847	24 Nov 1864	Owensboro KY	13th U.S. Colored Heavy Arty.
Hatuplon, George W.	Warren County, 1847	3 Apr 1865	Bowling Green KY	12th U.S. Colored Heavy Arty.

Name	Born At	Enlisted On	Enlisted At	Regiment
Hayden, David	Bowling Green, 1846	7 Mar 1865	Covington KY	13th U.S. Colored Heavy Arty.
Hayes, Charles	Warren County, 1846	14 Nov 1864	Bowling Green KY	12th U.S. Colored Heavy Arty.
Hayes, Heliary T.	Bowling Green, 1845	1 Dec 1863	Gallatin TN	14th U.S. Colored Infantry
Hays, Charles	Warren County, 1846	14 Nov 1864	Bowling Green KY	12th U.S. Colored Heavy Arty.
Hill, Manuel	Warren County, 1845	26 Apr 1865	Bowling Green KY	12th U.S. Colored Heavy Arty.
Hill, Pleasant	Warren County, 1838	4 Sep 1864	Bowling Green KY	6th U.S. Colored Cavalry
Hill, Robert	Bowling Green, 1847	18 May 1865	Bowling Green KY	13th U.S. Colored Heavy Arty.
Hitchins, John	Warren County, 1836	27 Sep 1864	Vicksburg MS	3rd U.S. Colored Cavalry
Hobson, Rickard	Warren County, 1840	27 Mar 1865	Bowling Green KY	12th U.S. Colored Heavy Arty.
Hoover, Henry	Warren County, 1844	15 Nov 1864	Owensboro KY	6th U.S. Colored Cavalry
Jackson, Michael	Warren County, 1823	10 Oct 1863	Natchez MS	6th U.S. Colored Heavy Arty.
Jackson, Thomas	Warren County, 1844	15 Nov 1863	Gallatin TN	14th U.S. Colored Infantry
Jarboe, Louis	Warren County, 1844	28 Jan 1864	Leelanau MI	5th U.S. Colored Cavalry
Jenkins, Albert	Warren County, 1837	3 Sep 1864	Bowling Green KY	6th U.S. Colored Cavalry
Johnson, Henry	Warren County, 1845	6 Aug 1864	Honnea, Louisiana	10th U.S. Colored Heavy Arty.
Johnston, Washington	Bowling Green	1863	Nashville TN	13th US Colored Infantry
Jones, Jacob	Warren County, 1849	13 Apr 1865	Bowling Green KY	12th U.S. Colored Heavy Arty.
Keel, Henry W.	Warren County, 1845	1 Aug 1864	Bowling Green KY	6th U.S. Colored Cavalry
Keel, James H.	Warren County, 1828	15 Dec 1863	Gallatin TN	14th U.S. Colored Infantry
Kelley, John	Warren County, 1845	25 Nov 1863	Stevenson	17th U.S. Colored Infantry
Kelley, Melvin	Warren County, 1846	3 Dec 1864	Springfield TN	15th U.S. Colored Infantry
Kelly, George	Warren County, 1842	29 Jun 1864	Bowling Green KY	5th U.S. Colored Cavalry
Kelly, John	Warren County, 1845	25 Nov 1863	Stevenson	17th U.S. Colored Infantry

Name	Born At	Enlisted On	Enlisted At	Regiment
Kelly, Prince	Warren County, 1837	5 Apr 1865	Bowling Green KY	12th U.S. Colored Heavy Arty.
Kimball, Moses	Warren County, 1847	6 Apr 1865	Bowling Green KY	12th U.S. Colored Heavy Arty.
Kirby, Yancey	Warren County, 1833	1 Jan 1864	Gallatin TN	14th U.S. Colored Infantry
Kurd, Zachariah	Warren County, 1839	25 Apr 1864	Fort Donelson	8th U.S. Colored Heavy Arty.
Lavayelle, Peter	Warren County, 1846	19 Feb 1865	Lebanon KY	6th U.S. Colored Cavalry
Lewis, Peter	Warren County, 1841	15 Feb 1864	Gallatin TN	14th U.S. Colored Infantry
Lively, George	Warren County, 1840	1 Feb 1864	Gallatin TN	14th U.S. Colored Infantry
Loveyell, Peter	Warren County, 1846	19 Feb 1865	Lebanon KY	6th U.S. Colored Cavalry
Lyne, James M.	Warren County, 1846	12 Aug 1864	Bowling, Green KY	6th U.S. Colored Cavalry
Lynn, Samuel	Warren County, 1826	2 Aug 1864	Bowling Green KY	6th U.S. Colored Cavalry
Mansfield, Richard	Warren County, 1841	23 Jun 1864	Bowlin Green KY	5th U.S. Colored Cavalry
Martin, Charles	Warren County, 1847	1 Apr 1865	Bowling Green KY	12th U.S. Colored Heavy Arty.
McCormick, George	Warren County, 1846	12 Aug 1864	Bowling, Green KY	6th U.S. Colored Cavalry
McElroy, Daniel	Warren County, 1838	30 Dec 1864	Lebanon KY	13th U.S. Colored Heavy Arty.
McElroy, Henry	Warren County, 1841	30 Dec 1864	Lebanon KY	13th U.S. Colored Heavy Arty.
Meaux, Chesterfield	Warren County, 1823	27 Jan 1865	Columbus OH	12th U.S. Colored Heavy Arty.
Mobbs, Danniel	Warren County, 1823	18 Nov 1863	B R Bridge	2nd U.S. Colored Light Arty.
Moore, Richard	Warren County, 1842	15 Jan 1864	Gallatin TN	14th U.S. Colored Infantry
Moore, Robert	Bowling Green	1864	Columbus OH	27th United States Colored Infantry
Morehead, Isaac	Warren County, 1842	11 Feb 1865	Bowling Green KY	12th U.S. Colored Heavy Arty.
Murry, Joseph	Bowling Green	1863	Circleville, Ohio	5th US Colored Infantry
O'Daniel, Francis	Warren County, 1845	22 May 1865	Lebanon KY	13th U.S. Heavy Arty.
Ogden, Wesley	Warren County, 1841	11 Sep 1864	Bowling Green KY	6th U.S. Colored Cavalry

Name	Born At	Enlisted On	Enlisted At	Regiment
Orndorf, Wesley	Bowling Green, 1841	11 Aug 1864	Bowling Green KY	6th U.S. Colored Cavalry
Parsons, Peter	Bowling Green	1864	Quincy IL	29th U.S. Colored Infantry
Pendleton, John	Warren County, 1847	3 Sep 1864	Louisville KY	5th U.S. Colored Cavalry
Phelps, Albert	Warren County, 1836	28 May 1864	Union County KY	8th U.S. Colored Heavy Arty.
Phillips, Benjamin	Warren County, 1842	22 Aug 1864	Bowling Green KY	6th U.S. Colored Cavalry
Phillips, James	Warren County, 1845	12 Aug 1864	Bowling Green KY	6th U.S. Colored Cavalry
Phillips, Lewis James	Warren County, 1846	23 Sep 1864	Camp Nelson KY	5th U.S. Colored Cavalry
Polk, James K.	Bowling Green, 1843	1 Nov 1863	Gallatin TN	14th U.S. Colored Infantry
Potter, Calvin	Warren County, 1846	30 Jul 1864	Bowling Green KY	6th U.S. Colored Cavalry
Potter, Henry	Warren County, 1848	1 Aug 1864	Bowling Green KY	6th U.S. Colored Cavalry
Potter, John	Bowling Green, 1845	18 May 1865	Bowling Green KY	13th U.S. Colored Heavy Arty.
Prewitt, George	Warren County, 1830	22 May 1865	Louisville KY	13th U.S. Colored Heavy Arty.
Redmond, George W.	Warren County, 1846	22 Mar 1865	Bowling Green KY	12th U.S. Colored Heavy Arty.
Reese, Authur	Bowling Green	1864	Crawfordsville IN	28th U.S. Colored Infantry
Reese, Robert	Warren County, 1820	29 Feb 1865	Cairo, IL	8th U.S. Colored Heavy Arty.
Richison, Edward	Warren County, 1840	13 Aug 1864	Rome OH	9th U.S. Colored Heavy Arty.
Rickets, Willis	Warren County, 1846	15 Jan 1864	Gallatin TN	14th U.S. Colored Infantry
Robertson, Berry	Warren County, 1820	4 Jun 1863	Columbus KY	4th U.S. Colored Heavy Arty.
Robertson, Nathan	Warren County, 1825	21 Apr 1865	Bowling Green KY	12th U.S. Colored Heavy Arty.
Robinson, Frank	Bowling Green	1863	Readville MA	54th Massachusetts Infantry (Colored)
Robinson, John	Warren County, 1835	26 Oct 1863	Union City TN	4th U.S. Colored Heavy Arty.
Sharp, James	Warren County, 1845	1 Aug 1864	Camp Nelson KY	6th U.S. Colored Cavalry
Smith, Andy	Warren County, 1846	2 Feb 1864	Knoxville TN	1st U.S. Colored Heavy Arty.

Name	Born At	Enlisted On	Enlisted At	Regiment
Smith, Charles	Warren County, 1848	22 Aug 1864	Bowling Green KY	6th U.S. Colored Cavalry
Smith, Fountain	Warren County, 1847	1 Apr 1865	Bowling Green KY	12th U.S. Colored Heavy Arty.
Smith, George	Warren County, 1823	26 May 1865	Paris KY	6th U.S. Colored Cavalry
Smith, George	Warren County, 1825	12 May 1865	Camp Nelson KY	6th U.S. Colored Cavalry
Smith, Isham Malone	Warren County, 1836	2 Nov 1864	Bowling Green KY	12th U.S. Colored Heavy Arty.
Smith, Joseph	Warren County, 1842	2 Nov 1864	Bowling Green KY	12th U.S. Colored Heavy Arty.
Smith, Robert	Warren County, 1838	1 Apr 1865	Bowling Green KY	12th U.S. Colored Heavy Arty.
Smith, William H.	Warren County, 1839	17 Jun 1864	Knoxville TN	1st U.S. Colored Heavy Arty.
Smith, Zach	Warren County, 1835	25 Apr 1865	Bowling Green KY	12th U.S. Colored Heavy Arty.
Smith I, James	Warren County, 1847	1 Apr 1865	Bowling Green KY	12th U.S. Colored Heavy Arty.
Stephens, Archy	Warren County, 1840	12 Apr 1865	Hartford KY	13th U.S. Colored Heavy Arty.
Stephens, Charles	Warren County, 1845	28 Jul 1864	Paducah KY	8th U.S. Colored Heavy Arty.
Stephens, Thomas	Warren County, 1845	10 Sep 1864	Paduch KY	8th U.S. Colored Heavy Arty.
Stevens, Archy	Warren County, 1840	12 Apr 1865	Hartford KY	13th U.S. Colored Heavy Arty.
Stevens, Thomas	Warren County, 1845	10 Sep 1864	Paduch KY	8th U.S. Colored Heavy Arty.
Strow, Amos	Warren County, 1829	9 Sep 1864	Paducah KY	8th U.S. Colored Heavy Arty.
Sumpter, John	Warren County, 1844	22 Aug 1864	Bowling Green KY	6th U.S. Colored Cavalry
Thompson, Jerry	Bowling Green, 1847	20 Oct 1863	Memphis TN	3rd U.S. Colored Heavy Arty.
Vernon, Joseph	Warren County, 1846	29 Aug 1864	Warren OH	17th U.S. Colored Infantry
Washington II, George	Warren County, 1846	23 Sep 1864	Camp Nelson KY	6th U.S. Colored Cavalry
Waters, Moses	Bowling Green, 1838	26 Dec 1863	Clarksville TN	16th U.S. Colored Infantry
Weston, Richard	Bowling Green, 1834	14 Dec 1863	Ft Pickering TN	3rd U.S. Colored Heavy Arty.
Wheeler, Samuel Thelbert	Warren County, 1838	15 Jan 1864	Gallatin TN	14th U.S. Colored Infantry

Name	Born At	Enlisted On	Enlisted At	Regiment
Wiley, John	Bowling Green, 1850	17 Jan 1864	Murfreesboro TN	17th U.S. Colored Infantry
Williams, Lee	Bowling Green	1865	Chicago, IL	29th U.S. Colored Infantry
Williams, Spencer	Bowling Green, 1833	15 Nov 1863	Vicksburg TN	3rd U.S. Colored Cavalry
Williams, William H.	Warren County, 1842	27 Sep 1864	Alliance OH	15th U.S. Colored Infantry
Williams, Winsted	Bowling Green	1863	Chicago IL	29th U.S. Colored Infantry
Wilson, Alfred	Warren County, 1842	1 Feb 1864	Natchez MS	6th U.S. Colored Heavy Arty.
Winchester, Alexander	Warren County	1863	Nashville TN	12th US Colored Infantry

Chapter 15

Indentured African Americans, 1867-1882

Indentured Servants in Virginia

After the slaves in Kentucky were freed, there were African American children who had no one to care for them. This dilemma was caused by their separation from their parents. There were several reasons that these children, orphans in effect, had been separated. Perhaps the child had been bought or inherited away from their parents, or their parents sold away from them, or their parents were among the thousands of destitute refugees unable to support them after freedom came. Whatever the circumstance, there was no one who was legally obligated and financially able to care for them. The solution was to use indenture, a form of voluntary servitude.

Indenture was a contract that bound a person to work for another for a specific time period. Indentures were used by The Virginia Company in the earliest days of our country as a way to entice laborers to come to the colonies. The document specified the term of service, the dues that would be given at the end of that term, and that freedom would be restored when the terms were completed.

One of the terms of those early indentures was that the servant could receive land. For many, there was no other hope to own land and that was the strongest incentive for a white person to indenture themselves to another or to The Virginia Company for a period of several years.

By the mid 1600s, from 30 to 40 percent of the Virginia colony's landowners were freed indentured servants. The indenture had served its purpose for both parties to the agreement. It provided needed labor to one and ownership of land to the other.

The introduction of slaves into Virginia doomed the indenture system. There was no provision of land to slaves and the servitude was perpetual rather than short lived. As a result, the flow of white indentured servants virtually ended by 1708 as the flow of black slaves increased.[1] In effect, the enslavement of blacks replaced the voluntary servitude of whites.

Indentured Freedmen in Allen County

The indenture of slave children in Allen County, as elsewhere in Kentucky, differed from that of the early colonial days. It was a means of assigning responsibility for the children until they became adults. Freed African American children were bound by indenture to white citizens by the Allen County Court when no parent or guardian was available. In a few cases, dire poverty could cause an African American relative to approve the indenture of a child. The contract required training of the child as an apprentice in some particular work. It also required that there be a "good and just master" to provide care and training of the child. As in slavery, the quality of life of the servant was commensurate with the quality of the master.

Indenture documents of apprenticeships for 25 freed slave children were examined. The ages at the time of the indenture ranged from four to eighteen. There were 9 girls and 16 boys. That difference is interesting. It recalls the fact that more male than female slaves were bought but no evidence exists to allow that conclusion in this case.

The 1860 census recorded that James A. Brite (spelled Bright elsewhere) had seven slaves: a 33 year old female, a 22-year-old male, a 14-year-old girl, an 11-year-old boy, an 8-year-old boy, a 6 year-old girl, and a 2-year-old boy. He had acquired four of them since the census of 1850: the 22-year-old male and the three youngest children. It is clear that Brite's slaves were not all part of the same family.

All of his slaves were freed after the end of the war. Only the two oldest males remained with Brite according to the 1870 census. The disposition of the others is unknown except for Caroline, who

[1] Ringer, Benjamin B. 1983. *"We the people" and others: duality and America's treatment of its racial minorities*. New York: Tavistock Publications.

was the 6 year-old slave girl in 1860. She was 12 in 1866, when she was indentured to her former owner, James A. Brite. That document was transcribed by Sharon Tabor and her transcription appears in Figure 41.

Figure 41

Transcription of an indenture of apprenticeship for Caroline 9 April 1866

Indenture of Apprenticeship
The Commonwealth of Kentucky

This Indenture made this ninth day of April one thousand eight hundred and sixty-six between CAROLINE a free girl of color who was 12 years old the ___ day of ___ 1866 by J.H. COLLINS, Clerk of the county court of Allen County, in the State of Kentucky, of one part, and JAMES A. BRITE of the other part;

Whereas, by an act of the General Assembly, the Judge of said Court is empowered to bind out orphans and poor children, which parents are incapable of bringing them up in moral courses, therefore the Court made the following order, to-wit:
On motion and at the request of JAS. A. BRITE It is ordered that CAROLINE a free girl of color who was ___ years old the ___ day of ___ 1866 be bound as an Apprentice to sd . BRITE who was the former owner and a suitable person until she arrives to the age of 18 years to be taught the art and business of Housewifery. And that the clerk of this county court prepare and enter into suitable Indenture with said BRITE in behalf of said girl

Now, therefore, this Indenture Witnesseth, that the said J.H. COLLINS, clerk of said Court, as above recited, hath put, place dna bound, and by these presents, doth put, place and bind the said girl Caroline apprentice to and under the said Brite with him to dwell, and him to serve, in the condition, duty, and character of an apprentice, until the said Caroline shall arrive at the age of Eighteen years, fully to be completed and ended— that, during all the said period, the said girl Caroline shall faithfully serve the said Brite as her master, in all lawful business, according to the best of her wit and ability, and in all things honestly, orderly and obediently demean and behave herself ; and the said J.A. Brite doth for himself heirs, executors, and administrators, covenant and agree with the said . Collins that he, the said J.A. Brite will teach the said Caroline the trade, art, and business of Housewifery and will find, provide for, and allow to the said girl Caroline sufficient diet, wearing apparel, washing, lodging, proper medical attention, and all other things usually allowed to apprentices by good and just masters, and will treat her with humanity — that he the said J. A. Brite will At the end of said apprenticeship of said girl Caroline to give her a new good suit of clothes and pay her fifty dollars: Provided however that of the sd Brite shall teach said Caroline to read & write then he shall not be bound to pay said $50

In witness whereof, the said Caroline by the said J.H. COLLINS, Clerk as aforesaid, and the said J.A. Brite have hereunto set their hands and seals, on the day and year first above written

/s/ J.H. Collins Clerk ACC
/s/ James A. Brite

The terms of the indentures for girls were completed when they turned eighteen, boys when they turned twenty-one. Girls were to be instructed in the "trade, art, and business" of housewifery. Boys were similarly trained, except that the trade was usually farming. At the end of the indenture period, girls were to be provided a "good suit of clothes" and were to be paid $50. That payment could be avoided if the girls had been taught to read and write. Boys were to receive $100 and clothing. Exemption from a cash payment would occur if the children could read and write. The reading and writing skills that would suffice for such exemptions was not defined.

Caroline is interesting because four years later, in the 1870 census, she was not living in the Brite household. Her period of indenture still had about two years left until completion, but she had moved away. She was recorded as being in the household of Dr. A. S. Walker, a Scottsville physician, and was using the name Caroline Walker. She had not taken the Brite surname, her last owner, but had chosen another. This illustrates another difficulty of tracing African American slave ancestry.

Caroline's reason for moving to Dr. Walker's household is unknown. Even so, one wishes to believe that she was there to attend the school for former slaves (see Chapter 16).

Caroline Walker's saga was not a singular experience. There were four other indentured children in the Brite household. Sharon Tabor transcribed the indenture documents and data from her transcriptions are presented in Table 38. Note that several of the children, including Caroline, had not yet chosen a surname when they were indentured.

Fifteen of the children were indentured to their previous owner. Of those, six had not chosen the former owner's name. Three more were indentured to a son of their former owner. Seven were indentured to someone other than a previous owner.

Slavery had ended but servitude had not.

Table 38

Allen County Indentured African Americans 1865-1882

In Alphabetical Order					
Date	Indentured Name	Age	Apprentice To	Former Owner	
				Yes	No
8 Jul 1867	Alexander, Sam L.	4	Mitchell, F. G.		X
13 Mar 1865	Bob	11	Woodcock, G. B.	X	
14 Jun 1869	Brockett, Henry	8	Anderson, Andrew		X
14 Jun 1869	Brockett, James	6	Anderson, Andrew		X
14 Mar 1870	Bruce, George	9	Harris, Robert D.		X
20 Nov 1882	Bush, Noah T.	7	Brite, J. A.		X
9 Apr 1866	Caroline	18	Brite, J. A.	X	
8 Jul 1866	Gatewood, Caroline Bell	11	Walker, A. S.		X
14 Aug 1866	George, Ann	6	Bruce, Mary J.	X	
9 Apr 1866	Hannah	18	Brite, J. A.	X	
8 Feb 1869	Manion, Amanda	3	Manion, Thompson	X	
8 Feb 1869	Manion, Martha	9	Manion, Thompson	X	
8 Feb 1869	Manion, Simon	7	Manion, Thompson	X	
9 Apr 1866	Mary	16	Ritchey, A. J.	X	
10 Dec1866	Moore, Joseph	-	Moore, Simpson		*
10 Dec 1866	Moore, Milvinah		Moore, Simpson		*
10 Dec 1866	Moore, Newton		Moore, Simpson		*
10 Jun 1875	Motley, William E.	12	Landers, John		X
9 Apr 1866	Nelson	11	Richey, A. J.	X	
14 Aug 1866	Sam	3	Bruce, Mary J.	X	
8 Oct 1866	Settle, Asa	5	Settle, G. M.	X	
8 Oct 1866	Settle, Christopher	8	Settle, G. M.	X	
8 Oct 1866	Settle, Sarah E.	10	Settle, G. M.	X	
9 Apr 1866	Simon	8	Brite, J. A.	X	
9 Apr 1866	Taylor	17	Brite, J. A.	X	
	* Son of former owner				

Chapter 16

Scottsville Freedmen School

Freedmen's Bureau

The Freedmen's Bureau was initiated by Abraham Lincoln and established by Congress on 3 March 1865. Its purpose was to protect and assist the former slaves in becoming productive free citizens. The surrender at Appomattox Court House, Virginia ended the war in April 1865 and the Freedmen's Bureau began its work in the seceded states. Meanwhile, Kentucky's slaves were left in a dilemma. The Federal Government considered them freed, the State Government declared that they were still slaves. The issue was settled legally when the slaves were freed by the ratification of the Thirteenth Amendment to our constitution. However, Kentucky refused to ratify the Thirteenth Amendment and the future of its slave population was uncertain. In December 1865, the Freedmen's Bureau declared that they would assume supervision over Kentucky's freed slaves. That action outraged white Kentuckians at a time when the state was still under martial law. Shortly thereafter, the Bureau opened its Kentucky office. Five District offices were soon added, one of which was in Bowling Green.[1]

One of the Bureau's primary objectives was to educate the freedmen to prepare them to be contributing citizens. It established schools for former slaves throughout the southern states of the Confederacy and the four slave states that had not seceded.

Secret Schools

In Virginia, some secret schools for slaves had begun as early as 1830. However, such schools were against the law and, as a result, were rare.

[1] Lucas, Marion B., 1992. A history of blacks in Kentucky from slavery to segregation 1760-1891. Kentucky Historical Society,

When the Civil War ended, the desire for an education was unleashed. In Lynchburg, Virginia, three black teachers opened two schools for Freedmen only one month after Appomattox. It is evident that slaves understood the importance of education, even though they had meager experience with it. One slave said, "There is one sin that slavery committed against me that I will never forgive. It robbed me of my education."

Freedmen's Schools

The Freedmen's Bureau provided books like the Primer, Third Reader, and Spelling Book (Figure 42). They also provided almost all of the funding for the schools.[2]

Figure 42
Spelling book used by students at Freedmen Schools

Freedmen Schools in Kentucky

Freedmen's Schools were established in Kentucky beginning in 1866. By November 42 schools were in session across the state, including one in Bowling Green. Kentucky's Legislature was very hostile toward the Bureau and its Freedmen's Schools. That hostility showed when the Legislature allocated tax revenues for its schools. It decreed that only tax revenues collected from black citizens could be used to support black schools, hardly wholehearted support. The impoverishment of the former slaves, many of who were refugees, assured that the amount of those tax revenues from blacks would be very small.[3]

The Freedmen's Bureau continued to add new schools. By

[2] Stennette, Janice S., 1996. *Teaching for the Freedmen's Bureau, Lynchburg, Virginia 1865-1871.* Dissertation. University of Virginia, Chancellorsville, VA

[3] Kleber, John E. 1992. The Kentucky encyclopedia. Lexington, KY: University Press of Kentucky.

April 1867, the State Superintendent of Freedmen's Schools added Scottsville to the list of places where new schools should be established. He estimated that forty pupils would attend if a school were to be provided.[4] That was quite an under estimation, as it turned out.

Freedmen School in Scottsville

The Scottsville Freedmen School opened in June of 1868. It was sustained by the Freedmen's Bureau and used a building provided by Dr. A. S. Walker of Scottsville through the remainder of the year. He had been the owner of fourteen slaves in 1860. He lived in a house made of logs hewn by slaves, which had a dungeon in its basement for stubborn slaves. He also had two slave houses. His home was at the corner of Second and Maple Streets. He owned the entire block between the Public Spring and Second Street. There were barns and stables on the property too. The location of the school is not known but it seems likely that it would have been somewhere on this property.

Dr. C. H. Alexander, who was another physician in Scottsville, provided a building for the second location of the School in February 1869. It was unusual that he and Dr. Walker did so. The Freedmen's Bureau's Superintendent in Kentucky said that "....places of worship are almost the only available school houses in the state." Dr. Alexander's home was located on North Court Street about two blocks north of the Square. The location of the building he provided for the school is not known.

The support by Dr. Walker and Dr. Alexander may help explain why Allen County did not record the open hostility to the Freedmen Schools that was experienced in other counties. Everywhere in Kentucky, the Freedmen schools were spoken of with scorn and contempt and the teachers were "spared no prejudices."[5] The school in Tompkinsville was burned on 10 October 1868 to break up that school. Several other schools in Kentucky suffered that same

[4] Noble, J. K., 1867. Letter dated 16 April 1867 from the State Superintendent of Freedmen's Schools, Bureau of Refugees, Freedmen, and Abandoned Lands to the General Inspector of Schools, J. W. Alvord, in Washington DC

[5] Noble, J. K., 1867. Letter dated 11 February 1867 from the State Superintendent of Freedmen's Schools, Bureau of Refugees, Freedmen, and Abandoned Lands to the General Inspector of Schools, J. W. Alvord, in Washington DC

fate. In Franklin, a detachment of army troops was sent to rescue a teacher whose house was surrounded by people who were hostile to the Freedmen's school there. Elsewhere, pupils were harassed, the pupils' parents were physically attacked, and teachers were insulted, beaten, and threatened with assassination.[6]

The attitude of many white Kentuckians toward the Freedmen schools was described as "bitter hostility." Some objections may have been based on the fear that the Freedmen would become better educated that the whites. There were fewer troubles in the deep south, perhaps because their time was occupied with the rebuilding of their economy instead of hindering the education of former slaves. The 1860 census had columns to indicate whether whites had attended school during the previous year and another column for whites that could read and write. The small numbers from that census indicate that education of whites had not been highly successful.

The new Freedmen school in Scottsville opened with one African American teacher. The school had nine male pupils and 19 female pupils. All the pupils were African American, and none of them had been freed before the war. Fifteen of the pupils were older than 16. The Scottsville School operated both as a day school and as a night school. Younger and unemployed children attended the Day School. Parents and other working people attended the Night School. In addition, one Sabbath School existed in Scottsville with 25 pupils in 1868, but that number increased to 69 in 1869. Sabbath Schools were held in churches and taught reading and Christianity. These religious organizations were reluctant to report their data to the Freedmen's Bureau and the numbers attributed to them may not be accurate.[7]

White students could attend the Freedmen's Scottsville School but, significantly, none of them chose to do so during the existence of the school. One report discussed why that was the case in Kentucky as a whole.

---

[6] Noble, J. K., 1868. Letter dated December 1868 from the State Superintendent of Freedmen's Schools, Bureau of Refugees, Freedmen, and Abandoned Lands to the General Inspector of Schools, J. W. Alvord, in Washington DC

[7] Peirce, Paul Skeels. 1904. The Freedmen's bureau; a chapter in the history of reconstruction. Iowa City, IA: The University.

> *Public sentiment towards the schools may be stated as covertly or openly hostile. Nothing can be done for the education of the poor whites by the Bureau for they are too proud and too hostile to its work to accept its aid. Assistance will be required for the education of children of the freedmen until just laws are passed by the state allowing the taxes collected to be used in support of the schools.*[8]

Regardless of the opposition, the Scottsville Freedmen School's pupil population dramatically increased to 28 males and 39 females by October of 1868. Minnie Smith, an African American, was the first teacher in the school and in October had 17 pupils who were taking spelling and reading lessons, 17 were in writing, 9 in arithmetic, 15 learning the alphabet, 9 in geography, and 9 in advanced reading.

The increase in enrollment continued through March 1869. During the previous month, 25 new pupils had enrolled and only seven pupils had left school during that period. The enrollment was 107 but the average attendance was 121. Of that number, 120 of them were always present and always punctual. These numbers tell us of those pupils' assessment of the value of education. It is believed that assessment was likely greater among school age African American than among whites.[9]

It is worth remembering that the former slave children had no prior experience with schools. They did not know what school was like, how to behave, how to sit motionless, or how to be attentive; all attributes unnatural to the natural behavior of children. They may have had even more difficulty adapting than our modern day first graders have. But, it is clear that they were eager to learn.

The Scottsville School was not graded, as public schools would later become. Few if any of these pupils had been in school before because no public schools existed for slaves. All the slave states, except Kentucky, Maryland, and Tennessee, passed and enforced laws that forbade instruction of slaves. Kentucky law didn't forbid

[8] Noble, J. K., 1868. Letter dated 10 November1868 from the State Superintendent of Freedmen's Schools, Bureau of Refugees, Freedmen, and Abandoned Lands to the General Inspector of Schools, J. W. Alvord, in Washington DC

[9] Ibid

teaching slaves, but it neither supported nor encouraged that instruction. Even so, the slaves' desires to learn were strong and their urge to read was strong. A study of 350 of Kentucky's runaway slave advertisements revealed that 71 of them could read and 37 could write. Clearly, the more a slave learned, the more likely he was to run away.[10]

Another African American, F. R. G. Pisani, became the teacher in November 1868, though Minnie Smith returned in December. Pisani taught again from February to May 1869. In May 1869, Lucy Tiller, also an African American, became the teacher. Albert P. Cox replaced her in February 1869. He was an African American who had taught in Bowling Green in a black school in 1860.

The teachers of the Freedmen schools in former Confederate states were mostly white and from the north. Whites citizens particularly disliked them and, in some cases, refused to provide them a place to live.

In contrast, eighty percent of the teachers in Kentucky Freemen schools were African Americans. That may explain why in the 17 states that had Freedmen schools, Kentucky usually ranked first or second in the percentage of school age former slaves who enrolled and third or fourth in attendance.[11] The former slaves found little in common with white teachers but took pride in the achievements of the African American teachers. Most of the African American teachers came from the northern states and from Canada.

It was difficult for former slaves to support the schools, but they paid tuition if could. They paid for the board of the teacher in some cases in Kentucky. In other cases, rent paid for the school building was returned by the building owner and the money was used to pay tuition for the poorest students. The Freedmen's Bureau also provided tuition assistance. One objective of the schools was to give African Americans experience in organizing and sustaining their schools.

---

[10] McDougle, Ivan E. 1917. Slavery in Kentucky. Lancaster, Pa., etc: The Association for the study of negro life and history, mc.

[11] Harrison, Lowell Hayes, and James C. Klotter. 1997. A new history of Kentucky. Lexington, Ky: University Press of Kentucky.

End of Freedmen Schools

In July 1868, Federal support and funding for the Freedmen schools was reduced. By then, the Freedmen's Bureau had established 219 schools for the former slaves in Kentucky over the objections of the state government. These schools had 10,422 former slaves attending.

A group of the leading African Americans of Louisville were convened by Brevet Colonel Ben P. Runkle on 7 April 1869 after it became clear that the good work of the Freedmen Bureau in Kentucky that he headed was coming to an end. Teachers from the schools and white friends joined them to address the future. At the end of that meeting, a remarkable statement was prepared (Figure 43).

Similar feelings must have been present among the former slaves in Scottsville, who had been given a taste of education before the Scottsville Freedmen School closed in June 1869. The periodic reports on the Scottsville School resumed in January 1870, but the Freedman's Bureau was no longer in charge of the school. It was then under the control of the State Board of Education. The handwriting on the wall was apparently visible to the students because only 14 males and 6 females were enrolled, and the average attendance was down to 18. Most state offices of the Freedmen Bureau were closed by the middle of 1870. In April 1870, the last report of the Scottsville School was submitted.

Kentucky did not create a uniform black school system until 1874, but only supported it with allocated tax revenue that came from blacks. Funding of black and white schools from a common fund began after April 1882. Even then, the per-pupil funding remained grossly unequal.

The census of 1860 recorded 63,000 whites in Kentucky who admitted to being illiterate. The degree of literacy for the others who claimed literacy is unknown but no doubt was limited. That was the monumental challenge that faced Fletcher Gatewood, the Allen County School Commissioner. He and Robert Y. McReynolds were appointed by the Allen County Court as Allen County's Commissioners of Common Schools in December 1854.

Figure 43

Plea to the colored people of Kentucky

To the Colored People of Kentucky.

We are called Freedmen, the chains which bound us in actual physical slavery have been broken, but we are *not yet free.*

Three conditions have combined to make us slaves—political power has been held by our former masters, leaving us helpless. The immortal Proclamation was followed by the amendment to the Constitution of the United States, and slavery was banished forever from American soil; and now, this is to be followed by a second amendment declaring that there shall be no longer taxation without representation—that no longer we shall be called to bear arms in defence of our country, and yet be excluded from the rights and privileges of citizens. It may follow, we trust it is our destiny and the will of God, that it shall follow, that we may be taxed as other men are taxed, and the taxes we pay appropriated for the education of our children. Much has been done for us, now let us act for ourselves.

Education has been confined to the white race—we and our ancestors had groped in darkness and ignorance for hundreds of years. We were held in bondage and toiled for the task-master—we made the land to bloom and blossom like the rose; the aristocracy of the land were lords upon the proceeds of our labor.

[illegible] Kentucky and Virginia waved in ripening luxuriance, and the cotton fields of the [illegible] weary and white [illegible] very little hope in this world, and indeed little in the next, ignorant, degraded, even the word of God a closed volume—our teachers who held out the bread of life often ignorant as we; and they called us happy—happy and contented. Contented we may have been, as the savage who knows not God, but happy we never were. Gleams of sunlight broke through the thick darkness now and then like the first faint rays at dawn.

There was a longing within us—a voice that said there is something better than this. And in secret and in silence, in the rice, the cotton and tobacco fields, in the crowded cities and in our plantation cabins, by night and by day, we waited and wished for the coming of the better time, the morning that arose at last.

But now we are told that we are inferior to the white race; that we are ignorant—it may be true, but why is it true? The ways of knowledge have been closed to us; no one has dared to educate us, lest they should incur the penalties of unjust laws. Mind is not the growth of a day or a year, but of centuries! We may be ignorant, but now that our chains are broken, and we must stand up and make our way through the world, we ask but an even chance; we only ask that our children may be educated, and prepared for the struggle of life. We want them to be intelligent, law-abiding, christian men and women. We are willing to be taxed, we only ask that the taxes we pay may be appropriated for this purpose.

The Government of the United States has been very kind to us, though Kentucky, the State where we must make our homes, among whose people we hope to live in peace and quiet, neither asking nor desiring social equality, but only equality before the law, has made no provision for us; yet we have 290 schools, and 14,000 of our children gather there day by day.

This the United States has done, but this must soon cease. The State has made no provision to continue these schools, we must do it ourselves; let us make one united and determined effort to help ourselves, and it may be that just men will rise up and plead our cause, and it will triumph in the end. And we ask for but simple justice, sooner or later we will secure it.

Again, we are poor, but there is no reason that we should remain so. We made our masters wealthy, we can do the same for ourselves. Throughout the length and breadth of this land, wherever there is a stately mansion, a broad plantation, or a beautiful city, we can point to it as reared by the proceeds of our labor, and the labor of our fathers, who toiled before us. Then, if we educate ourselves and our children, that we may labor intelligently, we may build up homes for our families, and come to be not only tolerated but respected by the people among whom we live.

Certainly all good men will wish us God's speed in our endeavors. Therefore, in view of all this, and for the purpose of making some provisions for the future, we the undersigned, a committee appointed by a meeting called together to consider the interests of our people, hereby call an Educational Convention to meet in the City of Louisville, on Wednesday the 14th day of July, 1869, and we ask the people of every town and neighborhood to send one or more good, earnest men to co-operate and consult with us:

H. J. YOUNG, Pastor Quinn, Chapel,
WM. H. GIBSON,
D. STRAKER, Jg. Reader of St Mark's E. P.,
M. J. DAVIS,
G. W. BROWN,
J. H. MERIWETHER,
R. G. MORTIMER, Pastor of Asbury Chapel,
ISAIAH MITCHELL,
JOHN Q. ADAMS,
A. HETH,
GEO. A. SCHAEFER,
NELSON C. SHAMBER,
Bishop J. W. LOQUEN,
Rev. RICHARD BRIEDWELL,
SAMUEL ELLIOTT,
SAMUEL SHERMAN,
ANTONY BUNCH,
JAMES B. JOHNSON,
YARMOUTH CARR,
E. H. CURRY,
J. B. COX,
LEROY BRANHAM,
W. T. BIDDLE,
L. B. STANSBERY, Pastor 15th St. Church,
ABR'M WARTHAM,
JOSEPH IRVING,
H. FIRST,
B. B. ROCHESTER,
JAMES IRVIN,
ADAM BROWN,
PETER HALL,
CHASTINE STURN,
ROBT. PARMER,
GREEN COOPER,
J. H. TAYLOR,
JAMES ADAMS,
THOMAS MANSON,
H. COZZENS,
H. ADAMS.

In 1870, there were 18 male and 10 female teachers for the white students in Allen County. According to the 1870 census, Jacob B. Walker and Nancy C. Watkins were schoolteachers in Scottsville, but the census identified only five boys and three girls attending school there. These eight white students were between thirteen and nineteen years old. That is an incredibly small fraction of the total number of the white children in Scottsville at that time.

There is no way of knowing if the census taker's numbers were correct. Even if the numbers of whites in school were ten times greater than the actual numbers recorded, it still would have been only 64 percent of the number of African Americans who were attending school just one year earlier.

White illiteracy rates had increased over the previous few decades but the efforts of the Sabbath Schools and the Freedmen's Schools had arrested the increase in black illiteracy that had prevailed throughout the decades of slavery.[12] There had been a beginning of enlightenment. It did not last very long.

The so called "Jim Crow" laws were passed beginning in the 1870s to legally segregate schools and other services in Kentucky. Those laws created separate white and black schools that were said to be equal, but were judged to be unequal decades later. African Americans from Allen County were bused daily to a segregated High Street High School in Bowling Green during the period after World War II.

The Brown v. Brown ruling of the Supreme Court of the United States in 1954 did not have the opposition in Kentucky as it did in the states that had been in the Confederacy. By 1956, 75 percent of Kentucky's school districts had desegregation plans.[13]

Table 39 contains data about the Scottsville School gleaned from reports made periodically to the Freedmen's Bureau about the all the schools in Kentucky.

---

[12] United States. 1870. Report of the Commissioner of Education made to the Secretary of the Interior for the year ... with accompanying papers. Washington: G.P.O.

[13] Kebler, John E., 1992. *The Kentucky encyclopedia.* The University Press of Kentucky, Lexington, Kentucky

Table 39

Scottsville Freedmen School reports 1868 - 1870

	1868				1869					1870			
	Jun	**Oct**	**Nov**	**Dec**	**Feb**	**Mar**	**Apr**	**May**	**Jun**	**Jan**	**Feb**	**Mar**	**Apr**
Nunber of Day Schools	1	1	1	1	1	1	1	1		1	1	1	1
Number of Night Schools	1	0	1	1	0	1	1	1		0	0	0	0
Name of School	Scottsville								**Closed**	Scottsville			
Date Opened	Jun	Sep 1868								Jan 1870			
Patron	Freedmen Bureau								State Board				
Number Sustained by Bureau	2	1	2	2	2	2	2	1		0	0	0	0
Bureau Furnished School Building	1	1	1	1	1	1	1	1		1	1	1	1
White Teachers	0	0	0	0	0	0	0	0		0	0	0	0
Colored Teachers	1	1	1	1	1	1	1	1		1	1	1	1
Male Pupils	9	28	48	43	48	50	50	20		14	16	18	15
Female Pupils	19	39	33	15	62	75	60	10		6	6	6	9
Number Enrolled Last Month	0	25	58	93	81	107	125	110		0	20	24	24
Number Left School this Month	0	0	0	0	0	7	15	80		0	2	0	0
Number New Scholars this Month	28	42	23	35	26	25	0	0		20	4	0	0
Average Attendance	28	40	81	54	107	121	110	27		18	18	16	15
Number Pupils Paying Tuition	13	35	12	0	0	0	0	0		15	15	14	10
Number of White Pupils	0	0	0	0	0	0		27		0	0	0	0
Number Always Present	28	40	81	54	107	120	110	27		17	15	16	15
Number Always Punctual	28	40	81	54	107	120	110	15		17	15	16	15

	1868				1869					1870			
	Jun	Oct	Nov	Dec	Feb	Mar	Apr	May	Jun	Jan	Feb	Mar	Apr
Number Older than Sixteen	15	10	40	2	70	50	50	10		7	8	8	0
Number in the Alphabet	3	15	12	7	28	17	30	5		4	0	0	0
Number in Spelling and Reading	4	17	22	8	26	35	30	10		16	24	24	5
Number in Advanced Readers	6	9	0	6	2	5	0	5		0	4	5	4
Number in Geography	6	9	2	6	7	8	8	0		0	0	1	0
Number in Arithmatic	6	9	12	8	14	19	20	0		0	0	1	5
Number in Higher Branches	0	0	0	0	0	2	2	0		0	0	0	5
Number in Writing	6	17	18	8	13	21	20	0		3	3	4	10
Number Free Before the War	0	5		1	0	0	0	0		0	0	0	
Number of Sabbath Schools	1	1		1	1	1	0	1		1	1	1	
Teachers in Sabbath Schools	1	2		1	3	4	5	3		4	4	4	
Pupils in Sabbath Schools	25	45		6	69	65	80	24		23	30	35	
Buildings by Owner	Dr. Walker				Dr. Alexander								
Name of Teacher	Minnie Smith		F. R. G. Pisani	Minnie Smith	F. R. G. Pisani			Lucy Tiller		Albert P. Cox			

Chapter 17

Slave Membership in Integrated Churches

Prior to 1867

Christianity was a solace to slaves because it promised a judging God and a personal savior. Their beliefs brought self-respect amid a demeaning life, spiritual strength during acts of injustice, and hope for eventual relief — all attributes necessary for survival through a life of slavery.[1] Some of those beliefs and feelings were expressed in song, spirituals spawned from sadness but written with an anticipation of freedom either in this life or the next. Thus the spiritual that said, "tell ole Pharaoh to let my people go," let slaves voice their belief that they would be delivered in this life just like the Hebrew children had been. But, deliverance was a long time coming.

In Allen County, the dominant churches were Baptist, Methodist, and Presbyterian.[2] All three, and other denominations as well, were constrained by Kentucky's 1850 constitution that reaffirmed that slavery was legal and that made advocating emancipation difficult. The decision of Kentucky in 1861 to remain in the Union as a slave state did not make the churches' stands any easier.

A few churches were organized before Allen County was established (Table 40).

---

[1] Boles, John B. 1995. *Religion in antebellum Kentucky*. Lexington, Ky: University Press of Kentucky.

[2] Harrison, Lowell H., 1978. *The antislavery movement in Kentucky.* Lexington, Ky: University Press of Kentucky.

Table 40

Allen County churches organized before 1866

Church	Organized
Bethel Baptist	1802
Bethlehem Baptist	1801
Big Spring Baptist	1847
Concord Methodist	1806
Harmony Baptist	1844
Liberty Baptist	1843
Mount Union General Baptist	1864
Mt Gilead Baptist	1829
Mt Union Methodist	1832
New Salem Baptist	1843
Old Buck Creek Methodist	1806
Pleasant Ridge Methodist	1850
Puncheon Baptist	1804
Rough Creek Baptist	1851
Scottsville Baptist	1841
Scottsville Methodist	1846
Smyrna Presbyterian	1840
Stony Point Methodist	1807
Trammel Fork Baptist	1802
Sulfur Springs Baptist	1798
Walkers Chapel Methodist	1850

Regardless of the difficulties resulting from Kentucky's decisions, the churches in Allen County were integrated from the beginning by choice, not by legal decree. The Methodist Episcopal Church formally voiced a strong condemnation of slavery as a great evil. It prohibited any preacher from owning slaves, directed expulsion of any member who sold slaves, and opposed the purchase of slaves by members.[3]

The early Methodist churches in Allen County welcomed and encouraged slave membership. The Methodist Episcopal Church's Scottsville Circuit recorded slave members in all their years from 1839 through 1866. Both white and slave membership varied, as

[3] Methodist Episcopal Church, 1804. *The doctrines and discipline of the Methodist Episcopal Church.* 13rh Edition,W. C. Robinson, Printer

did the number of churches. But, there was always a significant slave membership. Dr. Richard Weiss of the Kentucky Wesleyan Archives in Owensboro compiled the data used in Table 41. These data confirm the welcoming attitude of Allen County's Methodists toward their enslaved brethren.

Table 41

Slave membership in the Scottsville Circuit, Methodist Episcopal Church

Year	White Members	Colored Members	Churches
1839	434	8	6
1840	726	24	12
1841	460	20	8
1842	585	39	10
1843	641	18	11
1844	608	18	10
1845	608	18	
1846	735	18	
1847	683	15	5
1848	774	15	
1849	764	14	
1850	779	33	
1851	910	65	12
1852	975	64	14
1853	1103	22	11
1854	1087	33	6
1855	914	32	12
1856	591	55	8
1857	476	49	5
1858	541	48	3
1859	1161	16	12
1860	497	11	5
1861	163		
1862	834	12	12
1863	827	8	12
1864	880	10	12
1865	950	5	12
1866	378	9	9

Minutes from the church meetings record the acceptance of slaves as members. For example, Bethlehem Baptist Church accepted two "servants" [slaves], Judith and Fanney, "by experience" on 12 June 1819. On 10 November 1821, the minutes from Bethlehem recorded that there were "8 white and 2 blacks" present (Figure 44).

Figure 44

Minutes of meeting at Bethlehem Baptist Church on 10 November 1821

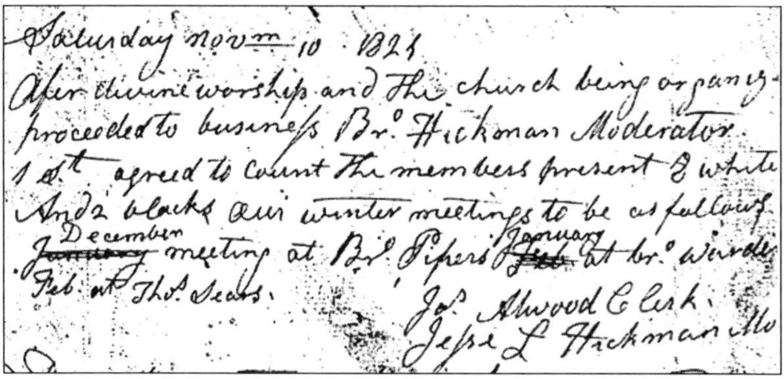
Saturday Novm 10 1821
After divine worship and the church being organiz-
proceeded to business Br. Hickman Moderator.
1st agreed to count the members present 8 white
And 2 blacks our winter meetings to be as follows
December meeting at Br. Pipers January at br. Wirdle
Feb at Thos. Sears.
Jos. Atwood Clerk
Jesse L Hickman Mo

At that same meeting, the church recorded a grievance lodged against a white member for "his speculation in the slave business." Clearly, ownership of slaves and being a slave trader were viewed differently. Slave ownership was common but slave trading was considered by most people to be abhorrent.

The Bays Fork Baptist Church[4] met in February 1861 in the Harrison School building. Members were not listed, but one of the early entries was that Mariah, a slave of T. W. Burton, was accepted as a member by letter from another church. Soffa, a slave of B. Neal was excluded in 1866 with no reason given.

When Mt. Gilead Baptist church was first organized, Samuel Carpenter and one of his slaves, Dolly, became charter members. Of the first 49 members of the new church, 11 were slaves. In September 1830, a slave named Dicy was tentatively accepted at Mt. Gilead awaiting a letter from her former church in Simpson

[4] This is not the same church as the one that was formed later with the same name in neighboring Warren County

County. Slaves, like the white members, were expected to move their membership when they moved to a different location. (Dicy had to wait until the following April for unqualified membership, the church had not held meetings until March because of a smallpox outbreak.)

One must remember that the churches did not have a separate and dedicated building at first. Mt. Gilead, for example,was organized in 1829, but did not have a church building until later. For several years, church services for all of the early churches were held in the home of one of its white members, the next host home being decided at each business session of the church. That practice gave rise to the name "Meeting House" for the home that would be used for the next service. The term persisted for decades as a synonym for the church building long after a dedicated church structure was constructed. Mt. Gilead slave membership is shown in Table 42.

Table 42

Slave membership in Mt. Gilead Baptist Church

Year Joined	Slave Name	Slave Owner Name
1829	Dolly	Samuel E. Carpenter
	Leah	
	Merry (a male)	Samuel E. Carpenter
1830	Felice	
	Dinah	
	Violet	
1831	Mariah	William Holder
	Dicy	Mrs. Whitney
	Nelly	
	Judy	
	Juda (Frank's wife)	
	Peter	Mrs. Whitney
1832	Joe	
	Frank (Juda's Husband)	
1843	Delila	Samuel E. Carpenter
	Rebecca	Samuel E. Carpenter
	Henna	John Calvert

1849	Edy	F. D. W. Harlen
	Bici	William Fitzpatrick
	Calvin	John Holder
	Fillis	
1850	Lucy	Edward Holder
	Phillip	
	Nancy	Willis Austin
	Jefferson	Matthew Johnson
	Burchey	Matthew Johnson
	Drury	S. E. Carpenter
1851	Richard	Joseph D. Carpenter
	Ambrose	Uriah Whitney
	Lucretia	Henry W. Hudson
	Elbridge	J. L. Siddens
	Marian	Uriah Whitney
	Delila	Ned Celser
	Dolly	S. E. Carpenter
	Mary	Benjamin Carpenter
1856	Phillip	Edward Holder
	Mandy	S. E. Carpenter
	Ishum	Matthew Johnson
	Delila	J. R. Dixon
	Rebecca	John Calvert
	Polly	Edward Holder
	Matilda	Herman Whitney
	Henry	S. E. Carpenter
	Richard	J. D. Carpenter
	Phillis	John Holder
1865	Merry	S. E. Carpenter
	Caroline	
	Betsy	Benjamin Carpenter
	Plura	S. E. Carpenter

During the services in the meeting house or later in the church, participants referred to each other as brother or sister. That seems to indicate recognition that slave and master were equal in the sight of God. At the same time, most churches did not support abolition, the Presbyterians being one exception.

Smyrna Presbyterian Church was organized in 1840. Their minutes contain the names of 99 white members and 31 "colored" members (Table 43). Although the charter members are not specifically identified, the clerk's handwriting and quality of ink indicate that there were 11 slave members recorded in the first entry. For the first ten years, they met in members' homes.

Table 43

Slave membership in Smyrna Presbyterian Church

Year Joined	Slave Name	Slave Owner Name
After 1840	Saul	Herrel
	Edward	Herrel
	Caroline	Brackin
	Kitty	Brackin
	Hannah	Chaney
	Alsey	Eubank
	Flora	Gaines
	Mandy	Gaines
	Eliza	Gaines
	Mahaley	Gaines
	Sarah	Gaines
	Angeline	M. C. Hobdy
	Kile	Lee Anthony
	Anthony	H. Harris
	Bob	William Walker
	George	Milliken
	Elizabeth	Gaines
	Linday	Anthony
	Milvinah	Anthony
	Liney	Harrell
	Alfred	Harrell
	Peter	Milleken
	Carrell	T. Hunt
	George	Harris
	Hiram	Harris
	Mary	Harris
	Eady	Ellis
	Sopha	Tavelsted
	Lucinda	Henley
	Josaphine	Childer
	Charles	Biren

It was common in most churches to exclude members when they offended the church's principles. Churches provided a moral compass for their members and maintained standards of morality, ethics, and behavior among them. Among those were exclusions for profanity, intoxication, fornication, and infidelity. The rules seem to have been applied equally to white and slave members.

Liberty Baptist church was organized in 1842 and had two slave members who were accepted for membership within the next year (Table 44).

Table 44
Slave membership in Liberty Baptist Church

Year Joined	Slave Name	Slave Owner Name
After 1842	Minny Porter*	
	Fanny Porter*	
1845	Lizzie Petty	James Petty
	Brittania Petty	M. Petty
1854	Daniel Porter	
	Toona Porter	
	Jackson Burton	
1857	Samuel Porter	M. Porter
	Linn Meridith	
	Susan Jewell	
	Edney James Petty	
	Mandy H. Ritchy	
	Richard Williams	
	James Sears	
	Sarah C. Linnin	
	Mira E. Stark	
	Cely Ann Stark	
	Rilda T. Stark	
	Dolly A. Williams	
	Eliza Porter	
	Ellas Porter	
	Eliza Porter	
1849	Mary Jane	James Petty
Before 1853	Winny*	M. Porter
1854	Brittanie	M. Porter
1856	Jackson	John Burton

* Minnie, Fanny, and Winny were removed from the church membership list on 31 January 1857 because they had been "sent off by their master," presumably sold.

Members were dismissed if they joined another church or, in the case of slaves, were sold away to another area without transferring their membership. The period near the end of the Civil War in April 1865 and before the ratification of the Thirteenth Amendment in December 1865 presented a problem. Legally, Kentucky slaves were not free but they must have known that slaves elsewhere in the United States were. It became a period of considerable unrest and uncertainty. During that period, one church dismissed two of its slave members, a man belonging to one owner and a woman belonging to another owner, because they had run away without permission from either the owners or the church. One slave was excluded in October 1865 because he had been sold away from the area several years earlier and had not asked for a letter to transfer membership to a church in that area.

Some of the twenty churches listed in Table 37 are no longer active. Most others have not donated copies of their pre-Civil War church minutes to the Historical Society. However, the minutes of a few have been. Those were researched to identify the names of slave members and those are the sources of data are presented in Tables 42, 43 and 44.

Chapter 18

African American Births and Deaths in Allen County

Death records have been continually issued in Kentucky since 1911. Before that date, only two extant datasets contain information that would help researchers of African American heritage. One was a special census in three decadal census years, the other was mortality lists that Kentucky required to be recorded beginning in 1852.

African American Deaths During 1860, 1870 and 1880

Each of the U.S. Federal Censuses from 1850-1880 included a mortality schedule that listed the individuals who had died in the year previous to the census year.[1] For Allen County, the year 1850 was not available for unknown reasons. The data were collected about all deaths and did not exclude slaves. The data included the name, age, gender, color, free or slave, marital status, state of birth, place of death, month of death, occupation, cause of death, and number of days ill. Although these records present data about the deaths during just one year of a decade, they are important glimpses of our ancestors, both black and white.

African American Deaths 1852-1878

Kentucky began recording deaths in 1852.[2] These records included slave deaths, although there is reason to believe that the record may not be absolutely complete. Regardless of its degree of completeness, it offers an avenue for genealogical researchers to reach back into the days of slavery to identify slave ancestors. This dataset included the name of the deceased, the age, sex, marital status, occupation, residence, state of birth, place of death, date of

---

[1] Ancestry.com. *U.S. Federal Census Mortality Schedules, 1850-1880* [database on-line]. Provo, UT, USA: The Generations Network, Inc., 2008.

[2] Kentucky. Kentucky Birth, Marriage and Death Records – Microfilm (1852-1910). Microfilm rolls #994027-994058. Kentucky Department for Libraries and Archives, Frankfort, Kentucky.

death, and cause of death. For whites, the names of the parents were recorded. For slaves, the name of the slave owner was listed instead of the parents, yet another indication of slavery's disregard of slave families. The letter "B" in the original record indicated a slave.

This dataset from Kentucky is unusual for this period of time. Few states have such records. That makes it all the more remarkable that slave information was included.

The record was interrupted during the Civil War. The data for Allen County slaves are missing after 1859 for all but five African American deaths, presumably because the others were not recorded. Data for white deaths are missing from 1865 through 1873 and are inconsistently recorded thereafter.

Slave Names on Death Records

The death data for African Americans' deaths (all but five were or had been slaves) during the 1852 to 1878 period that were extracted from recorded Kentucky data available from Ancesty.com. These data are presented in Table 45.[3] Many of the deaths of slaves were recorded using only first names because surnames were not usually acknowledged. (Surnames imply family relationships and those relationships were not recognized by slavery.) For example in these death entries from Kentucky, only two men were recorded with surnames. Contrary to the usual custom, surnames were often accorded the females whose deaths were being recorded. The reason is not clear because, in all cases, the entries were made by whites who chose to either enter only the first name or to assume and assign a surname. When surnames were listed, they have been included in the tables herein.

Table 46 presents the death data collected by the Census Bureau during the census year. Only those who were born into slavery (that is, before 1866) were extracted. Note that none of the slaves were accorded surnames in 1860. Surnames were only used in the post slavery census years of 1870 and 1880.

[3] Ancestry.com. Kentucky Death Records, 1852-1953 [database on-line] in Provo, UT

Table 45

African American Deaths in Allen County 1852-1878

Alphabetical by Surname						
Name	**Death**	**Location**	**Residence**	**Birth**	**Color**	**Gender**
Allen, Jon W.	Mar 1859	Allen	Allen	1835	Black	Male
Anthony, Caroline	7 Jan 1858	Allen	Allen	1828	Black	Female
Anthony, Mary	5 Aug 1859	Allen	Allen	1829	Black	Female
Austin, Jane	10 Jan 1855	Allen	Allen	1835	Black	Female
Black, Delilah	Mar 1878			1861	Black	Female
Black, Lucy Ann	20 Jul 1874	Allen	Allen		Black	Female
Boucher, Adaline	12 Mar 1859	Allen	Allen		Black	Female
Burton, Sam	11 Nov 1856	Allen	Allen	1840	Black	Female
Carpenter, Dinah	12 Oct 1856	Allen	Allen	1796	Black	Female
Carpenter, Martha	5 Apr 1854	Allen	Allen		Black	Female
Carpenter, Violet	16 Aug 1857	Allen	Allen	1813	Black	Female
Caruth, Anna	Aug 1856	Allen	Allen	1826	Black	Female
Chany, No Name	Jun 1859	Allen	Allen		Black	Female
Chany, Sophia	1 Jan 1858	Allen	Allen	1831	Black	Female
Donning, Violet	24 Oct 1854	Allen	Allen	1770	Black	Female
Downing, Elizabeth	20 Jan 1858	Allen	Allen		Black	Female
Dun, Pherily	Sep 1858	Allen	Allen	1835	Black	Female
Fant, Viollet	20 Mar 1854	Allen	Allen	1774	Black	Female
Fitzpatrick, Lenah	1 Nov 1856	Allen	Allen	1776	Black	Female
Gatewood, Milly	18 Jul 1874	Allen	Allen	1862	Black	Female
Gatewood, No Name	Dec 1859	Allen	Allen		Black	Female
Goodnight, Maria	2 Jun 1858	Allen	Allen	1832	Black	Female
Goody, No Name	Mar 1859	Allen	Allen		Black	Female
Graham, James T.	12 Jun 1854	Allen	Allen	1830	Black	Male
Hecter, No Name	14 Jan 1859	Allen	Allen		Black	Female
Hoon, Sellie	16 Mar 1859	Allen	Allen		Black	Female
Hughes, Mariah	9 Jul 1854	Allen	Allen	1834	Black	Female
Humbles, James	4 Oct 1854	Allen	Allen	1843	Black	Female
Hunt, Sarah	1 Jun 1858	Allen	Allen	1818	Black	Female
Jackson, Rhody	15 Apr 1856	Allen	Allen	1781	Black	Female
Milican, Lucy	10 Jul 1859	Allen	Allen	1836	Black	Female
Moore, Manerva	5 May 1857	Allen	Allen	1812	Black	Female
Motly, Eliza	18 Jul 1858	Allen	Allen		Black	Female
Neal, Sarah	10 Apr 1854	Allen	Allen		Black	Female
Neal, Sopha	Dec 1859	Allen	Allen	1819	Black	Female
Neal, Sopha	21 Jul 1861	Allen	Allen	1860	Black	Female
Newman, Lucy	Feb 1859	Allen	Allen		Black	Female

Name	Death	Location	Residence	Birth	Color	Gender
Page, Alis	Oct 1859	Allen	Allen		Black	Female
Pairheirs, Mary	Aug 1855	Allen	Allen	1837	Black	Female
Petty, Harret	20 Jul 1874	Allen	Allen	1856	Black	Female
Pulliam, Adaline	26 Nov 1856	Allen	Allen		Black	Female
Ritchy, Caroline	Feb 1858	Allen	Allen	1829	Black	Female
Russell, Lucy	15 Mar 1859	Allen	Allen	1819	Black	Female
Seares, Jane	Apr 1859	Allen	Allen		Black	Female
Seares, No Name	Apr 1859	Allen	Allen		Black	Female
Seares, No Name	Apr 1859	Allen	Allen		Black	Female
Sears, Judia	15 Apr 1856	Allen	Allen	1825	Black	Female
Sears, Lucy	28 Jun 1856	Allen	Allen		Black	Female
Sears, Mary	1 Sep 1854	Allen	Allen	1809	Black	Female
Sears, Mary	7 Apr 1857	Allen	Allen	1839	Black	Female
Sears, Pilly	Jul 1854	Allen	Allen	1809	Black	Female
Smith, Fanny	12 Jan 1852	Allen		1802	Black	Female
Spencer, Missourie	Jun 1858	Allen	Allen	1822	Black	Female
Stark, Alsy	Aug 1856	Allen	Allen	1796	Black	Female
Stark, Easter	Sep 1857	Allen	Allen	1822	Black	Female
Walker, Chany	27 Jan 1856	Allen	Allen	1803	Black	Female
Whitny, Mayland	Aug 1858	Allen	Allen		Black	Female
Williams, Mary	28 Aug 1854	Allen	Allen	1827	Black	Female
Williams, Sarah	3 Nov 1854	Allen	Allen		Black	Female
Wood, Letha A.	15 May 1854	Allen	Allen	1839	Black	Female

First Name Only	Death	Location	Residence	Birth	Color	Gender
Alexander	Nov 1856	Allen	Allen	1855	Black	Male
Alexander	Oct 1854	Allen	Allen	1849	Black	Male
Allen	May 1854	Allen	Allen	1853	Black	Male
Amanda	7 Jan 1855	Allen	Allen	1851	Black	Female
Andrew	10 Feb 1855	Allen	Allen	1854	Black	Male
Ann	Aug 1856	Allen	Allen	1847	Black	Female
Baler	10 Apr 1857	Allen	Allen	1802	Black	Male
Benjamin	Mar 1858	Allen	Allen	1831	Black	Male
Billey B.	6 Apr 1859	Allen	Allen		Black	Female
Billy	28 Apr 1854	Allen	Allen		Black	Male
Carol	29 Apr 1854	Allen	Allen	1833	Black	Male
Cato	Nov 1856	Allen	Allen		Black	Male
Charels	Apr 1859	Allen	Allen	1858	Black	Male
Charls	15 Sep 1854	Allen	Allen	1794	Black	Male

First Name Only	Death	Location	Residence	Birth	Color	Gender
Charly	16 Mar 1857	Allen	Allen		Black	Male
Dallis	10 Mar 1855	Allen	Allen	1853	Black	Male
Daniel	17 Jul 1858	Allen	Allen		Black	Male
Dolly	15 Oct 1856	Allen	Allen	1855	Black	Female
Edmuno	28 May 1857	Allen	Allen	1832	Black	Male
Eliza	1 Feb 1857	Allen	Allen	1845	Black	Female
Ephraim	10 Oct 1858	Allen	Allen	1831	Black	Male
Frank	4 Jul 1858	Allen	Allen		Black	Male
Freland	5 Sep 1854	Allen	Allen	1794	Black	Male
George	16 Oct 1856	Allen	Allen	1846	Black	Male
George	16 Oct 1856	Allen	Allen		Black	Male
George	27 Ded 1861	Allen	Allen	1827	Black	Female
Harman	1 Dec 1858	Allen	Allen	1857	Black	Male
Harry	30 Jul 1854	Allen	Allen	1846	Black	Male
Hary	Apr 1859	Allen	Allen	1858	Black	Male
Hecter	14 Jan 1859	Allen	Allen	1836	Black	Female
Helm	Apr 1859	Allen	Allen	1839	Black	Male
Henderson	15 Jan 1859	Allen	Allen	1838	Black	Male
Henderson	7 Jul 1858	Allen	Allen		Black	Male
Henry	12 Oct 1859	Allen	Allen	1846	Black	Male
Henry	3 Feb 1857	Allen	Allen	1851	Black	Male
Henry	6 Dec 1856	Allen	Allen		Black	Male
Ira	Jul 1856	Allen	Allen	1854	Black	Male
Isaac	22 Sep 1858	Allen	Allen		Black	Male
James	Aug 1858	Allen	Allen	1853	Black	Male
Jane	4 Jul 1858	Allen	Allen	1818	Black	Female
Jennette	15 Mar 1854	Allen	Allen	1852	Black	Female
Jick	31 Sep 1859	Allen	Allen	1772	Black	Male
John	10 Sep 1856	Allen	Allen	1844	Black	Male
John	7 Aug 1856	Allen	Allen		Black	Male
John	Mar 1858	Allen	Allen	1851	Black	Male
John	Mar 1859	Allen	Allen	1835	Black	Male
John	May 1856	Allen	Allen	1838	Black	Male
Josephine	Sep 1857	Allen	Allen	1856	Black	Female
Lewis	14 Feb 1859	Allen	Allen	1842	Black	Male
Lewis	26 Feb 1858	Allen	Allen	1839	Black	Male
Lewis	31 Jul 1854	Allen	Allen	1847	Black	Male
Lucinda	1 Nov 1854	Allen	Allen	1853	Black	Female
Lucinda	25 Aug 1854	Allen	Allen	1851	Black	Female
Luny	Sep 1857	Allen	Allen	1856	Black	Female

First Name Only	Death	Location	Residence	Birth	Color	Gender
Martha	10 Oct 1856	Allen	Allen	1849	Black	Female
Mau	Apr 1859	Allen	Allen	1858	Black	Male
Nelley	Sep 1854	Allen	Allen	1848	Black	Female
No Name	6 Aug 1859	Allen	Allen		Black	Male
No Name	Apr 1854	Allen	Allen		Black	Male
No Name	Dec 1856	Allen	Allen		Black	Male
No Name	Jul 1859	Allen	Allen		Black	Male
No Name	Jun 1858	Allen	Allen	1854	Black	Male
No Name	May 1857	Allen	Allen	1856	Black	Male
No Name	Nov 1854	Allen	Allen		Black	Male
Pompey	Jan 1857	Allen	Allen	1767	Black	Male
Rachel	Oct 1854	Allen	Allen	1853	Black	Female
Riley	3 Dec 1856	Allen	Allen	1825	Black	Male
Samul	Feb 1858	Allen	Allen	1783	Black	Male
Sarah	5 Feb 1856	Allen	Allen	1855	Black	Female
Sarah	Aug 1858	Allen	Allen	1848	Black	Female
Sherman	23 Jan 1859	Allen	Allen	1821	Black	Male
Smith	Jun 1855	Allen	Allen	1835	Black	Male
Susan	15 Aug 1857	Allen	Allen	1843	Black	Female
Tarnar	5 Aug 1854	Allen	Allen	1819	Black	Female
Tom	19 Apr 1857	Allen	Allen	1844	Black	Male
Washington	8 Oct 1856	Allen	Allen	1848	Black	Male
William	7 Jul 1854	Allen	Allen	1853	Black	Male
William	Jul 1854	Allen	Allen	1852	Black	Male
Wilson	27 Jul 1856	Allen	Allen	1855	Black	Male
Winny	4 Jul 1858	Allen	Allen		Black	Male

Table 46

African American deaths during census years

Census Years 1860, 1870, and 1880							
Name, Alphabetical	Death Location	Census Year	Birth Year	Birth State	Color	Gender	Age
No Name, Agnes	Allen County	1860	1797	VA	B	F	63
No Name, Alice	Butlersvlle, Allen County	1860	1858	TN	B	F	2
No Name, Amanda	Allen County	1860	1827	KY	B	F	33
No Name, Betty	Allen County	1860	1826	KY	B	F	34
No Name, Bill	Allen County	1860	1859	KY	B	M	2 months
No Name , Charlie	Allen County	1860	1859	KY	B	M	1
No Name, Daniel	Butlersvlle, Allen County	1860	1817	TN	B	M	43
No Name, Dellemar	Butlersville, Allen County	1880		KY	M	F	
No Name, Delpha	Allen County	1860	1805	KY	B	F	55
No Name, Elizabeth	Allen County	1860	1860	KY	B	F	6 months
No Name, Elizabeth	Allen County	1860	1859	KY	B	F	9 months
No Name, Francis	Allen County	1860	1860	KY	B	F	1 month
No Name, Franklin	Allen County	1880	1879	KY	B	M	1
No Name, Hannah	Butlersvlle, Allen County	1860	1839	TN	B	F	21
No Name, Henry	Allen County	1860	1846	KY	B	M	14
No Name, Horonit	Butlersvlle, Allen County	1860	1842	TN	B	F	18
No Name, Jack	Allen County	1860	1859	KY	B	M	9 months
No Name, Jane	Allen County	1860	1859	KY	B	F	9 months
No Name, Jo	Allen County	1860	1859	KY	B	M	9 months
No Name, Jock	Allen County	1860	1859	KY	M	M	1
No Name, John	Allen County	1860	1859	KY	B	M	6 months
No Name, Jude	Allen County	1860	1854	KY	B	F	6
No Name, Lucy	Butlersvlle, Allen County	1860	1827	TN	M	F	33
No Name, Malissa	Allen County	1860	1834	KY	B	F	26
No Name, Margarit	Allen County	1860	1859	KY	B	F	6 months
No Name, Mary	Allen County	1860	1859	KY	B	F	9 months
No Name, Mary	Allen County	1860	1859	KY	B	F	4 months
No Name, May	Butlersvlle, Allen County	1860	1832	KY	B	F	28
No Name, Ponds	Allen County	1880	1880	KY	B	M	10 days
No Name, Richard	Butlersville, Allen County	1860	1852	KY	B	M	8
No Name, Rubin	Allen County	1860	1805	VA	M	M	55

Name, Alphabetical	Death Location	Census Year	Birth Year	Birth State	Color	Gender	Age
No Name, Stark	Allen County	1860	1859	KY	M	M	1
No Name, Susan	Allen County	1860	1860	KY	B	F	1 month
No Name, Sydda	Allen County	1860	1795	VA	B	F	65
No Name, Thomas	Butlersvlle, Allen County	1860	1825	KY	B	M	35
No Name, Tom	Allen County	1860	1859	KY	B	M	5 months
No Name, Richard	Butlersvlle, Allen County	1860	1852	KY	B	M	8
Anthony, Mary	Allen County	1880	1871	KY	B	F	9
Bell, Fanny	Butlersville, Allen County	1880	1879	KY	B	F	1
Brown, Edwin D.	Precinct 1, Allen County	1870	1869	KY	B	M	1
Burton, Jane	Precinct 3, Allen County	1870	1843	KY	M	F	27
Carpenter, Elisabeth	Civil Dist 6, Allen County	1870	1843	KY	M	F	27
Carpenter, Fielding	Precinct 1, Allen County	1870	1845	KY	B	M	25
Carpenter, Henry	Precinct 1, Allen County	1870	1820	KY	B	M	50
Carpenter, Mary	Allen County	1880	1838		B	F	42
Carpenter, Mary E.	District 6, Allen County	1870	1853	KY	M	F	17
Dunivan, Dan'l	Allen County	1880	1815		B	M	65
Franklin, Jeff	Allen County	1880	1879	KY	B	M	1
Godley, Lucinda	Precinct 4, Allen County	1870	1856	KY	B	F	14
Granger, Buddy	Allen County	1880	1880	KY	B	M	24 days
Holder, Unnamed	Allen County	1880	1880	KY	B	M	1 month
Infant	Butlersvlle, Allen County	1860	1860	KY	B	F	3 months
Infant	Allen County	1860	1860	KY	B	M	1 month
Infant	Allen County	1860	1859	KY	B	F	9 months
Infant	Allen County	1860	1859	KY	B	F	4 months
Infant	Allen County	1860	1859	KY	B	F	1 month
Infant	Allen County	1860	1860	KY	B	M	1 month
Johnson, Thomas	Allen County	1880	1880	KY	B	M	1 month
Landrum, Rosa	Allen County	1880	1828	KY	B	F	52
McHenry, George	Butlersville, Allen County	1880	1879	KY	B	M	1
Merit, Augustus	Allen County	1860	1812	TN	M	M	48
Milliken, Nola	Allen County	1880	1880	KY	B	F	1 month
Pope, Haney	Butlersville, Allen County	1880	1879	KY	B	F	1

Name, Alphabetical	Death Location	Census Year	Birth Year	Birth State	Color	Gender	Age
Porter, Nickademis	Precinct 2, Allen County	1870	1858	KY	M	M	12
Price, Edward	Precinct 2, Allen County	1870	1813	VA	B	M	57
Russell, Annie	Allen County	1880	1855	TN	B	F	25
Sarver, Not Named	Allen County	1880	1880	KY	B	M	10 days
Seares, Gilford	Precinct 4, Allen County	1870	1835	KY	B	M	35
Seares, James Isam	Precinct 3, Allen County	1870	1866	KY	B	M	4
Sears, Elleseph	Precinct 3, Allen County	1870	1869	KY	B	F	1
Shea, Nancy	Butlersvlle, Allen County	1860	1814	KY	M	F	46
Stark, Bell	Precinct 3, Allen County	1870	1867	KY	M	F	3
Street, William D.	Allen County	1880	1879	KY	B	M	1
Stuart, Harvy	Allen County	1880	1880	KY	B	M	14 days
Tabor, Angaline	Allen County	1880	1840	KY	B	F	40
Tabor, Hollis	Allen County	1880	1870	KY	B	M	10
Tabor, Unnamed	Allen County	1880	1880	KY	B	M	1 month
Tucker, Danl	Butlersvlle, Allen County	1860	1846	KY	B	M	14
Williams, Martha A.	Allen County	1880	1879	KY	B	F	1

Chapter 19

Slave Cemeteries

There are four different types of cemeteries in Allen County: family, church, communal, and secular. Of those, the family cemeteries are the oldest. The earliest explorers and settlers were probably buried near where they died. Another factor may be that few of the earliest settlers would have been old when they immigrated to Kentucky. As the settler families grew in size and aged, the necessity for a family burial ground would have become more urgent and those buried there would expand to include the extended family as well as the immediate one.

Churches didn't have buildings at first and therefore did not have cemeteries either. The church cemeteries would eventually replace the family graveyards as the preferred resting place. But only seven of the 20 churches (Table 40 in Chapter 17) during the slavery period existed before 1840. The transition from family to church burials was not completed before slavery ended.

Communal cemeteries became necessary as towns grew and the number of churches in them became more numerous. The Old City Cemetery in Scottsville is an example. When it filled, another communal cemetery (Crescent Hill) was established.

A secular cemetery is a recent addition to Allen County, but none existed during the period of slavery.

Most slaves were buried in private cemeteries maintained by the slave owners. Most likely, they would have been buried in or near the family cemetery of the owner. Grave markers for whites in all the earliest cemeteries were un-engraved fieldstones. The slave graves would have been similarly marked. As prosperity increased, it became more common for the tombstones of whites to be engraved with the deceased's names. Slaves, on the other hand, seldom, if ever, had names engraved. Most markers continued to be un-engraved fieldstones.

Some slaves lived long enough to enter the era of engraved tombstones. The marked graves of people who were born as slaves in Allen County are presented in Table 47. The research was done by B. S. Chambers, who extracted the data for African Americans who were born prior to 1866 from published inventories of Allen County cemeteries. The presumption is that they would have been born as slaves.

Table 47
African Americans born as slaves buried in Allen County Cemeteries

Allen County Death Certificates 1911-1915 by Michael Denning						
Name	**Born**	**Died**	**Father**	**Mother**	**Cemetery**	**Gender**
Borren, Ida	2 Mar 1821	20 Apr 1911	Sam Dunn	Mary Hall	Smyrna	F
Bridges, Josie	11 Jun 1829	24 Feb 1913	Phil Shipley	Tilda Franklin	Scottsville	F
Burr, Sim	1869	17 Feb 1914	Sim Burr	Tilda Wright	Scottsville	F
Burris, Elvira	1839	11 Mar 1914	Henry Bug	Elizabeth Bug	Burris	F
Colbert, James	1846	30 Sep 1912	Burl Calvert	Dolly Carpenter	Scottsville	M
Downing, Wesley	13 Jan 1829	30 Oct 1914		Mettie Carpenter	Scottsville	M
Everett, Jennie	1859	7 Sep 1915		Lettie Brown	Fountain Run	F
Goodloe, Eliza	28 Dec 1861	5 Jan 1913	Hayes Cook	Parelle Tarlic	Scottsville	F
Graham, William C.	3 Jun 1840	6 Feb 1911			Scottsville	M
Holder, George	1858	1 Feb 1913	Robert Fitzpatrick	Polly Holder	Caney Fork	M
Jackman, Emma	17 Dec 1837	24 Oct 1914	John Sarve	Charity Milliken	Sarver	F
Martin, Albert	16 Sep 1838	15 Jan 1915	Alfred Price		Scottsville	M
Mitchell, Alay	1834	28 Feb 1914	Dock Dunn		Scottsville	F
Thomas, Nancy	1811	2 Nov 1913			Scottsville	F
Tooly, Millie	1823	21 Aug 1913	Berry Meadows	Silva Oglesby	Scottsville	F

First Missionary Baptist Church Cemetery						
Name	**Born**	**Died**	**Father**	**Mother**	**Cemetery**	**Gender**
Downing, Major G.	1856	1924				M
Fishback, Hannah	4 May 1842	5 Nov 23				F
Hughes, Henry	1857	1932				M
Landers, Jerry	23 Feb 1823	1914				M
Tuley, Adeline	1856	1949				F

Greenville Baptist Church						
Name	**Born**	**Died**	**Father**	**Mother**	**Cemetery**	**Gender**
	11 Apr 1915	11 Apr 1915	W. H. Shipley	Ora Shipley	Greenville	F
Bracken, Chaney	1817	2 Apr 1915	Samuel Chaney		Greenville	F
Brown, Kittie	1825	1 Aug 1911	Matt Sid-dens	Nielie Lyons	Scottsville	F
Lee, Richard	1832	1 Jun 1913			Greenville	M
Stark, Celia	1846	31 Jul 1911	Andy Stovall	Sarah Hinton	Greenville	F
Stark, Louise Jane	1 May 1833	30 Apr 1913	Isaac Hopson	Caroline Stark	Greenville	F
White, Pleasant	Abt 1849	15 Apr 1866			Greenville	M
Willoughby, Helen	9 Jan 1909	30 Oct 1915			Greenville	F

The Greenville Cemetery at the church near Settle has a marker for Pleasant White who was a Private in Company B, 6th United States Colored Cavalry during the Civil War (Figure 45). He had been a slave of Uriah Porter when he volunteered and was enlisted on 8 August 1864 in Bowling Green. Less than two months later the 6th Colored Cavalry was engaged in battle at Saltville, Virginia. He must have been a respected soldier because he later served as an orderly in the Regimental Headquarters. His unit was part of the occupation force that occupied Arkansas during the reconstruction period after the war. All the members of the unit were mustered out of service on 14 April 1866 in De Vall, Arkansas.

Figure 45
Marker for Private Pleasant White, 6th Colored Cavalry, Greenville Cemetery

Chapter 20

Freedmen Marriage Certificates

Background

The Freedmen's Bureau (established in the War Department by an act of Congress on 3 March 1865) was responsible for "the supervision and management of all matters relating to the refugees and freedmen and lands abandoned or seized during the Civil War." It was to act as a modern day social services agency regarding a variety of problems that freedmen faced: food and clothing, employment, medical care, and formalizing slave marriages during servitude.

Slave marriages had no legal standing prior to 1866. Slave husbands and wives, without legal recourse, could be separated or sold at their master's will. The marriage ceremony for slaves, in most cases, was comprised only of the owner's permission, if that. The slaves often had their own ceremony, jumping over the broomstick, for example.

A surviving spouse and children could not inherit property owned by a deceased spouse. The children, in a legal sense, were not legitimate because the marriage was not legal. Such was the unintended consequences of freedom. The solution was to make those slave marriages legal.

Marriage Certificates

On 30 May 1865, the commissioner of the Freedmen's Bureau issued instruction for solemnizing former slave marriages. Bureau officials in Kentucky and elsewhere issued marriage licenses and certificates and registered freedmen marriages.

For Kentucky, there were marriage licenses and certificates issued for the sub-districts of Augusta (1866 and 1867), Bowling Green (1865–1867), Columbus (1866–1867), Cynthiana (1866), Mount Sterling (1866), Owensboro (1866–1868), Paducah (1865–

1866), and Winchester (1866). Slave couples form Allen County would have had to travel to Bowling Green to obtain their marriage certificate. The whereabouts and disposition of the certificates that were issued at Bowling Green and once were held in the Warren County Courthouse are unknown. They are neither at the Warren County Courthouse nor at the Kentucky Library.

Figure 46

Marriage Certificate issued by the Freedmen's Bureau in 1866

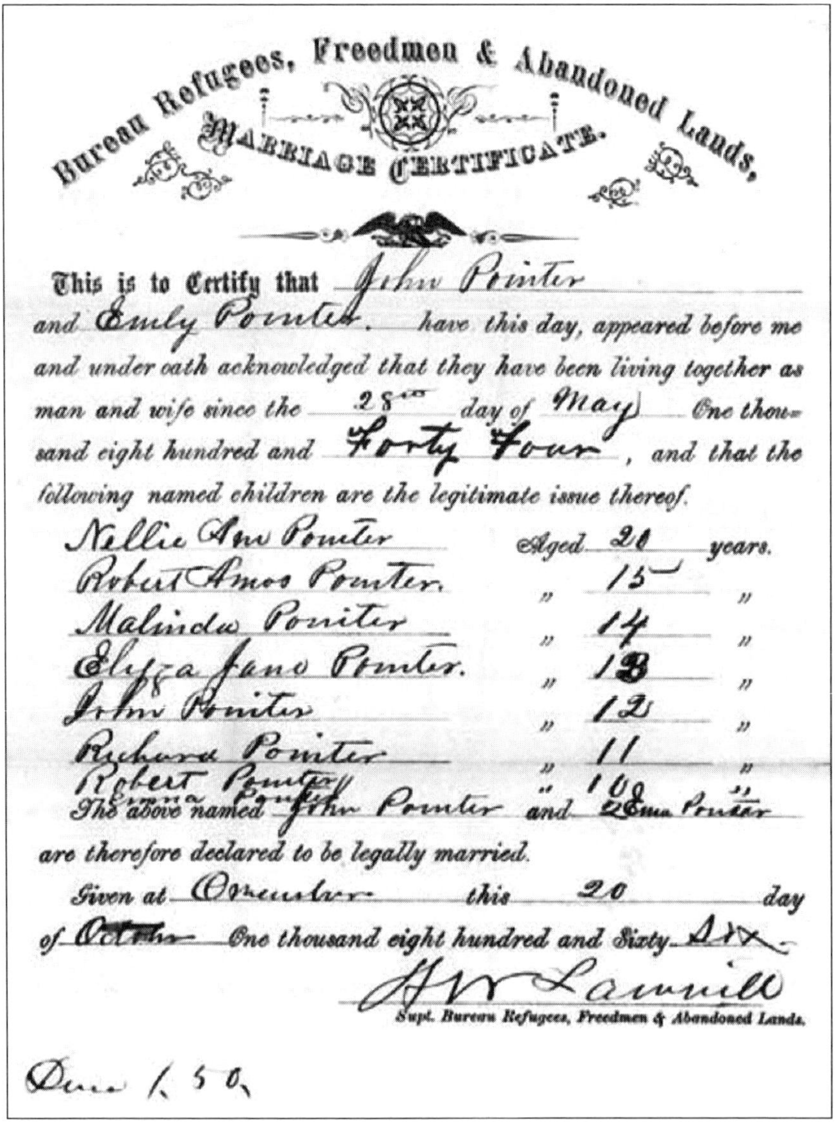

Bureau Refugees, Freedmen & Abandoned Lands,

MARRIAGE CERTIFICATE.

This is to Certify that John Pointer and Emily Pointer. have this day, appeared before me and under oath acknowledged that they have been living together as man and wife since the 28th day of May One thousand eight hundred and Forty Four, and that the following named children are the legitimate issue thereof.

Nellie Ann Pointer	Aged 21 years.
Robert Amos Pointer.	" 15 "
Malinda Pointer	" 14 "
Eliza Jane Pointer.	" 13 "
John Pointer	" 12 "
Richard Pointer	" 11 "
Robert Pointer	" 10 "

The above named John Pointer and Emma Pointer are therefore declared to be legally married.

Given at Owensboro this 20 day of October One thousand eight hundred and Sixty Six.

H W Lawrill
Supt. Bureau Refugees, Freedmen & Abandoned Lands.

Due 1.50

The National Archives and Records Administration (NARA) microfilmed the field office records for Kentucky. Those records are available on microfilm at the National Archives Building, Washington, D.C. and at each of NARA's regional facilities.

The marriage certificates issued by the Freedmen's Bureau are a rich source of genealogical information. Each one contains the names of the married couple, the date of their slave marriage, and the names and ages of each of their children. Figure 46 is a copy of a certificate issued in Owensboro. The ones issued in Bowling Green would have been on the same form.

Chapter 21

Civil War Pensions

Background

Discharge came soon after the end of the Civil War for most white soldiers in the Union army. Not so for many of the African American soldiers. The army considered them to be ideally suited to keep the peace and enforce the laws of Reconstruction as occupying troops in states that had joined the Confederacy. The sight of armed African Americans in uniforms was disconcerting to white southerners and comforting to the freed slaves. The result was that they served well in that role. So well, that some units like the 6th U.S. Colored Cavalry, were not mustered out until a year or more after Lee's surrender. In fact, thirteen of the Allen County-born soldiers were still in service into 1866. The last one to be discharged was Private James Anthony who was discharged in Nashville on 26 July 1866.

Pension Laws

Pensions had been paid to veterans who served in the Revolutionary War, the War of 1812, the Indian Wars, and the War with Mexico. The Civil War would be far different in the potential beneficiaries. On 22 July 1861, Congress authorized the building of an army of up to a half million men.[1] The pension rules had to be redefined and Congress did that the following year.[2]

Wounds or disease while on active duty qualified the veteran for a pension. The amount varied by rank from $30 per month for Captains and $8 for Privates. Widows, or children under sixteen, were eligible to continue the pension after the pensioner's death.

In 1879, the pension law was revised by the Arrears Act to

[1] Oliver, John W., 1915. *History of the Civil War military pensions, 1861-1885.* Bulletin of the University of Wisconsin, NO. 844, History Series, Vol 4 No. !, pp 1-120. Madison, Wisconsin

[2] U.S. Statutes at Large, Vol 12, 566-569

allow submission of claims more than one year after discharge. None of the Allen County born African Americans had submitted claims prior to that amended law. In all, 268,636 applications were filed within the first year.[3] The result was interminable delays in the decision process.

The Dependent Pension Act of 1890 made Civil War veterans who were disabled for any reason eligible for a pension. By 1910, 28 percent of American men over 65 years old were receiving pension benefits. Over 300,000 widows were on the rolls too.[4]

Pension Application and Certification Process

The processes for application and certification of pensions was difficult for white applicants, but was particularly so for African Americans. The Dependent Pension Act of 1890 made those veterans eligible for a pensions based on age alone. There followed a flood of applicants and the sheer quantity slowed the process. The success rate though was less for African Americans than for whites (Table 48).[5]

Table 48

Civil War Pensions 1861-1914

Pension Type	Percent Pensioned	
	White	Black
Veteran	92.6%	75.4%
Widow	83.9%	60.7%
Children	50.0%	50.0%
Parents	69.4%	35.5%

The difference in success did not seem to be from prejudicial reasons, but from the unintended results of the pension eligibility requirements. Most of problems for African American applicants who were born in Allen County arose from the fact that none of them could read or write.

[3] House Report, 46th Congress, 3rd Session, NO. 387, p 26

[4] Regosin, Elizabeth A. and Donald R. Shafer, 2008. *Voices of emancipation: Understanding slavery, the Civil War, and Reconstruction through the U.S. Pension Files.* .New York University Press, New York

[5] Shaffer, Donald R., 2004. *After the glory: the struggles of black Civil War veterans.* University Press of Kansas, Lawrence, KS

One of the most common problems was that the applicant's name did not match any soldier's name. The slaves who lived in Allen County when they enlisted had no surnames. They spoke a surname they chose or that they thought they had. The army clerk wrote what he thought he heard, essentially an attempt to spell the name phonetically. Years later, some pension applications were submitted using a corrected spelling or a change that the applicant had adopted since the war. For example, the soldier records listed Isham Stark but he applied for a pension using the name Isham T. Stark. The application was returned asking for proof that the two were the same person.

Another common problem for African American applicants related to dates. Slave owners usually did not record birth dates. Most enlistees knew only their approximate age, perhaps the year of their birth, but often not the month or day. The person filling out the application form would interpret the birth year from the age the applicant gave. Years later, when another form was filed, the interpreted or estimated year of birth could differ from the original record. That would cause it to be returned for clarification.

A special problem with birth dates occurred when pensions were authorized for veterans older than some age threshold. Jerry Landers' year of birth was estimated at the time of enlistment to be 1828. The pension bureau returned his application when he applied for full pension based on old age in 1907. He had then listed his birth date as 23 March 1830. The disparity of birth years caused it to be returned. He ultimately received pension approval.

Disability pensions required proof that the disability was caused by injury or disease while on active duty. That was a problem for both white and black soldiers but was much more difficult for Kentucky's African American veterans. Officers and surgeons in the Kentucky Colored units were white and did not reside locally. Their whereabouts were usually unknown, and obtaining verification from them of injury or disease was virtually impossible.

Illiteracy compounded the complicated process even more. The Allen County applicants had to depend on someone else to read the application forms, interpret what information was required, fill them out, and send them in. Many applicants relied on a Justice of the Peace, Court House clerk, or a Notary Public to complete the forms. Some paid fees to an attorney or agent for the work. In all cases, the illiterate applicant could not verify and assure that what was written was correct.

There were three types of applications from Allen County-born African American veterans. The most frequent applications were from veterans who claimed a disability. Those submissions were for what was called invalid pensions. Widows' pension claims were a second type. The third type was for orphan children of deceased veterans.

Prejudicial acts were not evident in the application and certification processes with one exception. A Pension Bureau Form "Index to Special Examiner's Report" that was required when the validity of an application was questioned, and a board of examiners appointed to adjudicate. That form listed the names of each witness in the questioned claim request and assessed their "Reputation" (Figure 47).

Figure 47

Examiner's Report regarding claim number 793377.

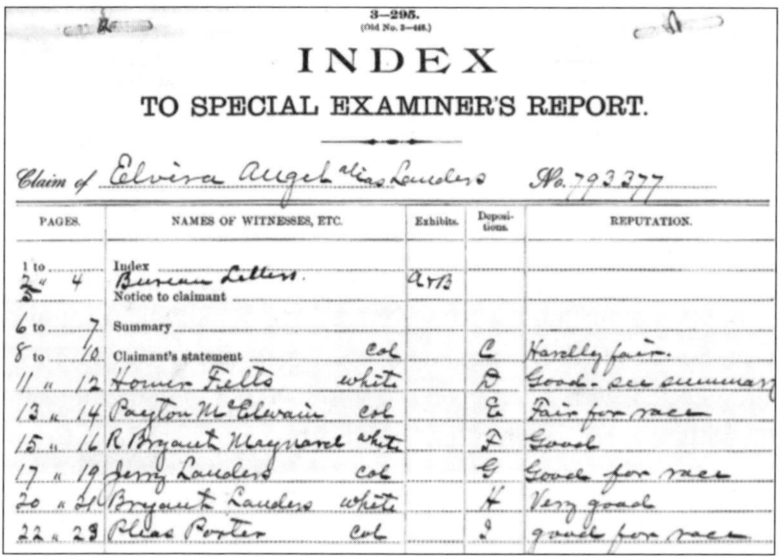

3—295.
(Old No. 3—448.)

INDEX

TO SPECIAL EXAMINER'S REPORT.

Claim of Elvira Angel alias Lauders No. 793377

PAGES.	NAMES OF WITNESSES, ETC.		Exhibits.	Depositions.	REPUTATION.
1 to	Index				
2 " 4	Bureau Letters.		A & B		
3	Notice to claimant				
6 to 7	Summary				
8 to 10	Claimant's statement	Col		C	Hardly fair.
11 " 12	Homer Felts	white		D	Good - see summary
13 " 14	Payton McElwain	Col		E	Fair for race
15 " 16	R Bryant Maynard	white		F	Good
17 " 19	Jerry Lauders	Col		G	Good for race
20 " 21	Bryant Lauders	white		H	Very good
22 " 23	Pleas Porter	Col		I	good for race

Note that all white witnesses were said to have unqualified good or very good reputations. All but one of witnesses listed as colored have qualified reputations like "good for race." The inference was that a good reputation of a white witness was better than a good reputation for a colored witness. In this case, the examiners in 1903 determined that Elvira's husband was not Allen County's Jerry Landers but someone else.

Invalid Pensions

Research revealed seven pension applications submitted by Allen County's African American veterans of the Union Army during the Civil War. There are probably others, but finding the records proved to be difficult. According to the law, only veterans who were invalids because of service related injuries or disease could apply. Typically, the pension process was long. Often, the applicant had to travel to face an examination by a surgical board that determined their disability. That was difficult, particularly for impoverished African American veterans.

Some of the pension application and certification files were examined and are described in the following paragraphs to illustrate some of those difficulties.

Sergeant Isham T. Stark

The earliest application was from Sergeant Isham T. Stark. He had been a slave of James and Granderson Stark of Allen County when he enlisted. He was about 25 years old when he was assigned as a Private to the 6th U.S. Colored Cavalry in 1864. He was promoted to First Duty Sergeant[6] on 1 November 1864.

Sergeant Stark was in Company B of the 6th U.S. Colored Cavalry that augmented the 5th U.S. Colored Cavalry in the dismounted attack on the Kings Salt Works at Saltville, Virginia on 1 October 1864. They charged and occupied the fortification. That charge ended with hand-to-hand combat. A Confederate soldier struck him on the left hip with the butt of a rifle. Unable to walk, he crawled into some bushes and was left on the battlefield when his unit was ordered to withdraw about two hours later.[7] That night

[6] The First Duty Sergeant was the second highest enlisted rank, only outranked by the First Sergeant

[7] Affidavit by George Anthony, 22 Nov 1888. National Archives pension files

after the battle, his troops went looking for him, found him crawling away from the fortification still unable to walk.[8] It was fortuitous that they found him because all the surviving wounded left on the battlefield were executed where they lay the next morning, the infamous Saltville Massacre.

His hip was so badly swollen that he could not mount his horse and had to be assisted into the saddle.[9] He rode in that condition with his unit back to Camp Nelson near Nicholasville, Kentucky. He said he was entirely incapacitated for five months from the injury.[10] Other soldiers reported the period of recovery was two or three months.[11,12]

He was mustered out of the army on 15 April 1866 in De Valls Bluff, Arkansas. He applied for a pension on 19 August 1879. The injury continued to make him unable to do much work after discharge.[13]

Because his company from the 6th U.S. Colored Cavalry was attached to the 5th U.S. Colored Cavalry for the battle, he knew none of their officers by name. The surgeon who treated him was Dr. Ryley (sic) but he was dead by the time of the pension application was filed.[14] The result was that Sgt Stark had difficulty in completing the pension papers to the satisfaction of the Pension Bureau. Ultimately, he did receive a pension.

Jerry Landers

The pension file #411690 for Jerry Landers was opened when he submitted a claim for disability on 21 October 1880 based on rheumatism and a big toe that was deformed by frostbite. Eleven documents were added to the file over the next five years. To claim a service caused disability, it was necessary to establish that the condition did not exist prior to enlistment. Concerning his prior health conditions, he stated that he could not send a statement

[8] Affadavit by Richard Cross, 11 March 1886. National Archives pension files
[9] Affadavit by Benjamin F. Ray, 16 January 1888. National Archives pension files
[10] Affidavit by Isham Stark, 19 August 1879. National Archives pension files
[11] Affidavit by Ferdinan Nichols, 23 September 1902, National Archives pension files
[12] Affidavit by Jerry Landers and Pleasant White, 26 January 1888. National Archives pension files
[13] Affidavit by Isham Stark, 2 December 1881. National Archives pension files
[14] Affidavit by Isham Stark, 17 February 1883. National Archives pension files

from a physician because he "never had any use for one." He also said that he had not seen a doctor since his discharge either. The only medical treatment he ever received was from Patsy Landers his "mistress" [owner] who once gave him some salve she had made. In 1885, a review board recommended a 2/18th pension. That amounted to $2 per month.[15]

He was living at Meador in Allen County in 1890. By then his wife, Becky, had died but their three children were alive: William B. born 7 January 1857, Alford born 22 December 1859, and Cynthy born 31 July 1862.[16]

It was common for illiterate veterans to hire attorneys to assist in the application process. In 1893, he employed P. B. Hawkins of Bowling Green for $10 to prepare a request to increase his pension amount. He also paid attorney E. Scott Brown of Scottsville to assist. That cost another $10. In December 1901, he employed attorney Joseph Hunter of Washington, D.C. In that case, the Bureau had disputed that he was 75 years old.[17]

In 1901, his pension was increased to $10 per month under certificate #321652.[18] The Pension Bureau in 1901 referred to him as Jeremiah Landers, the only such use of that name in his files. It appears that the first name was an assumption rather than a fact.

On 7 November 1901, a reviewer at the Bureau of Pensions wrote this note[19]:

> *Claimant is a colored man, raised in the south, enlisted in Louisville Ky*[20] *in 1864 and it is safe to assume that he does not know his age with accuracy, nor can he furnish testimony as to date of his birth. If the records should show that he would now be seventy-five years of age, we could hardly accept it as conclusive, in view of his numerous statements made during the pendency of his claims. It is my opinion that we must increase his pension as indicated by the medical referee, until such time as his disability from senility has increased so as to entitle him to the maximum rate, irrespective of his exact age.*

[15] Affidavit by Jerry Landers, 27 January 1883, National Archives pension files
[16] Affidavit by Jerry Landers, 27 Jun 1890, National Archives pension files
[17] Affidavit by Jerry Landers, 11 November 1901, National Archives pension files
[18] Approval of Claim of Jerry Landers, 10 October 1901, National Archives pension files
[19] Pension Bureau note re Jerry Landers, 7 November 1901
[20] This is incorrect, he actually enlisted in Bowling Green, Kentucky

By 1907, his pension was increased to $12 per month. Finally in 1908, he was accepted as being over 75 and his pension was raised to $20 per month. But that only occurred after he had been required to submit a notarized statement, "I can not write my name" to explain why he had not signed a submitted statement.[21]

Landers' pension file is voluminous, 37 documents in all. The accumulation of so many papers was caused by his persistence over a period of twenty-eight years. Nonetheless, the file is an indication of both the care with which the Pension Bureau evaluated applications, and the unintended hardship that was imposed on impoverished and illiterate veterans.

Anthony Hatfield

Anthony Hatfield was living in Chattanooga, Tennessee on 29 December 1881 when he applied for an invalid pension from service related injuries during July and August 1864. He broke two ribs from a fall while he was building a fortification in Chattanooga, Tennessee. His feet were injured during a twenty mile march over the crossties of a railroad track to Tullahoma, Tennessee. He did not know the whereabouts of Dr. F. W. Arms who treated him but thought he was in Minnesota. In 1887, his application was rejected because he had not submitted necessary supporting documentation from the physicians.

Levi Bryson

Levi Bryson was an Allen County-born slave who enlisted at Chicago, Illinois. He was a cook with the 29th U.S. Colored Infantry.[22] He was awarded a pension of $16 per month because of heart disease and rheumatism. In the spring of 1864, he had been injured while lifting logs to construct a fortification at Petersburg, Virginia. In 1880, he had a double curvature of the spine, was bent to a stooping posture, had a hernia, and had severe heart disease. The examining physician in Quincy, Illinois stated that his disability was the equivalent of the loss of a hand and a foot.[23]

---

[21] Notarized Affidavit by Jerry Landers, 4 January 1908, National Archives pension files

[22] Pension Application # 395383 filed by Levi Bryson 30 June 1880, National Archives pension files

[23] Physician's Evaluation of Levi Bryson, 5 February 1880, National Archives pension files

Other Invalid Pensioners

Nelson Brown applied for an invalid pension in 1880, Pleasant White in 1882, Lewis Heater and Daniel Whitney in 1889, and George Brown in 1890. Pension files exist for them but circumstances precluded access to them during research for this study. Table 49 at the end of this chapter contains the application and certification numbers.

Widow Pensions

Widows had to provide proof of either marriage or a comparable binding ceremony such as jumping over a stick.[24] Verifying dates was difficult for those who were married before the end of the Civil War.

Frances Porter had married Isham T. Stark in 1869 with Rev. Gilbert Graham performing the ceremony. She presented proof of that marriage when she applied for a widow's pension after his death on 3 August 1909. She was then 64 years and living near Hardcastle in Warren County.[25] Her pension of $12 per month was awarded on 9 December 1909 and retroactively commenced on 13 August 1909.

The earliest pension application filed by a widow was by Orphy Sears' widow after his death in 1890. The widow of Lewis Heater applied after he died and Daniel Whitney's widow applied on 28 October 1921. Table 49 presents the application numbers and certificate numbers for them.

Minor Pensions

Orphans of deceased veterans who were under sixteen years old were eligible for support by a pension. Only one record of application for a Minor's benefits was found. He was Theodore Godley who was Chiropodist in Brazil, Indiana by then. Theodore D. and Solomon H. Godley submitted a claim on 30 April 1913. They were the only children of Isaac Godley who had served in the 6th U.S. Colored Cavalry. Their father died 15 August 1875 when

---

[24] Regosin, Elizabeth and Donald R. Shafer, 2008. *Voices of emancipation: unstanding slavery, the Civil War, and Reconstruction through the U.S. Pension files. 2008.* University Press of New York, New York

[25] Declaration for Widow's Pension by Frances Stark, 6 August 1909, National Archives pension files

they were four and five years old. They initiated a claim for the support they should have gotten, in their view, from their father's death until they were sixteen.[26] The Bureau of Pensions asked for evidence that their father's death was the result of a condition that was present before he was discharged.[27] They responded that the doctors who could have provided that information were long ago dead.[28] The claim was rejected because they had failed to furnish evidence that his death was the result of his military service.[29]

Table 49 presents the application numbers and certificate numbers for African American veterans from Allen County.

Table 49

Allen County-Born African American Civil War Pensions

Soldier					Invalid		Widow		Children
Name	Approx Birth Year	Colored Regiment	Discharge Date	Discharged At	App. #	Cert. #	App. #	Cert. #	App. #
Anthony, James	1828	Co D, 14th Infantry	26 Jul 1866	Nashville TN					
Brown, George	1837	Co A, 27th Infantry	9 Sep 1865	New Bern NC	833366				
Brown, Nelson	1837	Co L, 6th Heavy Artillery	13 May 1866	Natchez MS					
Bryson, Levi	1828	Co B, 29th Infantry	5 Nov 1865	Brownsville TX	395383	293270			
Flippin, Adam	1837	Co K, 14th Infantry	16 Jan 1864	Gallatin TN					
Follas, Bird	1845	Co F, 6th Cavalry	15 Apr 1866	De Valls AR					
Godley, Isaac	1848	Co B, 6th Cavalry	15 Apr 1866	De Valls AR					1007097
Hatfield, Anthony	1820	Co C, 14th Infantry	26 Mar 1866	Nashville TN	436268				
Heater, Lewis	1833	Co C, 13th Heavy Artillery	18 Nov 1865	Louisville KY	713466	552054	768541	581308	
Hurston, Robert	1847	Co B, 13th Heavy Artillery	18 Nov 1865	Louisville KY					
Landers, Jerry	1828	Co B, 6th Cavalry	15 Apr 1866	De Valls AR	411690	321652			

[26] Godley, Theodore D., 1913. *Affidavit filed from Clay County, Indiana, 30 April 1913*
[27] Bureau of Pensions, 1913. *Letter to Theodore D. Godley, dated 8 August 1913*
[28] Godley, Theodore D. 1913. *Affidavit filed from Clay County Indiana, 28 August 1913*
[29] Bureau of Pensions, 1913. Letter to Theodore D. Godley, dated 4 September 1913

Soldier					Invalid		Widow		Children
Name	Approx Birth Year	Colored Regiment	Discharge Date	Discharged At	App. #	Cert. #	App. #	Cert. #	App. #
Page, George	1824	Co E, 13th Heavy Artillery	18 Nov 1865	Louisville KY					
Paris, John	1842	Co A, 14th Infantry	18 Jul 1864	Gallatin TN					
Parish, Richard	1824	Co D, 15th Infantry	3 Jun 1865	Nashville TN					
Porter, Thomas	1846	Co B, 6th Cavalry	1 Sep 1864	Bowling Green KY					
Pulliam, Farrew	1829	Co A, 12th Heavy Artillery	24 Apr 1866	Louisville KY					
Pulliam, Sam	1838	Co I, 6th Cavalry	19 Oct 1865	Lexington KY					
Sears, Isham	1841	Co F, 6th Cavalry	15 Apr1866	De Valls AR					
Sears, Orphy	1845	Co F, 6th Cavalry	15 Apr 1866	De Valls AR	422140	386351			
Stark, Isham T.	1846	Co B, 6th Cavalry	15 Apr 1866	De Valls AR	304714	664760	925429	693489	
Stoval, Cuba	1847	13th Heavy Artillery	18 Nov 1865	Louisville KY					
Walker, Robert H.	1848	Co C, 14th Infantry	2 May 1865	Nashville TN					
White, Pleasant	1849	Co B, 6th Cavalry	15 Apr 1866	De Valls AR	452303	717052			
Whitney, Daniel	1850	Co A, 12th Heavy Artillery	24 Apr 1866	Louisville KY	402528	673827	1180684	424086	

Chapter 22

Summary

Slavery in Allen County existed for forty-five years after the County was created and for a decade or so before. During that time, there was a steady increase in the total population and an increase in both the number of slaves and the number of slave owners (Table 50).

Table 50

Numbers of slaves and slave owners in Allen County 1820-1860

	1820	**1830**	**1840**	**1850**	**1860**
Enslaved African Americans	697	864	936	1312	1514
Slave Owners	175	199	238	278	282
Average Slaves per Owner	4.0	4.3	3.9	4.7	5.4

The increases in the number of slaves and owners as shown in Table 50 were not as consistent as they at first appear. Perhaps a better way of looking at these data is to examine the percent of increase from one decade to the next. In 1830 for example, there had been a 24 percent increase in the number of slaves compared to the number in 1820. There was a prohibition against importing slaves into Kentucky that caused the decadal increase in 1840 to drop to 8 percent over the 1830 total. It still increased, just not as rapidly. The lifting of that prohibition allowed the decadal increase in 1850 to jump to 39 percent before falling again to 15 percent in 1860 (Table 51). The latter slower increase may reflect the economic uncertainty that existed just prior to the Civil War.

Table 51

Decadal increases of slaves and slave owners in Allen County

	1820	1830	1840	1850	1860
Enslaved African Americans		24%	8%	39%	15%
Slave Owners		14%	20%	30%	3%
Average Slaves per Owner	4.0	4.3	3.9	4.7	5.4

The number of slave owners increased in each decade (Table 50), but 1860 had a dramatically smaller percentage of increase (Table 51) than the others. Perhaps the swirling winds of war were making potential owners leery of such investment of capital. Not everyone was leery because the average number of slaves per owner had reached the highest number of 5.4 slaves per slave owner.

There were some slaves who were emancipated or manumitted during each decade. Some of Freedmen remained in Allen County but many did not, choosing instead to migrate where they would not be subject to restrictions placed on them by Kentucky law. Their numbers had decreased between 1850 and 1960 (Table 52).

Table 52

Number of Freedmen in Allen County by decade

1820	Unknown
1830	7
1840	19
1850	44
1860	36

The numbers of Freedmen in Allen County were never very high ranging from under one percent of all African Americans in 1820 to a high of three percent in 1850. There was a significant drop to two percent in 1860. The percentages for all of Kentucky were significantly smaller (Table 53).[1]

[1] Cramer, Clayton E. 1997. *Black demographic data, 1790-1860: a sourcebook.* Westport, Conn: Greenwood Press.

Table 53

Percent of African American Freedmen in Kentucky by decade

	1790	1800	1810	1820	1830	1840	1850	1860
Kentucky	0.2%	0.3%	0.4%	0.5%	0.7%	0.9%	1.0%	0.9%

Slavery came to an end amid great turmoil, rancor, and hatred. Across Kentucky, many former slaves became refugees when they fled to the larger cities and to army encampments seeking assistance. The 1870 census recorded the flight of about 14,000 former slaves out of Kentucky during the prior decade. Others, who had been sold away from their family, came back seeking to find them and reunite with them. The soldiers who survived the war came back. Jerry Landers, who had fought with the 6th Kentucky Colored Cavalry, came home to Allen County to find that his wife and three children had been sold to Georgia. Fortunately, the circumstances prevented them from being delivered and he was reunited with them.[2]

The most immediate problem for freed slaves was food. The Methodist Episcopal churches operated missions to provide food, as did other charitable organizations. At the same time, former slaves were randomly beaten and whipped. In particular, African American veterans of the Union Army were targets of such action. It has been said that the post Civil War period was the most lawless in Kentucky's history.

Children, orphaned by slavery, were destitute. Medical care for all was difficult to acquire. The future was uncertain. African American families, who had endured the hopelessness of slavery, the indignities of poverty, and the unbearable hardships of the transition to freedom, somehow found the strength and faith to preserve their families. By 1880 for example, 75.8 percent of African American households in Louisville had both parents present, a remarkable achievement.[3]

[2] Landers, Douglas, 1991. *In the blood: History of the Starks-Landers-Stark families, Hickory Grove and Greenville.* Manuscript held by the Allen County Historical Society, Scottsville, Kentucky

[3] Howard, Victor B., 1983. *Black liberation in Kentucky: emancipation and freedom, 1862-1884.* Lexington, KY: University Press of Kentucky.

Conclusion

Allen Countians who have traced their roots back before 1866 in Allen County are likely to have ancestors who were either slaves or slave owners. Considering 25 years as a generation, six generations have passed since 1860. Parents who were born between 1960 and 1985 probably would have had 32 great-great-great grandparents living in 1860. Of those sixteen households in Allen County, it is probable that four would have owned slaves. The odds are that all of us have been touched by slavery in some direct way and for certain in many indirect ways.

How is it possible that our ancestors participated in slavery as either a slave or as an owner? We cannot understand it and we may become embarrassed to learn details about it. Everyone knows the famous quote from Patrick Henry that stirs our heart when we repeat it, "Give me liberty or give me death."

Patrick Henry was a slave owner when he said it and he died years later without having set them free. Even he had difficulty understanding why there were such inconsistencies between his words and his deeds.

> *...Would any one believe that I am master of slaves of my own purchase? I am drawn along by the general inconvenience of living without them. I will not, I cannot, justify it; however culpable my conduct, I will so far pay my 'devoir' to virtue as to my own the excellence and rectitude of her precepts, and to lament my want of conformity to them. I believe a time will come when an opportunity will be offered to abolish this lamentable evil: everything we can do is to improve it, if it happens in our day, if not, let us transmit to our descendents, together with our slaves, a pity for their unhappy lot, and an abhorrence of slavery. We owe it to the purity of our religion, to show that it is at variance with that law which warrants slavery.*[4]

There can be little doubt that other slave owners wrestled with the dichotomy that Patrick Henry described. For example, there were slave owners in Allen County who served in the Union Army.

[4] Tyler, Moses C., 1887. *Patrick Henry,* Houghton, Mifflin & Co., Boston

During the debates regarding the language to be inserted into the U.S. Constitution, Patrick Henry again voiced his uncomfortable beliefs.

> *Slavery is detested: we feel its fatal effects, —we deplore it with all the pity of humanity.... As we ought with gratitude to admire that decree of Heaven which has numbered us among the free, we ought to lament and deplore the necessity of holding our fellow-man in bondage. But is it practicable, by any human means, to liberate them without producing the most dreadful and ruinous consequences?*[5]

Those terrible but inevitable consequences came anyway more that seventy-five years later, with over 110,000 Americans killed or mortally wounded in defense of the United States in a war that ended slavery once and for all. Over 36,000 African American soldiers died on active duty (Figure 48).

Figure 48

National Cemetery at Chattanooga, Tennessee

[5] Tyler, Moses C., 1887. *Patrick Henry,* Houghton, Mifflin & Co., Boston

For the African American soldiers who survived the war, the discharge from the army was their real first taste of freedom. Colonel James C. Brisbin, commander of the 6th U.S. Colored Cavalry, advised his troops before they were discharged, "Be civil, polite, industrious, frugal, just, and religious, and you will prosper."[6]

The men who came home had experienced what men can do though the cooperative efforts of a group dedicated to a common goal. In Washington, D.C., an African American Civil War Memorial (Figure 49) displays each name of the over 185,000 African Americans who served in the military to preserve the Union and eradicate slavery.[7] Names of the white officers are included as well. They served at risk too because the Confederates were directed to treat them as outlaws, not as soldiers, if they were captured.[8] Among those African American names are 17 Medal of Honor winners.[9]

Figure 49

Front view of the African American Civil War Memorial, Washington D. C.

Ed Hamilton of Louisville sculpted the memorial. He not only honored those who served but also those they left behind. That poignant part of the

[6] Shaffer, Donald R., 2004. *After the glory: the struggles of black Civil War veterans.* University Press of Kansas, Lawrence, KS, page 30

[7] Black, Wallace B., 1998. *Slaves to Soldiers.* Franklin Watts, New York, Groler Publishers, Danbury CT

[8] *Confederate War Department General Order 60*, dated 21 August 1862.

[9] Mays, Joe H., 1884. *Black Americans and their contributions toward Union victory in the American Civil War, 1861-1865.* University Press of America, Lanham, MD

memorial was fashioned on the other side of the sculpture. That view is in Figure 50.

Figure 50

Reverse side of the African American Civil War Memorial in Washington, D.C

There were 23,703 African American who enlisted from Kentucky, 38 of whom born in Allen County. They said goodbye to their families- as depicted in this sculpture- and left, just as all soldiers do, for an uncertain future.

On one of the name panels at this memorial are the names of the members of 6th U.S. Colored Cavalry. Among them were Sam Pulliam the draftee, James and John Sears, who were killed in combat, and Orphy Sears (Figure 51).

Figure 51

African American Civil War Memorial: some soldiers from the 6th U.S. Colored Cavalry

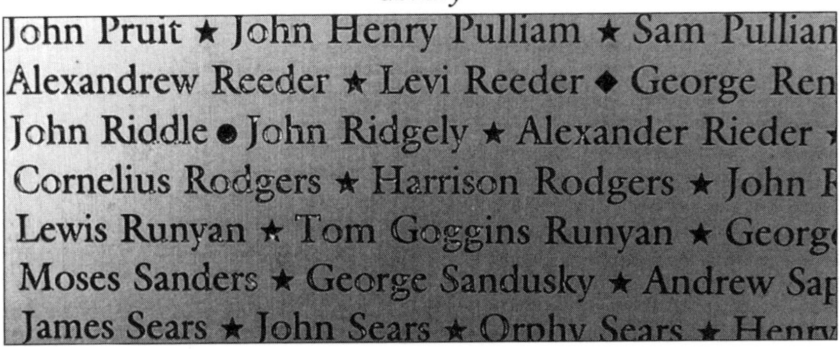

Grand Army of the Republic

The Grand Army of the Republic (GAR) was organized in 1866 as an organization, like that of the American Legion or Veterans of Foreign Wars, for those who served in the Union Army during the Civil War. For most white veterans, the Union had been saved and the war was over. For black veterans, the war was one of liberation and that struggle for equality had not ended.[10]

Gradually, during the years following the Civil War, white Union soldiers became forgiving of their Rebel counterparts for their role in the war. It was forgiveness to a degree that made Blue-Gray reunions not only acceptable but also an admirable display of compassion. To white soldiers, the reunions were a time when Union and Confederate veterans met to share their experiences as soldiers. African American veterans were by then encountering a disheartening surge in new Jim Crow laws that sought to subvert the precious freedoms they had fought for. They may have been less inclined to forgive.

A photograph taken of the GAR reunion held on 16 October 1909 in Scottsville shows only old white men. The list of Civil War veterans published in the paper listed only white soldiers. For whatever reason, the African Americans veterans were not there.[11]

---

[10] Shaffer, Donald R., 2004. *The struggles of black Civil War veterans.* University Press of Kansas, Lawrence KS

[11] Photograph is held by the Allen County Historical Society

Bibliography

Addington, Robert M. (1990). *History of Scott County, Virginia*. Salem, Mass: Higginson Book Co.

Ainsworth, Fred C., John S. Moodey, and Calvin D. Cowles.(1880*). The War of the Rebellion: a compilation of the official records of the Union and Confederate armies*. Washington, D.C.: Government. Printing Office.

Allen County Court Deed Book H, 1845-1850, page 426, provided by Harris Overholt

Allen County Court Order Book, 1858-1860. Allen County Court Clerk, Scottsville Kentucky.

Allen County Court Order Book, December 1826. Allen County Court Clerk, Scottsville Kentucky.

Allen County Court Order Book, January 1851. Allen County Court Clerk, Scottsville Kentucky.

Allen County Court Order Book, May 1850. Allen County Court Clerk, Scottsville Kentucky.

Allen County Court Order Book, October 1859. Allen County Court Clerk, Scottsville Kentucky.

Allen County Court Orders, January 1828. Allen County Court Clerk, Scottsville Kentucky.

Allen County Historical Society (1985). *A pictorial history of Allen County, Kentucky*. Allen County Historical Society, Scottsville, Kentucky.

American interregional migration, vital statistics, and manumissions, 1800-1860. Cambridge: Cambridge.

Ancestry.com. *Kentucky Death Records, 1852-1953* [database on-line]. Provo, UT, USA: Ancestry.com Operations Inc, 2007. URL: http://search.ancestry.com/search/DB.aspx?dbid=1222.

-- *U.S. Federal Census Mortality Schedules, 1850-1880* [database on-line]. Provo, UT, USA: The Generations Network, Inc., 2008.

Anthony, George, (1888). *Affidavit 22 Nov 1888.* Civil War pension files. National Archives and Records Administration, Washington, D.C.

Beecher, Henry Ward (1888). *Patriotic addresses in America and England, 1850-1885, on slavery, the Civil War, and the development of civil liberty in the United States.* New York: Fords, Howard & Hulbert.

Berkin, Carol, and Eric Foner (1999). *First generations: women in colonial America.* New York, NY: Hill and Wang.

Berlin, Ira and Joseph P. Reidy, and Leslie S. Rowland (1998). *Freedom's Soldiers: The Black Military Experience in the Civil War.* Edited by Cambridge, England: Cambridge University Press.

Black, Wallace B. (1998). *Slaves to soldiers: African American fighting men in the Civil War.* New York: Franklin Watts, New York, , Danbury CT.: Groler Publishers.

Boles, John B. (1995). *Religion in antebellum Kentucky.* Lexington, Kentucky: University Press of Kentucky.

Brown, Ohio History Central, Retrieved December 5, 2008, http://www.ohiohistorycentral.org/entry.php?rec=3375.

Bryson, Levi (1880). *Pension Application # 395383 filed 30 June 1880.* Civil War pension files, National Archives and Records Administration, Washington, D.C.

-- (1880). *Physician's Evaluation of Levi Bryson, 5 February 1880.* Civil War pension files, National Archives and Records Administration, Washington, D.C.

Bureau of Pensions (1913). *Letter to Theodore D. Godley, dated 4 September 1913.* National Archives pension files.

-- 1913. *Letter to Theodore D. Godley, dated 8 August 1913.* Civil War pension files, National Archives and Records Administration, Washington, D.C.

Columbia University (1891). *Studies in history, economics, and public law.* New York: Columbia University Press.

Confederate War Department (1862). *General Order 60*, dated 21 August 1862.

Cramer, Clayton E. (1997). *Black demographic data, 1790-1860: a sourcebook.* Westport, Conn: Greenwood Press.

Cross, Richard (1886). *Affidavit on 11 March 1886.* National Archives pension files.

Cunningham, Noble E. (2000). *Jefferson vs. Hamilton: confrontations that shaped a nation.* The Bedford series in history and culture. Boston: Bedford/St. Martin's.

Farman, Henry W. and Clive Day (2000). *Chapters in the history of social legislation in the United States to 1860.* Unoin, NJ: Lawbook Exchange.

Finkelman, Paul (1997). *Dred Scott v. Sandford: a brief history with documents.* The Bedford series in history and culture. Boston: Bedford Books.

Ford, Carin (2004). *African American soldiers in the Civil War.* Berkeley Heights, NJ: Enlow Publishing.

Frankel, Noralee (1999). *Freedom's women: Black women and families in Civil War era Mississippi. Blacks in the diaspora.* Bloomington: Indiana University Press.

Frazier, Harriet C. (2004). *Runaway and freed Missouri slaves and those who helped them, 1763-1865.* Jefferson, NC: McFarland & Co.

Gardner, Jeanetta S. (1999). *Allen County tax records.* Jeanetta Steenbergen Gardner, Collierville, Tennessee.

Gist, Christopher, and William M. Darlington (1893). *Christopher Gist's journals: with historical, geographical and ethnological notes and biographies of his contemporaries by William M. Darlington.* Pittsburg: J.R. Weldin & Co.

Godley, Theodore D. (1913). *Affidavit filed from Clay County Indiana, 28 August 1913.* Civil War pension files, National Archives and Records Administration, Washington, D.C..

-- 1913. *Affidavit filed from Clay County, Indiana, 30 April 1913.* Civil War pension files, National Archives and Records Administration, Washington, D.C.

Hadden, Sally E. (2001). *Slave Patrols: Law and Violence in Virginia and the Carolinas.* Cambridge, MA: Harvard University Press.

Hargrove, Hondon B. (1988). *Black Union soldier in the Civil War.* Jefferson, NC: McFarland.

Harrison, Lowell H. (1978). *The antislavery movement in Kentucky.* Lexington, KY: University Press of Kentucky.

Harrison, Lowell Hayes, and James C. Klotter (1997). *A new history of Kentucky.* Lexington, KY: University Press of Kentucky.

Horton, Louise (1975). *In the hills of the pennyroyal: a history of Allen County, Kentucky, from 1815 to 1880.* Austin, Texas: White Cross Press.

House Report, 46th Congress, 3rd Session, NO. 387, p 26.

Howard, Victor B. (1983). *Black liberation in Kentucky: emancipation and freedom, 1862-1884.* Lexington, KY: University Press of Kentucky.

Hunter, Tera W. (1997). *To 'joy my freedom: Southern Black women's lives and labors after the Civil War.* Cambridge, Mass: Harvard University Press.

Hurt, Billie (2009). *Verbal communication*, Scottsville, KY, 13 August 2009.

Jordan, Ervin L. (1995). *Black Confederates and Afro-Yankees in Civil War Virginia.* Charlottesville, VA: University Press of Virginia.

Jordan, Terry G. (1994). *Texas log buildings: a folk architecture.* Austin: University of Texas Press.

Kebler, John E. (1992). *The Kentucky encyclopedia.* Lexington, KY: The University Press of Kentucky.

Kennedy, Joseph C. G. (1864). *The United States in 1860 compiled from the original returns of the eighth census.* Washington, D.C., D.C.: Government Printing Office.

Kentucky General Assembly, *Resolution number 49*, approved 22 February 1864.

Kentucky Historical Marker Number 1990, located at 2nd and Main Streets in Louisville, KY.

Kentucky Historical Marker Number 31, located in South Portsmouth, Kentucky on KY highway 10 in Greenup County Kentucky.

State of Kentucky. *Kentucky Birth, Marriage and Death Records – Microfilm (1852-1910).* Microfilm rolls #994027-994058. Kentucky Department for Libraries and Archives, Frankfort, Kentucky.

Kleber, John E. (1992). *The Kentucky encyclopedia.* Lexington, KY: University Press of Kentucky.

Landers, Douglas (1991). *In the blood: history of the Starks-Landers-Stark families, Hickory Grove and Greenville.* Manuscript held by the Allen County Historical Society, Scottsville, Kentucky.

Landers, Jerry and Pleasant White (1888). *Affidavits on 26 January 1888.* Civil War pension files, National Archives and Records Administration, Washington, D.C.

Landers, Jerry (1883). *Affidavit on 27 January 1883.* Civil War pension files, National Archives and Records Administration, Washington, D.C.

-- (1890). *Affidavit on 27 Jun 1890.* Civil War pension files, National Archives and Records Administration, Washington, D.C.

-- (1901). *Affidavit on 11 November 1901*, Civil War pension files, National Archives and Records Administration, Washington, D.C.

-- (1901). Approval of Claim 10 October 1901, Civil War pension files, National Archives and Records Administration, Washington, D.C.

-- (1901). *Pension Bureau Note re Jerry Landers, 7 November 1901.* Civil War pension files, National Archives and Records Administration, Washington, D.C.

-- (1908). *Notarized Affidavit on 4 January 1908.* Civil War pension files, National Archives and Records Administration, Washington, D.C.

Larkin, Jack (2007) *The reshaping of everyday life, 1790 - 1840.* The everyday life in America series. New York, NY: Harper Perennial.

Lucas, Marion B. (1992). *A history of blacks in Kentucky from slavery to segregation 1760-1891.* Kentucky Historical Society, Frankfort, Kentucky.

-- (2003). *A history of Blacks in Kentucky: from slavery to segregation, 1760-1891.* Frankfort, KY: Kentucky Historical Society.

Mays, Joe H. (1884). *Black Americans and their contributions toward Union victory in the American Civil War, 1861-1865.* Lanham, MD: University Press of America.

Mays, Thomas D. (1995). *The Saltville Massacre.* Fort Worth, TX: Ryan Place.

McClelland, Peter D., and Richard J. Zeckhauser (2002). *Demographic dimensions of the New Republi.* American Interregional Migration, Vital Statistics, and Manumissions, 1800-1860, with Peter D. McClelland, New York: Cambridge University Press.

McDougall, Walter A. (2004). *Freedom just around the corner: a new American history, 1585-1828.* New York: Harper Collins Publishers.

McDougle, Ivan E. (1917). *Slavery in Kentucky.* The Journal of Negro History, The Association for the study of negro life and history, Lancaster, PA.

Methodist Episcopal Church (1804). *The doctrines and discipline of the Methodist Episcopal Church.* 13th Edition, W. C. Robinson, Printer.

Miller, Randall M., and John David Smith (1997). *Dictionary of Afro-American slavery.* Westport, CT: Praeger.

Minutes of the Trustees for the City of Bowling Green, 7 June 1825.

Nichols, Ferdinand (1902). *Affidavit 23 September 1902*, National Archives pension files.

Noble, J. K. (1867). *Letter dated 11 February 1867* from the State Superintendent of Freedmen's Schools, Bureau of Refugees, Freedmen, and Abandoned Lands to the General Inspector of Schools, J. W. Alvord, in Washington, D.C.

-- (1867). *Letter dated 16 April 1867* from the State Superintendent of Freedmen's Schools, Bureau of Refugees, Freedmen, and Abandoned Lands to the General Inspector of Schools, J. W. Alvord, in Washington D. C.

-- (1868). *Letter dated 10 November1868* from the State Superintendent of Freedmen's Schools, Bureau of Refugees, Freedmen, and Abandoned Lands to the General Inspector of Schools, J. W. Alvord, in Washington D. C.

-- (1868). *Letter dated December 1868* from the State Superintendent of Freedmen's Schools, Bureau of Refugees, Freedmen, and Abandoned Lands to the General Inspector of Schools, J. W. Alvord, in Washington D. C.

Oliver, John W. (1915). *History of the Civil War military pensions, 1861-1885.* Bulletin of the University of Wisconsin, NO. 844, History Series, Vol. 4 No. 1, 1-120.

Peirce, Paul Skeels (1904). *The Freedmen's bureau; a chapter in the history of reconstruction*. Iowa City, IA: The University.

Rabold, Mary M. and Elizabeth M. Price (1972). *Allen County Kentucky wills and settlements 1815-1902.* Published by authors.

Ransom, Roger L. (1989). *Conflict and compromise: the political economy of slavery, emancipation, and the American Civil War*. Cambridge [England]: Cambridge University Press.

Ray, Benjamin F. (*1888). Affidavit 16 January 1888*. National Archives pension files.

Regosin, Elizabeth A. and Donald R. Shafer (2008). *Voices of emancipation: Understanding slavery, the Civil War, and Reconstruction through the U.S. Pension Files.* New York: New York University Press.

Regosin, Elizabeth Ann (2002). *Freedom's promise: ex-slave families and citizenship in the Age of Emancipation*. Charlottesville: University Press.

Ringer, Benjamin B. (1983). *"We the people" and others: duality and America's treatment of its racial minorities*. New York: Tavistock.

Sears, Richard D. (2002). *Camp Nelson, Kentucky: a Civil War history.* Lexington, KY: University Press of Kentucky.

Shaffer, Donald R. (2004). *After the glory: the struggles of black Civil War veterans.* Lawrence, KS: University Press of Kansas.

Sheehan-Dean, Aaron (2007). *Struggle for a vast future.* Oxford, United Kingdom: Osprey Publishing.

Smith, Goldwin (1893). *The United States: an outline of political history, 1492-1871*. New York: McMillan and Company.

Smith, John David (2002). *Black soldiers in blue: African American troops in the Civil War era*. Chapel Hill: University of North Carolina Press

Speed, Thomas (1907). *The Union cause in Kentucky 1860-1865.* G. P. Putnam's Sons, New York.

Stark, Frances (1909). *Declaration for Widow's Pension by 6 August 1909.* National Archives pension files.

Stark, Isham (1879). *Affidavit on 19 August 1879*. National Archives pension files.

-- (1881). *Affidavit on 2 December 1881*. National Archives pension files.

-- (1883). *Affidavit 17 February 1883*. National Archives pension files.

Statistical View of the United States, 65: Statistics of the United States in 1860, 338.

Stennette, Janice S. (1996). *Teaching for the Freedmen's Bureau, Lynchburg, Virginia 1865-1871.* Dissertation. Chancellorsville, VA: University of Virginia.

Takagi, Madori (1999). *Rearing wolves to our own destruction: slavery in Richmond, Virginia 1782-1865.* Carter G. Woodson Institute of Black Studies: University Press of Virginia.

Taylor, Orville W. *(1958). Jumping over the broomstick: slave marriage and mortality in Arkansas*. Arkansas Historical Quarterly, Vol. XVII, No. 3. Van Buren, Arkansas: Arkansas Historical Association.

Thorpe, Francis Newton (1898). *A constitutional history of the American people, 1776-1850.* New York: Harper & Brothers.

Transcript (1824). *The trial of the British Soldiers of the 29th Regiment of Foot for the Murder of Crispus Attucks, Samuel Gray, Samuel Maverick, James Cladwell and Patrick Carr on Monday Evening, March 5, 1770.* Transcript of the hearing before the Justices of the Superior Court on 27 November 1770. Boston: William Emmons.

Tyler, Moses C. (1887). *Patrick Henry,* Boston: Houghton, Mifflin & Co.

-- (1898). *Patrick Henry.* Boston: Houghton, Mifflin & Co.

U.S. Statutes at Large, Vol 12, 566-569.

United States Government, Robert N. Scott, H. M. Lazelle, George B. Davis, Leslie J. Perry, Joseph W. Kirkley, Fred C. Ainsworth, John S. Moodey, and Calvin D. Cowles (1880). *The War of the Rebellion: a compilation of the official records of the Union and Confederate armies.* Washington, D.C.: Govrenment Printing Office.

United States Government (1870). *Report of the Commissioner of Education made to the Secretary of the Interior for the year ... with accompanying papers.* Washington, D.C.: Government Printing Office.

Watson, Thomas E. (1916). *Political and economic handbook.* Thomson, GA: Jeffersonian Publishing Co.

Weigley, Russell Frank (2000). *A great Civil War: a military and political history, 1861-1865.* Bloomington: Indiana University Press.

Williams, Heather A. (2005). *African American education in slavery and freedom.* Chapel Hill, NC: University Press of North Carolina.

Figures

Tables

Index

General

Full Names of Slaves

Note: Spellings often appear to be phonetic versions of names we have come to know in Allen County. The names are as they appear in the documents from which they came. No attempt has been made to alter them. Therefore, try alternate spellings if the surname you seek is not on this list. In particular, look for phonetic spellings.

First Names of Slaves without Surnames

Note: Surnames for slaves were uncommon before emancipation. Most often, only first names were recorded. This index lists first names that appear in the records without an associated surname. Spellings often appear to be phonetic versions of first names we have come to know in Allen County. The first names are as they appear in the documents from which they came. No attempt has been made to alter them. Therefore, try alternate spellings if the first name you seek is not on this list. In particular, look for phonetic spellings. The lack of a surname precludes multiple page listings for most individuals. In the few cases when records positively indicated that the first name was associated with an individual, multiple pages were listed. For all others, repetition of a first name may or may not be the same person.